THE
jAPANESE
BUSINESS
COMMUNITY
AND
NATIONAL
TRADE
POLICY,
1920–1942

THE JAPANESE BUSINESS COMMUNITY AND NATIONAL TRADE POLICY, 1920–1942

William Miles Fletcher III

The University of North Carolina Press
Chapel Hill and London

The paper in this book meets the guidelines for
permanence and durability of the Committee
on Production Guidelines for Book Longevity
of the Council on Library Resources.

Library of Congress Cataloging-in-Publication Data

Fletcher, William Miles, 1946–
    The Japanese business community and national
trade policy, 1920–1942.
    Bibliography: p.
    Includes index.
    1. Japan—Commercial policy—History.
2. Industry and state—Japan—History. 3. Japan—
Economic conditions—1918–1945. I. Title.
HF1601.F54   1989   380.1′3′0952   88-33854
ISBN 9780807857311 (pbk.: alk. paper)

CONTENTS

ACKNOWLEDGMENTS

Although scholarship depends much upon solitary effort, only the generous and able help of many people made this project possible. For advice and encouragement, I thank Awaya Kentarō, James B. Crowley, Hara Akira, Hosoya Chihiro, Igarashi Takeshi, Ikai Hisa, Imuta Yoshimitsu, Maeda Yasuyuki, Richard H. Mitchell, Nakamura Takafusa, Hugh Patrick, Takeda Haruto, and Takeuchi Kazuo. Financial support from several institutions proved crucial. Grants from the University Research Council of the University of North Carolina at Chapel Hill and from the American Philosophical Society allowed me to conduct research for this study at the Library of Congress and in Tokyo, Japan. A W. N. Reynolds research leave awarded by UNC-CH permitted me to complete a first draft of this book. Publication was aided by a subvention from the Endowment of the College of Arts and Sciences at UNC-CH.

I fear that if I try to list all of the people who aided me at various archives, I will by mistake omit a few names. Therefore, I will simply say that I appreciate greatly the generous help given by the staffs of the following libraries and archives: the Walter R. Davis Library at the University of North Carolina at Chapel Hill, the Perkins Library at Duke University, the Far Eastern Collection at the Library of Congress, the National Diet Library in Tokyo, the Libraries of the Faculty of Economics and the Faculty of Law at the University of Tokyo, the Archives of the Japanese Foreign Ministry (Gaimushō Shiryō Kan), the National Archives of Japan (Kokuritsu Kōbunsho Kan), the Mitsui Archives (Mitsui Bunko), the archives at the Mitsui Bank in Tokyo, the Mitsubishi Economic Research Institute (Mitsubishi Keizai Kenkyūjo), the Library of the Federation of Economic Organizations (Keizai Dantai Rengōkai), the Library of the Tokyo Chamber of Commerce, and the Institute for Research on the History of Industrial Policy (Sangyō Seisaku Shi Kenkyūjo).

Over the past few years I have benefited much from the comments that I have received when presenting aspects of my research in papers or talks. I am particularly grateful to the outside readers for the University of North Carolina Press for their diligence and constructive suggestions.

While working on this project, I profited greatly from the encouragement and help of the editorial staff at the University of North Carolina Press. I owe special thanks to Lewis Bateman, Ron Maner, and Mary Reid.

The staff of the Microcomputer Support Center at UNC-CH deserve credit for calmly and ably answering all of my questions, often posed in a tone of partially controlled panic over the telephone, about how to tame my PC.

The patience and support of my wife, Michèle, proved crucial to this project. During my research trips to Japan she had to juggle the demands of a job and childcare. Eric's non-negotiable requests for playtime with his Dad provided some helpful diversions.

In accordance with Japanese custom, Japanese names are written with the family name first and given name last. Macrons indicate long vowels, except in the case of the cities of Tokyo and Osaka, whose names are familiar to Western readers as written above.

THE
JAPANESE
BUSINESS
COMMUNITY
AND
NATIONAL
TRADE
POLICY,
1920–1942

INTRODUCTION

MAJOR ISSUES

The Japanese business community between the two world wars deserves careful analysis as a vital participant in shaping national economic policies. Major studies have focused on the influence of Japanese business groups and leaders since World War II,[1] but only a few articles have scrutinized the interwar period. Each of these has investigated the evolution of one particular policy, such as restoring the gold standard in 1929 and encouraging the iron and steel industry near the end of World War I.[2] No one has examined the role of the business community in helping the nation solve an unprecedented combination of economic challenges in the 1920s and 1930s: world depression, rampant protectionism, and war in Asia. Scholars have studied the impact on national policies of many other major groups in this twenty-year period—the imperial army, the imperial navy, the police, the Ministry of Foreign Affairs, and even the enfeebled political parties and labor movement. Surely the business community, which carried out the nation's surge to industrial power, commands equal attention.

In the absence of detailed studies, attention has focused on the responsibility of the business community for Japan's militarism, and extreme views have prevailed. Marxists have assumed that big business dominated the government and, eager to profit from arms sales and imperialist adventures, collaborated with the army to commit aggression abroad. Sakamoto Masako, for example, has contended not only that the large combines, the zaibatsu, reaped benefits from military expansion but also that their greed propelled the Japanese conquest of China and Manchuria. Writers have often blamed the zaibatsu for the government's oppressive domestic policies, even for the rise of fascism in Japan.[3]

Other scholars have depicted businessmen as politically weak advocates of peaceful trade whom fanatic generals and admirals intimidated into compliance. Mitani Taichirō has emphasized the efforts of bankers, especially Inoue Junnosuke, to promote economic cooperation with the United States and Britain during the 1920s. Forging a close personal bond with Thomas Lamont of J. P. Morgan and Company, Inoue as head of the Bank of Japan attracted considerable American investment to Japan. He also negotiated Japan's entry into the Four-Power Consortium which was supposed to supervise loans from the major powers to China. According to Mitani, the Manchurian Incident, planned and executed by the army, poisoned the atmosphere for such cooperation. The conquest of Manchuria heightened American suspicions of Japanese intentions in China and eliminated the political authority of cosmopolitan financiers. Morikawa Hidemasa has noted that few business leaders supported an aggressive policy toward China. Moreover, business leaders and groups in the late 1930s tried to induce Americans to invest in Manchuria and to promote goodwill with the Anglo-American powers.[4]

A careful analysis of important issues related to trade, though, yields an intricate mosaic of business attitudes and influence. Sometimes the goals of business groups opposed those of the military; sometimes they coincided. This study will argue that between the two world wars caution, ambivalence, and opportunism marked the attitudes of the business community toward Japan's subjugation of the Asian mainland.

Executives were most preoccupied with enlisting government help in expanding foreign trade without sacrificing the autonomy of the private sector. Tracing the development of trade policies illuminates the complex interaction that arose between various ministries and the business community. Because of the active role of officials in advancing Japan's rapid economic growth after World War II, the government-business relationship has fascinated American observers. Some have even called for imitation in the form of a coordinated national industrial policy in the United States.[5] Although most analyses of Japanese industrial policies have concentrated on the last forty years or so, some writers have recognized important continuities in the government's economic policies since the 1920s. The basic concepts of many policies toward major industries and trade have not changed.[6] Unfortunately, the activities of government officials have grabbed the scholarly spotlight. The business community's impact on national economic policies and its attitude toward the role of the government remain obscure.[7] An understanding of how the business-government relationship emerged requires an examination of the opinions and influence of the former. After all, refusal to cooperate or even dispirited participation by business leaders could have sabotaged any governmental policy.

This book takes trade policy as its subject for several reasons. Then, as now, the industrial economy could not function without foreign trade to gain the many raw materials that Japan lacked. During the interwar era business leaders and business groups became obsessed with finding ways of expanding trade along with ensuring a healthy balance of exports and imports. Determining trade policies involved a host of crucial issues pertaining to foreign relations as well as the organization of domestic industries. Finally, the travails of this period forged a new conviction, one that the Japanese business community maintained well into the 1980s as a guiding concept: the task of expanding Japan's international trade resembled a war in demanding a national strategy coordinated by the government.

The term "business community" needs clarification.[8] By the late 1930s, many business groups existed in Japan; these encompassed hundreds of local and national associations. This book uses the term to signify major business groups and leaders that during the 1920s and 1930s regularly expressed opinions on major economic issues and most actively sought to influence national policies. This definition accords with the scholarly use of the concept in recent decades. Ōgata Sadako, for example, has defined the post-1945 *zaikai* in this way: "It has come to refer to a group of major industrial and financial leaders who devote considerable time to the activities of one or more of the primary economic organizations. . . . Zaikai [*sic*] are generally regarded as a power elite who represent the interests of the business community as a whole rather than of individual businessmen."[9] During the interwar era the most vocal business executives worked for prominent companies. Some business groups represented primarily the interests of large companies, while others, such as the chambers of commerce, had a mixed membership. Those in Tokyo, Osaka, Nagoya, Yokohama, and Kōbe figure most prominently in this study, because they had large memberships and displayed great energy in tackling major economic issues.

The notion that the Japanese business community operated as a unified interest group might well provoke doubts. The term may imply a cohesion among groups that did or could not exist. Certainly no single organization embraced representatives of every sector of the economy. At times business groups and individual leaders differed sharply in their opinions on issues. Still, the interwar decades saw progressively effective attempts by business leaders to forge a consensus on important proposals. The means included national conferences, extensive surveys of executives' views by national business groups, and—in the case of the trade sector—the creation of organizations that encompassed all related groups. Even if members' levels of enthusiasm varied, the *zaikai* could speak with a united voice on a particular proposal.

The different backgrounds of business leaders also complicate the concept of a distinct business community. Inoue Junnosuke helped organize and manage major business groups during the 1910s and 1920s, yet he forged his career in the government's Bank of Japan. Gōdō Takuo, the president of the Tokyo Chamber of Commerce during the late 1930s, spent most of his professional life in the imperial navy. Gō Seinosuke, one of the most active leaders of the business world, hailed from an especially distinguished background. His father's service as the vice-minister of finance in the late nineteenth century earned the family entry into the hereditary aristocracy. Gō himself began his career in the Ministry of Agriculture and Commerce and belonged to the House of Peers. The case of Nakajima Kumakichi, the powerful leader of the Furukawa combine, bears similarities. The emperor bestowed aristocratic rank upon his father, Nobuyuki, a dynamic politician who had become the first president of the Lower House of the Diet. Inheriting the official title of baron, Kumakichi served twice in the House of Peers. Many business leaders entered cabinets, usually as minister of finance or of commerce and industry. Judging to what extent the views of such men derived from their ties to business or from other connections is often difficult. Except in cases where an executive in government office reversed a previous stand, this study will treat executives who spoke out on issues as representatives of the business community. One has to recognize, though, that the members of this interest group came from a variety of family and professional settings and that some of these involved close ties to the government.

One other caution deserves mention. A Japanese scholar warned the author that the custom of holding important negotiations between business leaders and government officials in teahouses, restaurants, or other informal settings would make the real evolution of policy decisions impossible to trace. Naturally no documents would survive to record such discussions. The conduct of unofficial consultation, however, can frustrate the study of the policy-making process in any political and economic system. Rarely do sufficient diaries and personal letters exist to explain an entire decision-making procedure. One must either abandon all efforts to probe how governmental policies are made or reluctantly accept the possibility that the reasons for some leaders' decisions will remain subject to speculation. In regard to trade policies in the 1920s and 1930s, available materials reveal the positions that various business groups and leaders took on disputes, indicate the sequence of decisions, and suggest lines of influence.

Five issues appeared most frequently in these debates. First, executives wanted governmental aid in the form of higher tariffs, subsidies for exports, and the streamlined administration of trade matters. Second, alarm at increasingly cutthroat foreign competition led to campaigns for a restructuring of the economy through national cartels organized by industry. Third, as cooperation between the government and business community grew, each side had to confront the challenge of creating a fair mechanism to devise national policies. How could businessmen have confidence that officials would not end up dictating regulations? How could public servants certify that businessmen would not scheme to gain excessive profits? Fourth, the future direction of Japan's trade—whether to attempt a regional autarky—presented another dilemma. Finally, full-scale war in China after 1937 presented the *zaikai* with the challenge of expanding exports and imports while feeding the military's voracious appetite for munitions and battling blatant efforts by officials to monopolize decisions on trade.

Analyses of how economic policy evolved in other industrial nations during the twentieth century have illustrated the pitfalls of assessing the impact that a particular interest group can have. Interpretations have generally divided into two camps—those that have accorded business leaders and/or groups vital influence and those that have not. Such studies have raised issues that demand attention. Those that have emphasized the influence of the business community have centered on its increased contact with the government. Some authors have described a naturally developing "corporatism," as government officials in European nations began to seek regular consultations with leaders of both business and labor organizations on various matters. Arenas where delegates of these interest groups could negotiate became crucial to resolving economic issues and easing domestic frictions.[10] This process proved even more significant than the actions of national elected assemblies. Keith Middlemas's case study of British economic policy describes the rise of a "corporate bias" in which the state admitted "representative bodies to its orbit rather than face a free-for-all with a host of individual claimants." Hence interest groups or "governing institutions," such as the Trade Union Council or the National Council of Economic Organizations, "became part of the extended state."[11]

Other writers have argued that business groups could gain benefits for particular industries without dominating the whole political structure or trying to determine broader policies. Grant McConnell has argued that in the United States after World War II a well-organized business group would often "capture" a unit of the government and determine its policy toward an industry. Businessmen could, in effect, regulate the regulators. In some cases, business and government had become so "closely meshed as frequently to be indistinguishable."[12]

Interpretations that have downplayed business influence have questioned the quality and results of government-business consultation.[13] Sometimes different business groups could not unite on a specific issue. Organizations representing small enterprises would conflict with lobbyists for large companies, or various industries would pursue separate interests. Sometimes executives did not want close cooperation with government officials. Finally, other lobbies could exert impressive political power. Case studies of Britain and West Germany have shown that once the elected national assembly began public debate on legislation, the leverage of business groups diminished rapidly. Because few elected officials could risk the appearance of yielding to special interests, the business community rarely stopped a bill that generated wide support. To have any effect, executives had to start negotiations in the early stages of drafting. Even then discussions with government officials dealt with details and methods of implementation rather than basic principles. One study observed that the post-1945 British government simply made "a ritual sacrifice at the altar of consultation" with business leaders. The authors called this policy-making process "pluralistic," because a variety of political and economic groups shaped the decisions of the government.[14]

This study examines the forms and frequency of business-government consultation in Japan and its results. The business community during the interwar era gradually became convinced of the need for what scholars would now label a corporatist relationship in order to pursue an effective trade policy. Business leaders and groups strived to reach a consensus on trade issues and to discuss them regularly with officials who, in turn, became increasingly responsive in playing a mediating role to help specific industries cope with problems and in composing new laws. The resulting legislation passed the Diet easily with little obstruction by other political forces.

By the mid-1930s executives envisioned a formal structure of mutual consultation with the government. The situation fit what Richard J. Samuels has called "reciprocity" in that "control [was] mutually constrained." Business had gained "systematic inclusion in the policy process" and "rights of self-regulation" while "grant[ing] the state some jurisdiction over industrial structure in the 'national interest.' "[15] Late in the decade, however, the policy process did not operate smoothly. The main problem for the *zaikai* came not from other private interest groups but from the fierce rivalries between government ministries. They stunted the growth of nascent corporatism. Hence the business community became a major participant in making trade policy but could not dominate it.

ONE

THE RISE OF THE
BUSINESS COMMUNITY

The late nineteenth century brought a radical economic transformation to Japan. The regime of the Tokugawa Shogun that had lasted for over two centuries collapsed in the Meiji Restoration of 1868. Until then the nation had had no mechanized industrial production. The new government, dedicated to strengthening the nation, decided that Japan's future depended upon the growth of industry. During the next decade officials brought in and ran foreign factories to show how they operated. This tactic aimed at luring wary Japanese merchants to shift investments from traditional commerce to large-scale manufacturing. In addition, the government helped build an extensive transportation and communication network within Japan and subsidized shipping companies that strived to end the monopoly of Western firms. Once these policies succeeded in prompting a number of new ventures in the private sector, the government shed most of its industrial facilities. By the next decade Japanese textile firms had already begun to penetrate the Chinese market.

The political structure changed too. As the leaders of the restoration assumed power, they dismantled the old regime that had delegated much authority to several hundred lords who each ruled a separate domain. In their place arose a Western-style centralized bureaucracy with national ministries and appointed governors for seventy-two prefectures. In 1889 the emperor proclaimed a constitution. It created a bicameral Diet: the House of Peers and an elected Lower House. These could pass laws and approve the budget. Immediately afterward political parties formed to dominate the Lower House. Japan's industrial and commercial pioneers soon took steps to make sure that officials and politicians heard their views on issues.

Business groups first formed on a regional or sectoral basis to represent the new enterprises. Each organization naturally tried to affect governmental policy toward its members. Later executives felt the need for broad-based national groups to increase the influence of business opinion. Business leaders created two such organizations, the Japan Industrial Club and the Japan Economic Federation. These marked important attempts to strengthen the business community's impact on major economic issues. Still, officials and executives lacked a set structure for discussing policies together.

THE FIRST BUSINESS GROUPS

The first major business groups in Japan formed at government insistence. According to the famous industrial pioneer, Shibusawa Eiichi, in 1877 oligarchs Ōkuma Shigenobu and Itō Hirobumi suddenly pressed him to develop chambers of commerce as quickly as possible.[1] These leaders cared little for the function of such bodies in the West as means for businessmen to advance their interests as a group at the local or national level. Instead, the oligarchs' motivation stemmed from diplomatic strategy and wounded national pride. They were then starting to renegotiate the humiliating commercial treaties that Japan had signed with the Western powers in the 1850s. These agreements not only mandated the principle of extraterritoriality—that Japanese courts could not try foreigners for crimes committed in Japan—but also limited the tariffs that Japan could place on imports. Because these restrictions might hinder the growth of industry, the Japanese government was eager to remove them. When diplomats told the British ambassador, Harry Parkes, that public opinion would not tolerate the treaties, Parkes had replied pointedly that no organized commercial groups existed in Japan to voice public opinion on economic matters! Hence arose the sudden fascination with chambers of commerce.

Inspired by Itō and Ōkuma's enthusiasm and the promise of a government subsidy of one thousand yen per year, Shibusawa set to work. He enlisted the help of friends, such as businessman Ōkura Kihachirō and journalist Fukuchi Gen'ichirō, to organize a Tokyo Chamber of Commerce by the end of the next year. It received both a subsidy and the free use of a new building from the government. By 1881 similar chambers spread to most major cities. These groups took as their goals consulting with the government on economic policy and representing business opinion.

Several years afterward the government tried to supplant these chambers with another set of more strictly supervised organs. In 1881 the Ministry of Agriculture and Commerce was established to unify economic policy and immediately created commercial and industrial consultative councils in each prefecture.[2] These comprised businessmen in each area, some appointed by the government and some elected by their peers. Government subsidies to the chambers of commerce ended.

This attempt to replace the chambers soon failed. The government's tight control over the membership of the councils rankled businessmen. Meanwhile, the chambers labored to better their position. In 1890 the Ordinance for Chambers of Commerce bestowed legal recognition on local groups. A new law spelled out their specific duties. They should deliberate on proposals to aid the "development of commerce," propose changes in laws and regulations relating to commerce, respond to officials' inquiries, provide economic data to the government, and mediate local commercial disputes. The Law for Chambers of Commerce in 1902 even granted the right to coerce eligible businessmen into becoming members. All individuals who paid income tax and administered some kind of business within a district qualified to join the local chamber. It could in effect levy a tax by compelling all of these residents to pay dues. The Ministry of Agriculture and Commerce kept some measure of control, as the minister had to approve the budget of each chamber and the means of revenue collection. Within each chamber democratic procedures prevailed. Members could vote for representatives to a governing council, and these in turn selected the officers of the organization.[3]

The chambers proliferated throughout the nation, with fifty-eight registering with the government by the turn of the century. In 1892 the first National Federation of Chambers of Commerce met in Kyōto. This conference decided to broaden membership in the individual chambers by permitting companies as well as individuals to join. The government ratified this change through ordinances issued in 1895 and through the legislation of 1902.[4] The passage of a navigation law in 1896 that provided special subsidies to overseas Japanese shipping lines demonstrated the close rapport that the government and individual chambers could achieve. The Tokyo chamber, which had requested such aid for two years, and the N.Y.K. (Nihon Yūsen Kaisha), a major shipping company, served as the "main architects" of the legislation.[5]

Despite this support from and cooperation with officials, the chambers became political thorns in the side of the national cabinet. The continuation of special taxes levied for the Russo-Japanese War of 1904–1905 first spurred the chambers to decry national policies. The government had borrowed heavily to pay for the huge military expenses incurred in the conflict. Several chambers passed resolutions calling for fiscal responsibility by quickly repaying the old bonds and refusing to offer new ones, and in October 1906 the National Federation demanded the abolition of emergency wartime taxes.[6] Business leaders argued that high taxes would rob the nation of its economic might, the pillar of the nation's power.

The cabinet had its own economic agenda. The party in power, the Seiyū-kai headed by Premier Saionji Kinmochi, advocated an aggressive economic policy of funding public works, both to prime the economy and to gain votes through pork-barrel politics. The military emphasized the need to expand, now that Japan had joined the ranks of the world's top military powers. Far from abolishing the recent war levies, the cabinet decided to impose new ones on the consumption of rice wine (*sake*) and sugar.

The total failure to influence tax policy did not daunt the chambers as they raised a storm of protest. In 1907 the National Federation petitioned the cabinet three times to complain about the new taxes.[7] During the next year the chambers directly confronted the government. Nakano Buei, the successor to Shibusawa as head of the federation, called an urgent meeting. There he proclaimed that mere pleas to the cabinet would not succeed; the situation demanded "power to the people." The assembly devised an ambitious plan for revamping government finances. The government should repeal the burdensome wartime taxes and reduce or eliminate many others: the business tax, the tax on consumption of woven goods, and the tax on subcontracting work. The chambers also favored budget cuts, deplored the government's salt monopoly and the recent nationalization of seventeen railroads, and requested a "reform of financial plans" for the military.[8] Even the venerable Shibusawa, who claimed the loftiest patriotic motives for his diverse business ventures, explained that because expansion of the military hindered industrial progress he opposed such "unproductive expenses."

The business community's attack did not bother the Saionji cabinet. Rural voters, the heart of the Seiyūkai's electoral support, remained indifferent to the antitax movement. Endorsing the movement did not keep the majority party's main opponent, the Kensei Hontō, from losing the Diet election of 1908.[9] When Saionji resigned in July for political reasons not related to the tax crisis, the next premier, General Katsura Tarō, proved more hostile. When the chambers persisted in clamoring for tax reduction and fiscal austerity, Katsura retaliated by revoking their authority to force local businessmen to pay dues.[10]

He justified the measure by asserting that the chambers had abandoned their original function of commenting on economic policy and had become political lobbies.

In response, the chambers' stance hardened. Four years later they still championed the cause of slashing the military budget. This time Saionji, once again premier, infuriated the imperial army by declining to fund a new division of troops. When the army's refusal to appoint a minister caused the cabinet to fall, the Tokyo Chamber of Commerce praised the premier's obstinacy and pledged opposition to the new Katsura cabinet. Many other chambers issued resolutions vilifying the arrogant actions of the army and lauding the ousted Saionji.[11] When Katsura indicated that he would approve increased military funding, criticism in the elected Diet and in the newspapers mounted. Several politicians and journalists organized a Movement for Constitutional Government that sponsored public demonstrations across the nation to protest the sly political maneuvering of the premier and the army. Eventually the latter received its extra division, but the wave of protests forced Katsura to resign. In 1916 Premier Ōkuma Shigenobu restored the precious right of local chambers to force payment of dues from eligible businessmen.

Meanwhile, chambers of commerce had taken on the role of representing the general interests of the business community. In 1916 the government convened a special conference to discuss national economic policy; twelve of thirty-nine business participants came as delegates from various chambers. Their broad membership gave them a strong base from which they could wield great political leverage. By 1941, for example, the six largest chambers could boast a total of 77,000 members, with Osaka alone having over 27,000.[12] Even in 1916, they could claim to embrace a huge constituency.

The breadth of membership, which ranged from huge modern combines to tiny shops, could also make forging a consensus on issues hard. For example, Gō Seinosuke, a major figure in the world of big business and president of the Tokyo chamber in the 1930s, complained about the divided interests of the members. Joining the Tokyo branch required only two years of business operation in the city; even owners of one-person stores were welcome.[13] A shopkeeper who paid an annual tax of only five yen had the same right to vote for delegates to the elected council as the head of the giant Mitsukoshi department store or the Bank of Japan. Even if candidates had to qualify for the elections by paying a certain amount of business taxes, those sympathetic to small businesses could monopolize the local council and determine its decisions. This problem had existed for a long while. In 1917 officials from large companies occupied only four of forty-nine seats on the Tokyo council.[14]

The chambers took some steps to safeguard the interests of large companies. National legislation in 1928 mandated that local councils have at least one representative for each major industry. In Tokyo and Kōbe, the local council had fifty members with ten slots reserved for delegates from designated sectors.[15] Often the heads of prominent firms dominated the top posts of such chambers. Still, the difficulties of reconciling the different concerns of large companies and small enterprises helped convince the former of the need to create their own organizations.

Moreover, the regional basis of each group hindered the chambers' impact on the government's policies. Although each group could represent local interests, they rarely cooperated in promoting their proposals. As evident from 1905 to 1916, the pronouncements of meetings of the National Federation could attract public attention. Still, no permanent structure or office existed to organize the study of national issues as they arose and to facilitate contact with officials.

Another business group that embraced different economic sectors, the Japan Trade Council (Nihon Bōeki Kyōkai), began in 1885. Founded by thirty pioneering importers and exporters, it encouraged foreign commerce by easing the exchange of information among traders and conducting research on foreign markets. Headquartered in Tokyo, the council drew most of its members from the nearby Kantō area and by 1912 counted 401 participants.[16]

Compared to the chambers of commerce, the Trade Council had far fewer members and more narrowly focused its activities on issues directly related to trade. For example, the council remained neutral during the fierce struggle between Premier Saionji and the army. Instead, the group petitioned the Ministry of Transportation about an increase in shipping fares for exports to Europe and proposed that the Diet eliminate the import tax on rice in order to lower the prices of domestic goods and thus, indirectly, of exports.[17]

Gradually the Trade Council grew in size, prestige, and sophistication. By 1916 it had divided into ten different sections to respond to the varied interests of members. A separate section dealt with each of the following areas: trade, transportation, immigration, overseas communication, foreign exchange, industry, insurance, magazines, entertainment, and membership requirements. When the council addressed an issue, only members of directly affected sections met to discuss recommendations.[18]

The Trade Council's proposals gradually became bolder, as seen in its imaginative reaction to the steep rise of shipping costs during World War I. Members reasoned that a growing shortage of cargo space to handle rapidly increasing exports and imports fueled this price explosion. Governmental controls on shipping prices would only discourage efforts of new companies to add to the nation's merchant marine. The government should thus permit price rises while directing the reinvestment of profits to insure the production of more ships and more cargo space. In addition, officials should requisition naval warships to carry goods for export and order naval shipyards to build freighters.[19] However visionary proposals like this may have seemed, government officials began to confer regularly with the council about trade policies. That three members were asked to join Japan's delegation at the Versailles Conference in 1919 indicated both the stature of the group and its distinguished membership.[20]

Several industrial cartels emerged during the late nineteenth century. The most durable and powerful turned out to be the Japan Spinners Association (Dai Nihon Bōseki Rengōkai), which started in 1882 and governed the sector that led Japan's industrialization. The association began with the goal of helping the exchange of information between the managers of the fifteen factories that joined first. By the mid-1930s the membership had grown to 60 companies and 261 factories, and the group exercised control directly or indirectly over most aspects of the textile business.[21] Some members only manufactured yarn, while others traded in raw cotton and cotton yarn as well.

The functions of this powerful group soon expanded. In addition to improving the general quality of products and manufacturing technology, members wanted to thwart the fledgling labor movement and protect companies' investment in skilled workers. The charter forbade one company from raiding the work force of another. In the event of a strike, the spinners pledged not to hire workers from the affected company and to lend workers if necessary.[22] Evidently these vows had limited effect, because companies' attempts to pry valuable production secrets from rivals' employees or to entice them away remained a problem even in the 1930s.[23]

Other policies had more success.[24] As the textile industry grew, the spinners began to realize that competition in the world market demanded a finely tuned and strictly enforced marketing strategy. The association in 1890 decreed for the first time a set number of production holidays in order to match more precisely the overall supply and demand for cotton yarn. Such actions became common. In 1900 and 1901, for example, members temporarily had to idle 40 percent of their production capacity. One observer's comment that the development of the textile industry comprised a "history of reduced operations" suggests the tight supervision imposed by the cartel.

In 1890 the group decided to enter the world market by shipping out 30,000 bales of yarn a year regardless of the losses. Members agreed to share these equally. In a similar move members resolved to bear together any losses from producing special yarn to replace the type that Japan imported from India. Several years later each member had to pay fees to support the export of yarn and cloth. Because the association's regulations stipulated that members must agree to such decisions with near unanimity, only a firm and widely held conviction that cooperation would speed the growth of the textile industry made these actions possible.

This ambitious cartel wielded great economic and political influence in matters relating to the cotton industry. In 1893 the association secured a contract with N.Y.K. for the transport of Indian cotton at cheap prices in return for granting the shipping company a monopoly on this trade. During the next year heavy lobbying led to the removal of the export tax on cotton yarn. Two years after that, the government eliminated tariffs on imported raw cotton despite the protests of domestic producers. When Japanese companies began to supply the market with yarn, officials obligingly raised tariffs on imported varieties. The spinners chalked up only one major failure: the cartel could not persuade the government to provide direct subsidies for exports of cotton products.[25]

The cartel determined basic policies for most aspects of the textile industry by the early twentieth century. The association arranged the transport of raw cotton to Japan, set quotas for the types of yarn to be manufactured, and ordered special inspections of goods for export. The production schedules of companies that manufactured cotton cloth depended upon the amount of yarn that the spinners decided to manufacture.[26]

Their bylaws granted the largest companies considerable authority while safeguarding the interests of smaller firms. An executive committee composed of delegates from the twelve largest companies formulated proposals. Because these companies collectively held over one-half of the productive capacity of the members, a decision by the committee to support a particular policy or recommendation carried considerable weight. Still, the general meeting (sō-kai) of members had to approve all decisions that needed an outlay of funds. Any plan to reduce manufacturing operations required assent from 90 percent of the members, who had to represent at least 90 percent of the total number of spindles possessed by all members. Special committees supervised and enforced policies that members approved for limits on production and for standards of quality. The lack of sanctions other than mere warnings indicated a strong reliance on consensus and peer pressure to assure voluntary compliance.[27]

The financial community also organized swiftly into powerful interest groups. By 1880 the two largest cities of Osaka and Tokyo each had a bank assembly (ginkō shūkai) that studied issues related to the banking industry and represented the views of local financial institutions.[28] By the turn of the century such groups had appeared in Yokohama, Kōbe, and Nagoya as well. In 1891 the Tokyo Bank Assembly created the first clearinghouse (tegata kōkan-jo) to handle financial transactions and to "plan the progress and reform of the general banking industry."[29] Any company that belonged to the Bank Assembly and had dealings with the Bank of Japan could join.

The budgetary strains of the Russo-Japanese War conferred new political prestige on the banking community. The sudden need to raise cash through massive offerings of national bonds put the government at the mercy of financiers' expertise. Without the extra funds the entire war effort might have collapsed. As if to pay his respects, the finance minister in 1908 started a custom of announcing each year's national budget at a meeting of the National Federation of Clearinghouses. Three years later a banker, Yamamoto Tatsuo, became the first businessman to enter the cabinet. His appointment as finance minister set a precedent for selecting executives to head the ministries that focused on economic policy.[30]

EFFORTS TO UNITE BUSINESS OPINION

By the mid-1910s many industrial leaders outside of the areas of trade, banking, and textile production resented their political frailty. The Trade Council, the Spinners Association, and banking groups focused on their own narrow interests; the other industrial sectors lacked powerful lobbies. The various chambers of commerce provided forums to express views, but, as explained above, proved frustrating for members from large firms. Seven prominent executives decided in 1915 to form a new group to represent large industrial companies. These leaders—Nakajima Kumakichi, Fujiwara Ginjirō, Uemura Chōsaburō, Ōhashi Shintarō, Wada Tōyōji, Yoshimura Tetsunosuke, and Moroi Tsunehei—came from a wide variety of industries, including textiles, electrical engineering, publishing, and the manufacture of paper, metals, fertilizer, and beer. In 1917 their plans culminated in the creation of the Japan Industrial Club (Nihon Kōgyō Kurabu). The head of the giant Mitsui combine, Dan Takuma, accepted the post of executive director. Wada, Nakajima, Ōhashi, and Gō Seinosuke assisted him as managing directors.[31]

The initial membership numbered 185, and within four years it had ballooned to 679. This figure encompassed 387 members who paid annual dues; they nominated 287 other members. Three traits of the membership stood out. Many members came from the newly developing areas of iron, steel, and chemical manufacturing and electrical power production. The banking sector had relatively few delegates. And the overwhelming majority of members, almost five out of six, resided near Tokyo.[32]

Members were determined to affect national economic policies. Nakajima wrote in the statement of purpose that the club would foster research on economic issues, aid industrial development, and help conduct "national diplomacy" in the international economy. The iron and steel industry became the group's first concern. Because demand in this new sector was outstripping supply, government officials were deliberating over policies to spur production. In June 1917 the club took a bold stance. The government should remove tariffs from equipment imported for iron and steel production, exempt iron works from all taxes, and grant ten-year subsidies to encourage the manufacture of certain products. Special tariffs should block the flood of iron and steel imports that many executives expected when the world war ended. Two weeks after receiving this recommendation, the cabinet submitted to the Diet a bill exempting large iron and steel companies from business and income taxes and excluding imports of vital equipment from tariffs.[33]

The Industrial Club's endorsement helped persuade an emergency session of the Diet to pass this law within six weeks of submission.[34] The government acted quickly for other reasons too. The United States' decision to cease all exports of iron products after its recent entry into the war had sparked alarm over inadequate supplies of steel. The provision for removing taxes on large enterprises had already received the support of a special study group on the steel industry that the government had established. The club's proposals had simply expanded that exemption to cover much smaller companies and had added the elimination of taxes on essential equipment. Finally, the rejection of some proposals showed the limitations of the new group's influence. The government adopted neither direct subsidies nor protective tariffs.[35]

Undaunted, the Industrial Club continued to advance its proposals. Convinced that the nation needed a healthy steel industry and that new and small firms deserved protection from market forces, Gō and Nakajima spearheaded efforts to rework the original suggestions and to convince the government to adopt them. By February 1919 Gō and Nakajima had drafted a new program. It demanded limits on imports of iron and steel products, penalties for foreign dumping on the Japanese market, and creation of a government-sponsored committee to plan the future development of the steel industry. The club favored as long-term policies more imports of raw materials from China, protective tariffs for Japanese products, and the merger of private factories with the government-owned Yawata Iron Works—the first and largest in Japan.

The government responded by referring this proposal to a special committee to study the iron, steel, and shipbuilding industries. As part of the Temporary Conference to Investigate the Economy and Public Finance that met in July 1919, the committee assembled officials and business leaders from all sectors of the economy. The final report approved the encouragement of mergers among iron and steel companies, exemption of entrepreneurs in the industry from all taxes for ten years, tariff protection for domestic pig iron and rolled steel products, and subsidies for shipbuilders who used domestic steel and iron. In 1921 the government amended the previously passed steel law to include the recommended subsidies and tariffs.[36]

The Japan Industrial Club, though, lost one major battle. As the fighting in Europe drew to a close, the government in 1918 sponsored legislation to ease the increase of munitions production if Japan entered another war. The recent experiences of the European powers had made officials realize that future conflicts might well demand the total economic resources of the nation. Awed by this prospect, officials wanted the legal authority to apply extensive controls over factory production in wartime.[37] The Industrial Club thundered its opposition by warning that bureaucratic controls could damage the nation's industry, which remained in an "infant" stage. Rigid regulations would "frustrate the industrial desire of private citizens" and hamper production. Instead, the law should mandate a "strong administrative organ [in which] many private citizens of knowledge and experience would participate to plan smooth mobilization under the cooperation of government and business." The original bill, despite the club's stern admonitions and avid defense of entrepreneurial creativity, passed easily.[38]

Within a few years domestic and international concerns prompted the formation of the most powerful economic body, the Japan Economic Federation (Nihon Keizai Renmeikai). The inspiration for this organization came from a special mission abroad by Japan's business elite. The British ambassador to Japan, Sir Charles Elliot, had suggested to Shibusawa Eiichi in April 1921 that a group of industrial leaders visit England to strengthen commercial ties between Japan and his nation. The Japanese decided to travel to the United States as well and to make the examination of the Western powers' economies a major goal.[39] Inoue Junnosuke, the head of the Bank of Japan, Fujiyama Raita, the president of the Tokyo Chamber of Commerce, and Nakajima Kumakichi, a top official of the Furukawa Electrical Industries Company and the Japan Industrial Club, chose twenty-four colleagues for the group.

The eight-month trip had important consequences. The cordial reception that the Japanese envoys received from American and British chambers of commerce and business leaders reinforced the image of Japan as a peaceful and important mercantile nation and helped forge close ties between some Japanese and Western executives.[40] Like the famous diplomatic and investigative mission to the West that Prince Iwakura Tomomi led in the 1870s,[41] this one returned with strong opinions about economic conditions abroad and the need for new policies. In May 1922 Dan Takuma alerted members of the Industrial Club to the dangers of increased industrial competitiveness from the Western nations. They were slashing military budgets and taxes, encouraging mergers and cooperation within industries, and raising productivity.[42] The mission perceived an immediate need for revamping business organizations. The political muscle of national business groups in the United States and England had clearly struck members of the delegation. Dan saw the Federation of British Industries and the United States Chamber of Commerce as effective lobbies that provided accurate information on national economic problems to their governments and constantly pressured officials. In October he argued in a speech to the Industrial Club that "in Japan too we must create one federation to embrace as much as possible each type of [business] organization."[43] Although Nakajima Kumakichi later disdained the mission as a public relations stunt to curry Western favor and as a waste of time, Dan's proposal helped spur planning for the Japan Economic Federation, which would soon overshadow the Industrial Club.[44]

Dan, a cosmopolitan executive who had been trained as an engineer at the Massachusetts Institute of Technology, also held a firm belief that Japan should cultivate closer ties with the Western powers. The business community needed a new organization to join the International Chamber of Commerce that had begun only two years before in Paris. That the United States, England, and France had already joined showed that this chamber would wield power. Participation would increase Japan's prestige and provide a formal international forum to settle foreign trade disputes. Membership, however, required a national body representing all business sectors.[45] The National Federation of Chambers of Commerce could have served this function, but Dan and others discounted this body's effectiveness. Because it met only a few times each year, the federation could not react quickly to issues.

The swift reaction of the *zaikai* to Dan's idea reflected the urgency that business leaders felt regarding the need for a powerful lobby at both the national and international levels. In August 1922 one hundred business executives met to discuss a new organization. The sponsors included Dan and other prominent figures from the industrial and financial world. Soon afterward, the Japan Economic Federation started operations with fifty members. The statement of goals proclaimed that because the "interests and welfare" of a "modern nation . . . exist in economic problems," the business community had to participate more in governmental decisions on such matters.[46] In recruiting members, the federation said that it wanted to "contribute to the establishment of national economic policy." "Fair proposals" would emerge from "discussing problems from a national viewpoint." Moreover, because of problems in foreign trade, business leaders had to "plan the unification of our opinions toward the outside world" in "facing the situation where the relations between Japan and foreign nations are becoming closer."[47] As later analysis will clarify, a belief that the future would bring unprecedented economic dilemmas and challenges underlay the conviction that the *zaikai* had to have a unified and comprehensive lobby.[48]

This strong sense of need inspired 330 members to join by 1924. These included 11 major economic groups, such as the Japan Trade Council, 64 companies, and 251 individuals. The federation emphasized the need for representatives from all major economic sectors and regions to participate. Hence the Osaka-based Spinners Association, the Tokyo and Osaka Bank Assemblies, and the Sumitomo zaibatsu—all of which had refused to enter the Japan Industrial Club—became members. The hefty minimum requirement for the capital owned by corporate members restricted this privilege to large enterprises.[49]

The procedures of governance granted a measure of democracy. Every member had the right to vote on the annual budget in the general meeting and to vote for delegates on the ruling council of 200. Reserving one-half of the council seats for candidates from business groups guaranteed significant influence to the largest sectors of the economy. The council selected the board of fifty directors, who each served a six-month term as one of the twelve executive directors. At first the directors chose the president; later the rules changed to permit the entire membership to elect him. The executive directors exercised much power, as they determined which issues deserved attention. Appointed committees would collect data and draft proposals to send to the appropriate ministries. After a recommendation had passed the scrutiny of both the executive directors and the ordinary directors, the full council had to give final approval.[50]

The federation quickly became the premier business organization in Japan. The prestigious Dan Takuma served as president; Inoue Junnosuke, finance minister from 1923 to 1924, and Tsuchikata Hisayoshi, vice-president of the Bank of Japan, provided close contact with the government. The group soon dominated the special national committee that formed to represent Japan in the International Chamber of Commerce.[51]

The Japan Economic Federation gradually took over many tasks of the Industrial Club. At first the two groups cooperated closely, as the club provided office space and many of its leaders became the initial executive directors of the federation. For the first decade the two organizations often collaborated on economic research projects, because the club had a much larger budget. In 1932, though, the club stopped drafting proposals on general economic policy and concentrated on preventing the Diet's passage of a bill that would extend legal recognition to labor unions.[52] Meanwhile, the federation continued its efforts in framing recommendations on various issues.

THE GOVERNMENT AND EARLY EXPORT POLICY

The Japanese government from the start of the Meiji era had viewed industrial strength and foreign trade as vital concerns. The importation of model factories, the granting of special subsidies and protection to strategic industries, such as shipping,[53] and the tolerance for cartels, such as the Spinners Association, had all aimed at nurturing a vibrant and competitive private sector. By the 1880s, forecasts of a flood of cheap and shoddy exports to foreign markets caused the government to consider aid of another kind, inspection to ensure the quality of products.

The government progressed cautiously toward such regulation by permitting the creation of regional trade associations (*dōgyō kumiai*). Allowed to form in 1884, over 1,500 groups sprang up in less than two years. Because the associations could limit the production of goods and set prices, price-fixing schemes spread rapidly. Concerned, the government enacted a new law in 1897 that defined the associations' main duties as the exchange of information and the administration of inspections to guarantee the quality of some exports. An association could form if two-thirds of the companies in an industry in a particular region agreed to do so and if the minister of agriculture and commerce approved. Such an association could force all companies eligible for membership to join and accept the inspection process. Later revisions of the law expanded these powers to cover not only exports but certain "important goods."[54] Doubts about the groups' effectiveness, however, led the government to take over the examination of some products. In addition, the persistence of price-fixing arrangements continued to displease officials. Legislation in 1916 mandated stricter supervision of the associations' activities.

The Kōbe Trade Association that organized in 1900 showed how a successful group operated. It inspected brushes for export, investigated opportunities for obtaining financial credit, and distributed information on overseas markets. The association fulfilled a parental role through mediating disputes and cautioning members about actions that could threaten credit ratings abroad for everyone.[55] The organization served as the voice of the city's trading community for four decades.

By 1920 the trade associations faced an uncertain future. After the onerous inspection duties imposed in 1897 had induced some 80 percent of the groups to disband, they had revived to number 1,455. In the larger cities, such as Tokyo, their merger into federations (*jitsugyō kumiai rengōkai*) that regularly submitted recommendations on economic policy to the government suggested an increasing desire to affect policy. Yet, the powers of the minister of commerce and agriculture checked the associations' independence. If he judged that an association's actions harmed the public welfare, he could rescind a group's decisions, remove its officers, and even dissolve it.[56] Moreover, without more authority the associations would continue to play only a minor economic role.

Businessmen after 1900 had made few efforts to alter or improve the basic export policies of the government. The huge government debt accumulated during the Russo-Japanese War had drawn public attention to the budget and taxes as the most vexing economic problems early in the century. Meanwhile, Japan's annual surplus of imports persisted despite the nation's impressive gains in industrialization.[57] Dependence on colonies and foreign nations for foodstuffs, especially rice and sugar, and for industrial raw materials, such as raw cotton and wool, had made a balanced trade difficult to achieve. For example, not even a fifty-five-fold increase in the export of cotton goods after 1890 had reversed an overall import surplus in that efficient industry. Fortunately, massive exports of raw silk, mostly to the United States, kept the trade imbalance from becoming a crisis.

The world war then brought an unexpected surplus of exports and unprecedented prosperity. Demand for Japanese goods throughout Asia soared as the Western powers abandoned foreign markets to concentrate on munitions production and bought more Japanese goods. These new markets encouraged the expansion of newer and more capital-intensive industries, such as iron, steel, and machine manufacturing. Only when business leaders considered the economic impact of peace in Europe did their thoughts turn to changing the government's trade policies.

By the 1910s the business community had grown in size, organization, and stature parallel with the rise of Japanese industry. In the 1870s the oligarchs could discuss economic issues on a personal level with a few entrepreneurs, such as Shibusawa. The late 1890s saw the government take a more formal approach in arranging a series of formal meetings, the High Level Conferences on Agriculture, Commerce, and Industry (Nōshōkō Kōtō Kaigi), to consult with business leaders about economic matters.[58] Chambers of commerce and the Japan Spinners Association began to lobby the government about taxes and tariffs with varying degrees of success. Finally the Japan Industrial Club and later the Japan Economic Federation arose as efforts to create a single, strong voice for the national business community. The *zaikai* became increasingly determined to influence national economic policy.

The community, however, remained diversified. Far from deferring to the Industrial Club or the Economic Federation, the chambers of commerce, the Japan Trade Council, the Spinners Assocation, and other industrial groups drafted their own proposals on issues and exerted pressure on the government separately. It, in turn, sought consultations with many different business groups for discussions of policy. By 1920 no recognized standard procedure existed for government and business to cooperate in deciding and implementing new economic policies. The growing ambition and power of the *zaikai* and the challenges of the postwar era, however, would compel energetic efforts to create such a structure.

TWO

LEARNING TO WIELD POWER,
1920–1931

Signs of major political changes within Japan increased as the world war ended. Among the original leaders of the Meiji era, those towering figures who had guided Japan's rise to the status of a world power, only Yamagata Aritomo remained, and he died in 1922. The radical doctrines of anarchism and socialism attracted intellectuals inspired by the idealism of the Bolshevik Revolution in Russia. Illegal unions proliferated and organized strikes. In 1918 spontaneous riots protesting the high price of rice swept the nation. Many activists called for universal manhood suffrage. The passing away of the old leaders and the increasing pressure to broaden the franchise portended a political system more open to influence from new interest groups.

Seeking more impact on policies, the business community carved out several avenues of influence. Requests from government ministries to express opinions on important issues gave major business groups frequent opportunities to draft detailed proposals. Executives and officials met often for discussions in formal conferences; some occupied a day, some lasted several weeks, and others spanned months or even years. Finally, business leaders serving in cabinet posts could promote policies that they favored.

Deciding when to reimpose a gold standard drew much attention. The *zaikai*'s response revealed important characteristics about how it operated. At times it could fragment badly on an issue, but at others members could compromise and achieve a unified stand. As long as business opinion remained divided, the government showed little inclination to act. In this case, executives' success in finally hammering out a consensus on how to create a convertible currency and prevent a short-term catastrophe in foreign trade cleared the way for a major change in policy.

Trade issues in general obsessed many businessmen during the decade. They seized the initiative in designing both broad and specific policies to solve what they saw as a chronic crisis for the nation. They realized gradually that Japan's foreign trade needed a national strategy in order to survive and prosper. This had to rest on a strong, cooperative relationship with the government. It, in turn, had to become more involved in promoting exports.

CONFRONTING THE POSTWAR TRADE CRISIS

The business community had good reason to worry. Peace in Europe delivered two blows to Japan's economy: the nation's foreign trade contracted while it registered a huge surplus of imports. Because the economy had grown so much during the wartime boom, demand remained strong for imported sundry materials—for example, leather, dyes, and photographic paper—to be sold as or used in producing consumer goods.[1] Woollen goods poured in, as did inexpensive foodstuffs, such as soybeans and eggs, from China. New industries— the manufacture of woollen goods, dyestuffs, fertilizer, glass, paint, rubber, metal, and machines—posed special problems. These enterprises required huge amounts of imported raw materials but could not yet compete on the world market. Inevitably they contributed a net loss to the national trade ledger. Even the mighty cotton industry, which would soon trouble Western competitors, could not export enough to cover the value of its imported raw cotton. The burden of redressing the trade debit fell on producers of raw silk, still by far the main earner of foreign exchange, and manufacturers of toys and pottery, whose exports began to climb steadily after a brief decline.

The leaders of the *zaikai* viewed this situation with mixed emotions. They took pride in Japan's recent ascension into the ranks of the major industrial powers of the world. Entering the International Chamber of Commerce seemed to signify this new status. The Japan Economic Federation described the International Chamber as a "powerful group uniting and embracing the major economic powers of the world."[2] Dan Takuma, as one of the founders of the federation, asserted that membership would demonstrate "Japan's [new] economic position." Participation would also improve Japan's opportunities for "development on the stage of the world economy." Devoted to expanding trade and negotiating solutions to international economic problems, the chamber would provide a valuable channel for businessmen to cooperate in building world peace. Proof of this came with the first conference in Rome in 1923 that drew over five hundred participants to discuss crucial issues affecting the world economy. According to the Economic Federation, these discussions laid the basis for the American Dawes Plan of 1924 that set a schedule for payment of German war reparations. The federation argued that because Japan's heavy dependence on imported raw materials made foreign trade a crucial concern, Japan must anticipate and settle trade disputes in multilateral discussions.

The prevailing international mood of peace and cooperation helped nurture the naive belief of Japanese business leaders that the International Chamber would make important decisions. The new League of Nations planned to use the principles of collective security to forestall armed conflict among members; the Washington Conference from 1921 to 1922 achieved large reductions in the battleship fleets of the five largest navies. Businessmen had reason to hope that calm and deliberate discussions among the industrial powers could resolve trade issues as well. Realizing that Japan must trade, the business community intended to show its commitment to peaceful cooperation.

The postwar period also produced deep pessimism and sometimes even panic over the future of the economy. Perhaps Inoue Junnosuke, the president of the Bank of Japan, voiced business leaders' worries most bleakly. Japan, he wrote, was trapped.[3] Exports to Europe had dwindled with the revival of its manufacturing. Statistics showed that by 1920 Japan's exports there had slipped by one-third from the level of 1918; a lopsided export surplus had turned into a deficit. Some traders hoped to compensate by selling more to other Asian countries. Inoue pointed out that those nations faced the same problem that stumped Japan. They had benefited by selling goods to Europe during the war; when these exports plunged, Asians could not afford to buy more imports.

As Inoue predicted, the overall volume of trade with Asia soon plummeted. Japan's exports became even more dependent on American purchases of raw silk. Meanwhile, in 1920 production fell 35 percent in shipbuilding, 20 percent in the manufacture of iron and steel, and 30 percent in the manufacture of woven goods.[4] A solution to Japan's trade predicament would require drastic measures.

Both national and regional business groups launched campaigns to alter the government's passive trade policies. The regional bodies included chambers of commerce, trade councils, and federations of local trade associations. Their overt tactics took the form of publicizing formal proposals and sending them directly to government officials. In 1921 the Osaka Trade Council, for example, distributed its suggestions to all prefectural governors, mayors of large cities, and officials of the national government, as well as presidents of major companies.[5] More often, organizations targeted cabinet ministers whose authority touched on trade matters. In the early 1920s the Ministry of Agriculture and Commerce and the Ministry of Finance received most of the petitions.

Several themes dominated the many plans offered in 1921 and 1922. They agreed that Japan faced a crisis. The Japan Trade Council said that the nation had entered a "new competitive era" in trade. The National Federation of Chambers of Commerce argued that Japan had to help itself, because the rest of the industrial world was struggling too. Creating new markets would require great efforts and substantial investments overseas.[6]

Many of the groups conceded that businessmen had to change their ways. Intoxicated with wartime prosperity, executives had become too complacent and ill-prepared to meet ferocious competition from the Western powers. The Japan Trade Council argued that only the "self-control of capitalists and businessmen" in lowering profits could solve the trade crisis. The National Federation of Chambers called for "reducing the standards of profit for capital" in order to lower the prices of goods.[7] The times demanded sacrifices to restore the nation's economic health.

Not surprisingly, groups debated bitterly over who had sinned the most. The Tokyo Federation of Business Associations, which comprised producers' associations (dōgyō kumiai) within the city, complained that visions of hefty profits had led exporters to flood foreign markets with "crude goods." Producers should try to bypass professional traders. The Japan Trade Council, composed of firms engaged in overseas trade, countered that during the war "manufacturers fell into the evil of a standard of greed." Citing the need to increase the volume of production, the council urged producers to switch to a standard of "thin profit and many sales." The Osaka Trade Council recommended stronger safeguards to prevent agreements among producers to limit production and maintain high prices. In addition, national profit controls would help: producers should be forced to "determine a proper profit and dividend [rate] and apply any surplus to the capital of the enterprise." The National Federation of Chambers sagely apportioned blame to all sectors: manufacturers had to avoid raising prices by artificial means, while "traders" had to curb their tendency to swamp markets with cheap goods to make a quick yen.[8] Everyone would have to accept less profit to make the nation's goods competitive.

A general conviction emerged that excessive competition, especially among small firms, hurt the economy as a whole. The early twentieth century had seen the rise of large, powerful combines or zaibatsu, such as the Mitsui, Mitsubishi, Sumitomo, and Yasuda companies. Still, factories of less than one hundred workers employed the majority of the work force and produced in aggregate well over one-half of the nation's industrial output. These firms manufactured many of the nation's exports. With few resources to withstand periods of slow sales, the small companies competed fiercely by slashing prices on exports. They flooded foreign markets with shoddy products that ruined the reputation of Japan's goods abroad. To expand exports, the small companies had to raise the quality of their goods to match Western ones while maintaining low prices.

Businessmen concurred that less competition and increased cooperation among manufacturers and exporters would help. Noting the prevalence of small household firms, the Nagoya Chamber of Commerce declared that industry must progress to the state of a "modern production organization" through the increased use of machines. The government should encourage mergers among companies within the same industry to encourage large-scale production and to regulate supply and demand. The Kōbe chamber championed enhancing the "efficiency of production," through the "unification of each type of business," and the "organization of production and sales associations." The Osaka chamber agreed that all companies involved in foreign trade should work together to find new markets. Proclaiming that "Japan must establish thorough policies and national principles" for trade, the Nagasaki chamber announced its agenda for reforms. These included the "reform of industrial organization" through mergers of producers, the creation of manufacturers' and exporters' associations, a structure to provide liaison between the two types of associations, and long-term financing for exporters. The National Federation of Chambers favored improving the quality of goods by "changing the small-scale factory system and moving to the management of large-scale factories." Forming "cooperative sales organs" and "links of associations for the export of goods" would prevent "improper competition among exporters." The Japan Trade Council believed that mergers of small firms and a "system of cooperative sales" would bring greater productivity. The Tokyo Federation of Business Associations hoped that joint sales organs created by manufacturers would allow them to keep prices down by eliminating the traders' profit.[9]

The business community expected help from the government too. Administrative changes would allow officials to concentrate more on trade issues. The Osaka Chamber of Commerce proposed a joint government-civilian agency to investigate trade problems and to collect information on foreign markets. The National Federation of Chambers recommended establishment of a new trade bureau to unify the supervision of trade matters that the Ministry of Finance and the Ministry of Agriculture and Commerce handled separately. A special civilian organ staffed by businessmen would consult on trade policy.[10] Financial aid for exports constituted another pressing issue. The Osaka Trade Council, the Osaka Chamber of Commerce, the Japan Trade Council, and the National Federation of Chambers all wanted the government to provide low interest loans to companies that exported goods. In particular, these firms needed "foreign exchange loans" to finance the shipment of products overseas. The Japan Trade Council proposed that exporters form associations for the purpose of receiving special financing from the government.[11] All of these organizations believed that the government had to take a more active role in trade policy.

This belief strengthened as the Japanese perceived that they lagged behind other nations in encouraging trade. The press in Japan publicized how new trade legislation in Europe and the United States, such as the British Trade Facilities Act of 1921 and the American Edge Act of 1919, aided exporters. In May 1921 the Nagoya Chamber of Commerce enviously summarized the results of a special survey of rivals' tactics. The British government had begun to guarantee promissory notes issued by exporters to banks. The Edge Act permitted the formation of federally chartered American banks to specialize in financing exports. In Germany companies had created federations to "respond to [the situation of] economic war with foreign nations by following a national policy and taking temporary measures necessary to advance." The National Federation of Chambers claimed that the British government spent 2,600 pounds each year to promote trade and, presumably referring to the Webb-Pomerene Act of 1918, noted that the United States had exempted export associations from antitrust legislation. Depicting the American government as continuously plotting export strategy with bankers and industrialists, the Japan Trade Council suggested that the policies of "first class exporting" nations deserved attention. The National Federation concluded that "all governments but Japan's" encouraged trade.[12] Dan Takuma's trip to America and Europe in 1922 prompted him to warn that "each nation in Europe was steadily presenting results in the rebuilding of [their] postwar economies" and that "preparation of our industrial world for the worsening of competition with other nations that can be predicted from now on is an urgent [concern]." Envisioning a national economic mobilization for trade, he called on leaders of the nation to "arouse the spirit of the people" to meet the challenge.[13]

Despite the *zaikai*'s own pleas for special subsidies and financing, it insisted that the government trim the rest of the national budget. Such frugality and sacrifice would set a good example for the private sector, prevent rises in taxes, keep fees low for transporting goods on the national railroads, and reduce prices through a general contraction of currency. Dan emphasized that Japan must imitate the West in cutting the national budget and taxes through curbing the expansion of "national defense." The Japan Trade Council pinpointed military expenses, which consumed 50 percent of the government's expenditures, as the fattest target. To businessmen, security issues paled in importance in comparison with the crisis in foreign trade. Their attitudes toward the Soviet Union revealed their priorities. In 1918 Japan had sent forces to Siberia as part of a joint expedition with the United States. Three years later some 70,000 Japanese troops still occupied parts of the territory in an apparent effort to encourage resistance to the Bolsheviks. Meanwhile, the National Federation of Chambers of Commerce clamored for an immediate restoration of trade with the Soviets.[14]

Finally, business leaders believed that the public at large must contribute to making Japan's exports competitive. Dan recommended that while executives learned to improve efficiency, all Japanese would have to eliminate luxuries and "wasted expenses." In August 1922 the Tokyo Chamber of Commerce decided to sponsor a series of "economy days." A special committee deliberated to devise ways to remind citizens twice a month to economize on purchases in order to lower the prices of goods in general.[15] Although no evidence exists to suggest that this campaign had any effect, the effort suggests the extent of executives' fears about trends in foreign trade.

The Ministry of Agriculture and Commerce, which in 1921 had officially solicited opinions on trade matters from business groups, responded to these proposals in several ways. Officials from the Ministries of Commerce, Finance, Foreign Affairs, and Communications began joint discussions on trade policy. By April they started to draft new legislation. The investigation of foreign models focused attention on the role of German cartels in raising productivity and reducing unnecessary competition. Meanwhile, officials promised to continue extensive consultations with private business groups.[16]

They persisted in demanding new government policies. In 1923, for example, Fujiyama Raita, president of the Tokyo Chamber of Commerce, argued that Japan could prosper only through the restructuring of inefficient small-scale enterprises. The Tokyo Federation of Business Associations emphasized the need for export associations and for syndicates in each industry to cooperate in purchasing raw materials abroad. The Tokyo Chamber of Commerce endorsed the general ideas of merging enterprises, increasing efficiency, and "reforming the organization of production." The chamber wanted a special agency for financing trade along with a trade bureau. Eliminating the income tax on profits from exports and overseas operations and cultivating a "love" for Japanese products at home to suppress imports would also help correct the trade deficit. In a special meeting with an official from the Ministry of Commerce, the Kōbe chamber recommended revisions of the Trade Association Law, presumably to increase the powers of local associations of businesses in various industries.[17]

A major economic council that convened in the spring of 1924 affirmed the need for changes. Under the direction of Premier Katō Takaaki the Imperial Economic Conference assembled over one hundred delegates from business and government to debate pressing economic issues. Committees in the trade section comprised leaders of the largest chambers of commerce and executives of major companies. Their discussions stressed the need for cooperation among exporting firms, increased efficiency of production through mergers of firms, and government subsidies for exports. Takigawa Gisuke of the Kōbe chamber argued that associations of small companies had to instill the "morality" of averting excessive competition among businessmen. As Fujiyama Raita noted, all participants agreed that the government should make low-interest loans available for exporters. The issue of whether such aid should focus on particular markets and products with the greatest potential for growth sparked a lot of debate. Many discussants favored such a targeting policy. The idea of increasing exports to China through special finance organs drew some support. Still, grave doubts emerged about this kind of approach. Isaka Takashi of the Yokohama Chamber of Commerce countered that fair judgments on which markets or goods would receive special treatment would prove too difficult. The disagreement led to a decision not to favor certain exports or markets.[18]

Participants had little trouble agreeing on the need for easier access to capital. Fujiyama, Isaka, Kodama Ichizō of the Tōyō Cotton Company, and Yukawa Kankichi of the Sumitomo Bank all suggested ways for the nation to free funds for investment in private businesses. The government could cut its spending, discourage private consumption, "reduce current private enterprises" through mergers, and entice foreign investment. Kaneko Naokichi of the Suzuki Trading Company favored legislation to encourage exports through special financing.[19]

Officials in the Commerce Ministry seemed sympathetic to these proposals. In January 1923 the head of the Trade Bureau declared the need to "aid in a pragmatic way joint councils in each industrial trade sector in order to promote mutual benefits [among companies]." By early 1924 the ministry was studying proposals for merging enterprises, increasing productivity, providing capital for export ventures, and granting tax breaks for exporters. Despite some signs that the Ministry of Finance abhorred the prospect of potential tax losses, commerce officials forged ahead. In August they consulted extensively with business groups in the Tokyo and Osaka areas to gauge reactions to plans of the Commercial Affairs Bureau for giving subsidies to groups of exporters. Meanwhile, the Industrial Affairs Bureau focused on a "reform of industrial organization" among manufacturers to promote the efficient production of high quality goods.[20]

By early October the ministry's plans had crystalized. Minister Takahashi Korekiyo would submit legislation to permit the creation of foreign trade associations that the government would aid in various ways. It would fund studies of foreign markets and help finance exports. Imitating British policy, the government would guarantee 70 percent of the credit that private banks would extend to members of the new associations of exporters. Regional industrial associations could form to inspect manufactured goods and to lower production costs through sharing information and facilities.[21]

These ideas met fierce resistance within the government bureaucracy. In particular, the Finance Ministry fretted about funding the special guarantees and subsidies. By late November it had voiced strong opposition to any special financing for the export associations. Not until January 21, 1925, did the Ministries of Commerce and Finance reach an accord on the new laws. The latter even hesitated to grant to the new associations the exemption from income and business taxes that the old trade associations had enjoyed. After cabinet approval on January 31, the Diet began its consideration of the bills.[22]

By the end of February the Diet had passed both the Export Association Law and the Important Export Industry Association Law. Several critics in the Lower House lamented the lack of financial help for exporters. Kanemitsu Tsuneo, president of the Chiyoda Trust Company and the Taishō Life Insurance Company, wanted Japan to copy British policy by creating a credit bureau for exports. Reminding his audience that the government had issued bonds to help the residents of Tokyo recover from the devastating earthquake of 1923, he asserted that the nation had an even greater stake in a healthy balance of trade. Takahashi, as the minister of commerce, defended the legislation by contending that excess competition posed the greatest threat to exporters. When other politicians complained that only a return to the gold standard could solve the trade imbalance, Takahashi replied that Japan had to move cautiously on that issue. The nation, for example, lacked the vast reserves of foreign exchange that had recently enabled Great Britain to resume free trade in gold.[23] Some members of the House of Peers protested the authority granted to each industrial association to compel nonmembers to comply with its policies. Although the legislation fell short of the expectations of many business leaders and Diet members, they accepted the bills as the most feasible alternatives at the time. Finance Minister Hamaguchi even made a small concession in permitting the Bank of Japan to discount promissory notes for purchasing foreign exchange issued by members of the new export or industrial associations.[24]

The Export Association Law permitted the formation of export groups by businessmen who sold similar products overseas or who sold different goods to the same foreign market. One-half of potential members had to agree to join an association, and it had to receive approval from the Ministry of Commerce. These groups could provide cooperative facilities for the storage and wrapping of exports and for the study and development of new markets. An association could also enact "limits of operation to correct obstructions in members' operations"; these could include limits on production and the regulation of minimum prices through cooperative sales arrangements for a particular market.[25]

Industrial associations had a similar structure and purpose. Created by manufacturers of similar goods for export, they would insure quality by inspecting both the facilities for manufacturing and the final products. An association could arrange for members to share production equipment and to cooperate in sales, hence allowing joint controls on the production of goods by members and on the prices of those goods. Organizing a group required agreement from two-thirds of possible members in a region and permission from the ministry. It could also force nonmembers to comply with the decisions of an association. Finally, the industrial associations could form national federations to help carry out their goals.[26]

Although Japan's export woes continued, these two laws marked an important turning point in trade policy. Chalmers Johnson has argued that they opened the way for creating cartels that soon became major instruments of economic policy for combating recessions and carrying out rationalization programs. Certainly the laws extended for the first time a blend of government supervision and companies' self-control to industrial groups organized on a national scale. These laws also reflected the growing influence of the *zaikai*. Johnson has ascribed responsibility for the legislation to "Yoshino [Shinji] and his colleagues in MAC [the Ministry of Agriculture and Commerce]."[27] However, the campaign of various business groups for changes in trade policy commenced well before the ministry considered major reforms in trade policy and persisted throughout the early 1920s. The success of the Finance Ministry in thwarting a total victory showed the power of bureaucratic rivalries, but the business community grew even more determined to influence economic policies.

The Japan Economic Federation immediately expressed its dissatisfaction with the legislation. Prior to January, the group's policy research committees had concentrated on budgetary and tax problems, and it had not commented publicly on the issue of encouraging cartels. The only hint of concern for industrial reorganization had appeared in a major report of 1922 that urged the government to take the initiative in "studying policies appropriate to planning an increase in productive capability and regulating the supply and demand of goods." Suddenly, on January 27, 1925, just as the Ministries of Commerce and Finance submitted the new trade laws without new major funding, the

Economic Federation announced the creation of a new committee to study trade policies. It included Ishii Akira of N.Y.K., Ikeda Seihin of the Mitsui Bank, Kadono Chokyūrō of the Ōkura Trading Company, and Inoue Junnosuke. Over the next month it collected information and testimony from a variety of government ministries and business leaders.[28]

When the Diet finished its deliberations in late February, the federation was ready to distribute the conclusions of its study to government officials. The group suggested two changes in the laws. Forming an export association should require the assent of two-thirds of potential members, instead of one-half. More importantly, firms that exported goods should receive financial incentives: low interest loans, an insurance system for specific sales overseas, reduced levies on imported raw materials used in exports, and discounts on railroad fees for their products.[29] The federation would champion these goals for the rest of the decade.

CONSIDERING A RETURN TO THE GOLD STANDARD

As business leaders groped for means of erasing the nagging trade deficit, their attention centered on restoring the gold standard. Having adopted it first in 1897, Japan had abandoned it twenty years later during World War I. In doing so, Japan followed the example of many European nations and of the United States, which halted exports of gold. Even though the American government resumed free trade in gold soon after the war ended, Japan hesitated to reinstate a convertible currency. In 1922 an International Economic Conference held in Genoa and sponsored by the League of Nations clearly expressed the conviction of Western governments by resolving that all nations should adopt the gold standard. Feeling pressure to conform once more to trends among the major powers of the world and to take advantage of a rising exchange rate, Finance Minister Ichiki Otohiko considered ending the embargo on gold.[30] The issue touched off a heated debate.

Mutō Sanji, a Keiō University graduate who had built the Kanegafuchi Company into Japan's largest cotton spinning enterprise, emerged as the most strident advocate of the gold standard. Only potent medicine like this could cure the sick economy; there should be no delay. He reasoned that removing the embargo on gold would bring deflation, which along with cuts in government expenses and interest rates would lower the prices of Japanese products.

This would help domestic consumers and spur exports.[31] Mutō believed fervently in the virtues of small government. Depicting government as the "greatest waster" of capital, he thought that channeling more capital into the private sector through lower taxes and expanding the freedom of entrepreneurs would bring prosperity. Free trade in gold would allow the economy to regulate itself in a natural way. This position placed Mutō at odds with the major business groups that favored export subsidies and increased cooperation between officials and executives in trade policy.

Mutō never sought influence in these organizations. Although he headed the Japan Federation of Business Associations, a loose grouping of *dōgyō kumiai* from all over the nation, he refused to join the Japan Economic Federation because of the dominant role of Inoue Junnosuke. Mutō thought that Inoue, who had always worked for the government, should not meddle in the affairs of private companies. Mutō also predicted that a strong lobby, such as the Economic Federation, would increase the regrettable tendency of Japanese businessmen to rely on the government for solutions to economic problems.[32] By 1923 Mutō had gained considerable national attention by speaking out often on the issue of the gold standard, publicly calling for the impeachment of Inoue as director of the Bank of Japan, and forming a political party, the Business Association (Jitsugyō Dōshikai).

This party wanted to cleanse the political world of professional politicians who, ignorant of Mutō's insights into basic economic principles, strived only to protect their political interests. The initial platform argued that because of the stagnating economy and unbalanced foreign trade, Japan faced a crisis even more momentous than those caused by the earlier wars with China and Russia; Japan was losing an economic war. The remedy had to come from reduced government expenses, less government intervention in the economy, and fewer taxes.[33] In the election of 1923, eleven of thirty candidates from the Business Association won election to the Diet.

The miniscule size of the party did not dampen Mutō's enthusiasm. As the Business Association quickly gained a reputation as a staunch advocate of the gold standard,[34] Mutō consistently censured the timidity of the Finance Ministry from the floor of the Diet. Meanwhile his political program for paring government profligacy grew more ambitious. He proposed streamlining the military by combining the Ministries of the Navy and Army into a single defense ministry. Because the government was becoming "communistic," it should terminate its ownership of all industries, including railroads and the Yawata Iron Works.[35]

Mutō's *bête noire*, Inoue Junnosuke, also wanted to sweep away the embargo on gold, because the resulting deflation would slash the prices of goods. He pointed out that if one set the index for Japanese prices in 1913 at 100, they had now reached 200, while American prices lagged at 144 and England's at 166. Japan also suffered from comparatively high interest rates because the supply of capital at home was lessened by the use of gold reserves—built up and stored abroad during the world war—to pay for extra imports. Lowering the prices of goods and interest rates would require the government, companies, and the public at large to cut their consumption of goods. To Inoue, this task posed a stern test of national character for the Japanese to sacrifice and discipline themselves for the nation's sake. He argued, "To correct the habits of laziness, waste, recklessness, and speculation that have been brewed in the past five years, we must become aware of much suffering." He disdained those who wanted to avoid this economic pain through "makeshift policies," "policies to turn the depression around," "positive industrial policies," and "prevention of imports."[36] These measures would only distract citizens from their proper economic duties.

By 1923 Inoue openly asserted that a healthy foreign trade demanded a gold standard, because it was "natural" and would bring economic stability. The manipulation of a nation's exchange rate through the use of overseas gold reserves—a tactic that some observers wanted Japan to adopt—was both impossible and "improper." A stable rate would help businessmen forecast future trends in foreign trade and devise successful strategies. The ability of individual politicians or governments to alter the value of a currency at will would complicate companies' long-term planning and inhibit trade. The exchange rate, Inoue concluded, was better left to "nature," determined solely by the balance of trade.[37]

Few businessmen shared the enthusiasm of Mutō and Inoue for the gold standard. Kadono Chokyūrō of the Ōkura Trading Company, Takigawa Gisuke of the Kōbe Chamber of Commerce, and Kodama Ichizō of the Tōyō Cotton Company supported immediate enactment with no hesitation. Others harbored serious doubts. Yatsushiro Norihiko of the Sumitomo Bank wondered whether the weak economy would permit all of the expected benefits of the gold standard—generally lower prices and hence increased exports—to occur. Itō

Takenosuke of the Itō Chū Trading firm asked rhetorically, "Can this drastic treatment really be endured by the [Japanese] economic world that is in the situation of a sick person?" Itō thought that the nation should first try to solve the problem of high prices by somehow contracting its currency and increasing production. Miyajima Seijirō of the Nisshin Spinning Company worried that a strong yen could lower the prices of imports that might threaten new and fragile industries now protected by tariffs. Kobayashi Ichizō, president of the Tokyo Electric Light Company, straddled the fence. The predictions by both sides—that a convertible currency would court economic disaster or usher in prosperity—left him unsure of what the future would hold. Most people agreed with Mutō Sanji's commonsensical theory, but "there was a deep logic regarding its not being implemented." Kobayashi pointed out that under the gold standard before 1917 Japan had regularly maintained an annual deficit in foreign trade.[38]

Some businessmen sought a compromise path: adoption of the gold standard under certain conditions. Kushida Manzō of the Mitsubishi Bank and Fujiwara Ginjirō of the Ōji Paper Company each insisted that the exchange rate should reach its old parity of fifty dollars per hundred yen before the embargo ended. Even so, Fujiwara admitted that the resulting deflation would damage the economy. Special measures, such as a steep tax cut, were needed to prevent a downturn in business activity.[39]

Finance Minister Ichiki consulted with leaders of the *zaikai* at his home in early September 1922.[40] Backed by a representative from the Ministry of Agriculture and Commerce, Mutō Sanji advocated the gold standard. Reminding others that it alone could deflate the high prices that had accompanied the wartime expansion of currency, he warned that keeping a weak yen would obstruct the rise of new industries by making imported raw materials and machinery more expensive. If the surplus of imports persisted, Japan would soon exhaust its overseas stores of specie. When those ran out, the nation would face the trauma of an abrupt curtailment of its imports. Ōyama Kenzō from the Sanjū-yon Bank in Osaka countered that a gradual lessening of public and private consumption could suppress the prices of goods without risking the disruption of returning to free trade in gold.

Most of the participants sought the middle ground. Fuji Spinning Company's Wada Tōyōji supported Mutō, while the Daihyaku Bank's Ikeda Kenzō sided with Ōyama. The two delegates from the Bank of Japan, Inoue Junnosuke and Kimura Seishirō, avoided active participation in the debate. The others—Iwai Katsujirō, a trader who headed his own firm, Iwai Shoten; Kimura Kusuyata from the Mitsubishi zaibatsu; Kodama Kenji from the Yokohama Specie Bank; Hara Tomitarō, a prominent businessman from Yokohama who specialized in trading raw silk; and Dan Takuma—favored implementing the gold standard only under special conditions or after a delay. Ending without any clear statement on lifting the embargo on gold, the conference signaled a lack of consensus.

In keeping with the doubts registered by these business leaders, Ichiki announced on September 16 that the unsettled financial situation did not bode well for permitting free trade in gold. Later, even Hamaguchi Osachi, a bitter critic of Ichiki's decision, stalled on enacting the gold standard after becoming finance minister in 1924. When Mutō grilled Hamaguchi in the Diet about this betrayal of his earlier convictions, he affirmed the need for preconditions, such as a high exchange rate, to prevent economic turmoil when the embargo ended. Unfortunately, the rebuilding of Tokyo after the Kantō earthquake of 1923 had caused massive amounts of imports that worsened the balance of trade and drove the exchange rate to a new low of \$41.50/100 yen.[41]

Discussions among government officials and business leaders in the spring of 1924 had also revealed continuing discord over managing Japan's currency. The Imperial Economic Conference created a finance section for the specific purpose of studying the gold standard and the exchange rate. Ikeda Seihin from the largest bank, Mitsui, and Gō Seinosuke of the Japan Economic Federation favored rapid enactment, as did Mitsubishi Bank's Kushida Manzō, who had dropped his previous qualms. Other prominent bankers, though, objected. These included representatives from the two next largest zaibatsu banks, Yukawa Kankichi of the Sumitomo Bank and Yūki Toyotarō of the Yasuda Bank, along with Sasaki Yūnosuke of the Daiichi Bank. They argued that the exchange rate had to stabilize at a high level before the embargo could end. A low rate would make Japan's gold reserves available to foreigners at bargain-basement prices, and the nation would soon find its stores of the precious metal depleted. The section's report recommended preparing for free trade in gold by reducing government and private consumption, reforming the organization of industry, suppressing imports, and developing exports. A special government-business committee should supervise the use of specie to pay for foreign goods and restrict such payments in order to slow the drain of overseas reserves. Finally, the government should institute the gold standard only when it would not "have unusual influence on the general business community."[42]

In contrast to the energetic campaign for industrial restructuring and aid for exports, business organizations did not lobby intensively for the gold standard in the early 1920s. Among the major chambers of commerce, only the Kōbe branch issued a clear call for a convertible currency. Most other groups, including the Japan Economic Federation, did not comment on the issue. Just before the Imperial Economic Conference, the Tokyo chamber argued against the gold standard by noting that it would increase imports. A depression would follow and "one cannot judge what kind of chaos [the economy] would fall into." The government should wait for a more propitious time. The National Federation of Clearinghouses also counseled patience: "[We] must expect not to miss the appropriate time to break the embargo on exports of gold." Meanwhile, austerity in the government's budget and the attainment of a high exchange rate would help prepare for eventual free trade in gold.[43]

By the mid-1920s business opinion remained badly splintered over the gold standard. One could find supporters and opponents in each major sector—for example, in both banking and textile manufacturing. Leaders of the various zaibatsu expressed differing opinions, and sometimes even executives of the same combine could not agree. The government backed away from decisive action as long as this dissension persisted.

THE CAMPAIGN FOR CARTELS AND AID FOR EXPORTS

While the movement to reinstate the gold standard languished, the consensus regarding the need for cartels and special assistance for exports intensified. Imaizumi Kiichirō, a steel executive and member of the Diet, explained the need for industrial cartels in 1924. He argued that Japan should follow the example of the "interest agreements" (*rigai kyōyaku*) that companies had formed in postwar Germany. These "alliances" (*dōmei*) had allowed German companies to cooperate in entering overseas markets and had encouraged mergers. The iron and steel industry, for example, had flourished, even though the peace settlement had stripped from Germany's control the major iron-ore producing area of Alsace-Lorraine and territories that contained much of the nation's iron-making capacity.[44]

Impressed by Germany's success in overcoming a lack of critical raw materials, Imaizumi thought that Japan should imitate its policies. Japanese industrial leaders, like their German counterparts, should take the initiative in proposing and campaigning for appropriate legislation. "World economic competition" demanded such a "resolute reform." As the technological pioneer Ōkōchi Masatoshi pointed out, protectionist policies provided the only alternative and these would damage the long-term prospects of the economy. If tariffs insulated companies from outside competition, Japanese industry "could not be active as a world industry."[45] By creating cartels Japan would replicate the efficient industrial organization of her competitors.

Nakajima Kumakichi reached similar conclusions. His varied experiences as a top executive of the Furukawa combine, an active leader of the Japan Economic Federation, and a member of the House of Peers gave him a broad perspective. Taking a sweeping view of recent trends in world politics, he concluded that in each industrial nation labor unions had garnered public support by attacking inequitable and inefficient aspects of the capitalist system. Hence, the people had demanded more forceful action by the state. Even in England, long a bastion of the values of individual freedom, citizens looked to the government to solve economic problems. Similarly, the future would bring more "meaningful intervention of the state" in the Japanese economy.[46]

The business community had to organize in self-defense. Nakajima cautioned that increased state interference could wreak havoc, that politics "has a power that [we] must fear." Inexperienced officials with only a "simple knowledge" could draft laws, and the Diet could pass them just to suit the "mentality of the masses." Thus, the chambers of commerce, the Japan Industrial Club, and the Economic Federation had to try harder to influence policy. Nakajima cited as his favorite model the National Association of Manufacturers in the United States. Its administrative bureau in Washington, D.C., had proved effective in advocating policies and blocking hostile legislation in the Congress. By noting that the group had even helped William Howard Taft defeat William Jennings Bryan for the presidency in 1908, Nakajima implied that Japanese businessmen had to become just as intrusive in the national politics of Japan.[47]

Nakajima believed that businessmen should not seek political power for the purpose of exploiting society. Opponents of free enterprise had perceptive criticisms that should inspire the creation of a "new era" of capitalism. "Scientific methods of organization" should insure products of good quality at reasonable prices for the ordinary consumer: "Now it is recognized that unchecked competition may not certainly be to the advantage of society in general." Nakajima advocated the national "regulation and distribution of production." Executives should strive to

> have the goal of avoiding disadvantageous competition in the same industry; merge and arrange operations together through certain means; at least through the means of trade associations limit the productive power of each industry; plan the adjustment of general supply and demand; prevent improper fluctuations in prices and support them in a moderate range; of course consult and make policy together; lighten the burden of capital for enterprises; eliminate waste in production; harmonize the general relationship of production and demand to an appropriate degree; and establish means to make products inexpensive.[48]

Trends at home and abroad suggested that cooperation within the national economy rather than competition would forge the new era of capitalism.

In September 1926 the first national conference to focus on foreign trade provided ample opportunities for business leaders to present their views to government officials. The meeting, which centered on issues related to trade with the South Seas (*Nan'yō*), lasted for ten days. It attracted sixty-eight officials as well as delegates from six chambers of commerce and fifty-three business groups and private companies.[49]

Several individual companies trumpeted the benefits of cartels. A position paper prepared for the conference by a member of Nakajima's combine, Furukawa Electrical Industries, offered a blunt proposal for "organizations at home and abroad similar to offensive and defensive federations." The company realized that critics would assail cartels in major industries as a means to monopolize profits and jack up prices "as if [we] are falling into delusions similar to the evils of trusts in America." Still, cartels in other nations had played a crucial role in nurturing new industries. The British cartel of electrical equipment manufacturers had helped that sector to thrive. "Now, in developing and expanding markets abroad, [the Japanese had to] abandon convention and [take] a national [perspective]." With cartels, citizens could "expect the stabilization of the industrial world because those [companies] in the same industry [would] plan together a great combination of organizations with a spirit of coexistence and coprosperity. On the other hand the state [would] protect and encourage this and simultaneously with the reform of industrial organizations [would] promote opportunities for the expansion of exports." Citing the problems of unproductive strife among producers, the huge Mitsui Trading Company also recommended associations of manufacturers to spur cooperation. "If manufacturers form[ed] associations and [if each industry] export[ed] through one channel, trade in Japanese goods could see a completely new situation."[50]

The question of governmental aid for exports attracted much comment. Furukawa Industries, citing British and German policies, favored an insurance system for exports and special "export banks" to provide capital. Mitsui Trading claimed that because banks in Germany had played a major role in increasing foreign trade prior to the world war, special agency banks (*kikan ginkō*) should form to advise overseas enterprises and help finance them.[51] The Osaka and Tokyo chambers of commerce pointed out "the need to establish a government-run system to insure credit for exports following the examples of Britain and Germany" because of the "danger that customers abroad will not be able to pay." The six largest chambers together recommended that the government assemble "powerful industrialists" to create a "South Seas company" along with entirely new "finance organs" to fund and carry out trade with the region. The chambers thought the government should share the risks of investing in Southeast Asia and the Pacific islands and expanding new markets there.[52]

Although the trade conference did not even try to reach any conclusions on trade policies, several ideas pervaded the discussions. Expressing optimism about the future of Japanese exports, many participants in the export section echoed the need for the government's help. Some wanted a stricter inspection of textile products and sundry goods destined for export, while others favored the promotion of cartels for manufacturers of electrical machinery. The Mitsubishi Trading Company thought officials should encourage a spirit of "fair play" among competitors to guarantee a plentiful supply of high quality exports at inexpensive prices.[53] One reporter summarized the conference's findings by observing that increased exports to a relatively new market, such as the South Seas area, required closer collaboration among firms within the different industrial sectors, lower costs for Japanese products, and more plentiful long-term financing to encourage selling on credit.[54]

The next few years saw major business groups insist that cartels held the key to the nation's economic health and potential for export growth. In 1927 the Japan Economic Federation completed a major report, "A Draft Regarding the Correction of Obstacles (*jihei*) to Japan's Industrial World." Declaring that the most urgent task was to "eliminate reckless and foolish competition born from the duplication of enterprises," the draft praised the Japan Spinners Association as a model cartel. "One can say that while many Japanese industries have suffered from the evils of reckless competition as described above, only the spinning industry, with good management of a cooperative organ and smooth control among member companies, has been building a strong base of operations. [This example] more than proves the need for such control." Accordingly, the federation wanted an "organ of control and association among businessmen in [each] industry for [ensuring] the rational regulation of production and the stability of market prices." Financial institutions should exercise prudence while investing in new manufacturing facilities to avoid the "frequent occurrence of imitative enterprises."[55] Tightly run cartels should dominate the economy.

The Tokyo Chamber of Commerce prepared an extensive set of recommendations on trade policy. These were submitted to a special government-business conference, the Council on Commerce and Industry (Shōkō Shingi-kai), that convened between 1927 and 1929. Spotlighting over-production as a major problem, the chamber proposed more intensive collaboration between government officials and business executives. The former would gather accurate statistics on the production of important goods and the anticipated demand for them, while the latter would use these data to create long-term plans. This approach would embody a fruitful combination of the "leading attitude of the government and the rational attitude of businessmen."[56] Encouraging associations and federations of companies to join together in purchasing raw materials and machines, selling finished products, and raising capital would lower the costs of production. To this end, a new industrial association law should permit participation by large firms.[57] Close collaboration in each industry would also boost sales of exports. Careful calculations of future foreign demand could prevent sudden and painful cuts in factory operations and induce the manufacture of exports to concentrate in the most efficient factories. Trade associations that would bring together manufacturers and exporters, both large and small, could most effectively analyze new markets, advertise products, and design new exports.[58]

The Tokyo chamber desired important changes in the government's trade administration. One bureau should supervise all trade matters as opposed to the current division of authority among five different ministries. Moreover, the Japan Chamber of Commerce, which a law of 1928 recognized as a permanent body representing all chambers, should guide the private sector's participation in a national trade policy. With branches all over the country, the national chamber's duties would range from organizing exhibitions of Japanese goods abroad and overseeing the inspection of exports to coordinating the activities of trade, export, and industrial associations.[59]

The idea of both streamlining government trade offices and reinforcing their contacts with private business groups quickly gained support. In 1927 the Council on Commerce and Industry asked the Japan Trade Council for its opinion on ways to revive the economy. The council underlined the need to unify the organs that administered foreign trade, rationalize industrial production, and correct "defects in industrial organization" in regard to foreign trade.[60] In 1929 the Japan Chamber of Commerce submitted an elaborate plan featuring a centralized trade structure that would have branches in each prefecture and major metropolitan area. The chambers of commerce would provide the sinews of this body. "Each chamber should spur the interest of related businessmen in the reform of [industrial] organization and management." Then, "under the unification (*itchi*) of government and business, [we] would pursue especially detailed studies of exports that are important now and which have prospects of future growth and establish policies regarding the production and revival of exports." The chambers would "respect mutual trust among businessmen in the same industry and encourage each related group to prohibit actions that obstruct deals [for foreign trade] and to cooperate closely in the development of new markets from a national viewpoint. When necessary, the chambers would more aggressively take effective measures to encourage cooperation and settle disputes."[61] The national control of trade would arise from the collaboration of government officials and the chambers.

BLUEPRINTS FOR NEW ECONOMIC POLICIES

On May 23, 1927, the government took a major step toward revamping its economic policies by organizing the Council on Commerce and Industry. Its creation followed a terrifying economic shock, the financial panic of April 1927. The failure of the Suzuki Trading Company, which had borrowed heavily from the Japanese Bank of Taiwan, had sparked a run on domestic deposits. The Bank of Japan's massive transfusion of new funds to banks and the hasty imposition of a moratorium on financial transactions brought the situation under control. The near catastrophe dramatized the underlying weakness of the economy and reinforced demands for fundamental changes.

As part of the new Seiyūkai cabinet that assumed power in May, Minister of Commerce and Industry Nakahashi Tokugorō[62] launched the council to assess the entire economic situation. A former bureaucrat, executive, and Diet politician, he gave participants a broad mandate while alluding to the need to avoid new expenditures. People held, he said, too many expectations toward government. It could help industry most effectively through indirect aid, by "eliminating barriers to industrial development." Four committees formed, with each studying one of the following topics: facilities for industrial recovery, facilities for heavy industry, policies for the improvement of productivity, and the reform of industrial administration. When the rival Minseitō assumed power in the summer of 1929, several additional committees were created to discuss industrial rationalization and supplies of fuel and energy. Over the next two years a total of forty-three officials and business leaders discussed all the above issues with the aim of making specific proposals on how to strengthen the economy.[63]

The few remaining records of committee meetings from this council indicate that both prominent businessmen and officials assumed that Japan's new industries needed special protection. For the soda ash industry, for example, Dan Takuma, Ōkōchi Masatoshi, and Kimura Kusuyata each favored subsidies to allow Japanese companies to compete with European imports. When Sakatani Yoshirō, a retired Finance Ministry official, argued for a less overt form of aid to avert criticism from foreign competitors, Dan and Kimura insisted on direct payments to companies.[64] Similarly, Dan and others favored giving subsidies and protection to firms that produced artificial salt, an important product for the developing dyestuff industry that was battered by German competition.[65]

Executives evinced great enthusiasm for industrial rationalization to improve efficiency. Confident that private ownership could accomplish this goal best, they urged the government to give up all of its factories. In one meeting, Dan, Gō Seinosuke, Sakurai Gunnosuke, and Yukawa Kankichi of the Sumitomo Bank even castigated attempts by the Commerce Ministry to justify continued government management of the Senjū factory that produced woollen goods for the army. Sakurai argued too that the government should open the telephone industry, a government monopoly, to competition from private companies. The executives agreed that efficiency required mergers of companies in all sectors except for the most successful, such as the manufacture of textiles and glass. Consolidation could benefit large companies as well as small enterprises. Gō, for example, chided the giant combines, Mitsui and Mitsubishi, for failing to combine their subsidiaries in the "electric industry." Participants wanted to create a national committee on rationalization that would publicize and coordinate efforts at eliminating waste in every factory.[66]

The final recommendations of the Council on Commerce and Industry echoed these sentiments. It affirmed the need for the rationalization of small and medium enterprises. Such firms also needed more financing. The government should give subsidies to enable members of industrial associations to build "cooperative factory facilities." The associations themselves had to become stronger by acquiring the authority to sell all goods produced by members and to plan the production of those goods. The groups should also have access to convenient credit from the government or a special central depository to which all associations could contribute.[67]

Exports required special aid: efforts to collect information on world trade should improve, the system of "merchandise halls" to advertise Japanese goods abroad should expand, and the government should fund an export compensation system. To entice exporters to try new markets, the government would guarantee 80 percent of a bank's losses when it gave credit to a company exporting to "dangerous" markets, such as Central America, South America, the Balkans, Africa, and Russia. Selecting the export associations as the main channel for granting this insurance would have the additional advantage of reinforcing the power of these groups. The government should acknowledge the importance of exports for the nation's welfare by eliminating all taxes on exported products and on profits earned abroad.[68]

Industrial rationalization became the yardstick for measuring the success of all policies. Mergers among firms and the creation of cartels were to increase cooperation in production, sales, and prices. Industrial efficiency would rise through the standardization of raw materials and manufacturing processes and the adoption of mass production. Ideally, the government would first empower a committee of businessmen to use efficiency ratings for licensing companies in regulated industries, such as electric power generation and insurance. Then this type of supervision would spread to "free" industries.[69]

The ultimate aim was to expand exports. All of the people had to mobilize to attain this goal. The government had to "make efforts to diffuse knowledge of the international economy in magazines, newspapers, and school conferences, as the Japanese generally [were] lacking in the spirit of overseas development." The average citizen had to alter individual habits of consumption in order to dampen the demand for goods and hence lower their prices. Housewives should abandon their reckless use of credit and shop together to find bargains. The Japanese had to "adopt methods of life by a budget" and "eliminate waste in consumption," such as wearing fancy clothes on ceremonial occasions, using too much electricity, and not eating all the food in the box lunches [bentō] that people ate on trains. "Planning the spread and nurturance of the thought of savings and insurance" would help too.[70]

Representing a consensus among Japan's top business leaders and economic bureaucrats, the council's proposals reflected and elaborated upon major ideas evident within the business community for almost a decade. The plans for mergers, industrial associations, and cartels to boost the productivity of firms and to slash the costs of production embraced not only small enterprises but also large companies. The specific plan to insure exports to new markets followed the principles of previous recommendations by business groups.

The proposals assumed a closer relationship between government and business. Business leaders, however, did not want the nationalization of industries; indeed, executives demanded that the government turn over the ownership of all its factories to the private sector. Nor did companies expect huge subsidies; the council estimated modest expenditures for new programs, such as export compensation.[71] Yet, the government would have to use its power to make sure that cartels formed and worked effectively to increase exports in each industry. In addition, the government would have to assist in calling attention to the trade crisis and motivating the people to respond. In the past they had mobilized for war; now they had to mobilize for exports. The council believed that only such a campaign could enable companies to achieve the low prices necessary to escape from the quagmire of a stagnating foreign trade.

TOWARD THE GOLD STANDARD

By 1929 the campaign for the reform of industrial organization and trade policies had combined with the movement to end the embargo on gold. Faith in the benefits of industrial rationalization helped mollify skeptics who had opposed the gold standard. They were persuaded that the economy might well strengthen to the point that it could withstand the shock of such a change. When business leaders decided to recommend both sets of policies, the government followed suit.

The return to the gold standard remained a central issue throughout the mid-1920s. In 1925 and 1926 Finance Minister Hamaguchi began gradual budget reductions in order to fortify the yen as preparation for free trade in gold. His successor, Kataoka Naoharu, drafted an "Outline of Measures to Prepare for an End to the Gold Embargo." He began redeeming bonds issued by the national government and introduced legislation to settle the promissory notes that had financed the economic recovery from the Kantō earthquake. The sudden eruption of the financial panic of 1927, however, obstructed further moves to bolster Japan's currency.[72]

Inoue Junnosuke outlined the most cogent argument for the gold standard. Oddly enough, he used the continuing crisis of the nation's economy to justify risking the obvious perils of the policy. He harped on the chronic woes of the government's debt and the surplus of imports to demonstrate that only a drastic change could prevent the further stagnation of this "unhealthy" and "irrational" condition. The government, as the largest single consumer in the society, had to pare expenses and balance its budget. This financial retrenchment would cause a recession, but he declared that "today's situation is a recession whose end is completely unseen. It is a recession from which there are no predictions for recovery." Left alone, the current troubles would worsen. Moreover, the Japanese could not rely on outside economic stimulation from overseas demand as they had in the past. Exhausted because of the world war, the Western nations were limiting imports and gaining a surplus of exports. Japan had to solve its problems by its "own power." A temporary setback induced by deflationary policies at least offered the hope of prosperity in the long run.[73]

Between 1927 and 1929 many business leaders rallied to defend the restoration of a gold standard. Some of them, such as Anamizu Yoshichi of the Fuji Paper Manufacturing Company, Takigawa Gisuke of the Kōbe Chamber of Commerce, and Matsunaga Yasusaemon of the Tōhō Electric Power Company, longed for a "normal economic situation." "Real prosperity," he predicted, "will not come if the zaikai does not suffer some deflation based on ending the embargo on gold, pass through [a period of deflation], and become healthy." These men acknowledged that instituting a convertible currency would cause problems, but they "recognize[d] that this [was] an extreme necessity for rescuing [the economy] through financial policy."[74]

Other businessmen gave more specific reasons. Yamamuro Sōbun of the Mitsubishi Bank thought that a stable exchange rate would make the prices of imports more predictable. This would help foreign trade and new businesses by easing long-range planning. Japanese banks could also invest their excess deposits abroad with much less risk. Hirao Hachisaburō, from the Tokyo Marine and Fire Insurance Company, expected that the stronger yen would mean lower prices for imported raw materials and hence would slash the costs of producing Japan's exports. As imported materials for daily necessities—raw cotton and wool, wood, and fertilizer—became cheaper, wages would fall and make Japanese companies even more competitive. Finally, the rise in interest rates caused by an outflow of capital to other nations would end up aiding Japanese industry by attracting investment.[75]

Two opponents of the gold standard in 1922 now rendered qualified support for the measure. Yūki Toyotarō of the Yasuda Bank speculated that ending the embargo could put the economy back on a "normal path." If the nation's trade attained a favorable balance, few problems would arise. Reversing his longstanding opinion that an exhausted business community could not withstand a jolt of deflation, Sumitomo Bank's Yatsushiro Norihiko finally decided that the time for free trade in gold had arrived. The recent decision of Norway and France to align their currencies with those of Germany, Italy, and

England meant that Japan alone among major industrial powers eschewed the gold standard. The trade situation was getting better, and the exchange rate was nearing parity. Yatsushiro preferred to wait until the outlook for exports brightened, but he realized that the delay could prove indefinite.[76] Japan might as well try the gold standard soon.

A few critics stood their ground. Kiyomizu Bunnosuke from the Taiyō Life Insurance Company believed that deflation would aggravate the current recession. The economy could continue its slow rebound without radical changes in policy. Kodama Ichizō of the Tōyō Cotton Company wanted to maintain a low exchange rate to help exports. Mori Heibei, vice-president of the Osaka Chamber of Commerce, worried about the expected outflow of gold and the constriction of investment capital.[77]

A survey of the Japan Industrial Club in 1928 uncovered much apprehension about the possible results of a gold standard, although a majority of companies favored such a move. Trading firms and manufacturers of paper and rayon voiced the most optimism. The manufacturers foresaw a drop in the price of imported pulp that would help their products meet international competition. All of the trading firms in the survey approved the change despite their prediction of a wider trade gap immediately afterward.[78] Executives from other sectors of the economy were more wary. Anticipating only temporary problems, some textile concerns looked forward to plunging prices for raw materials and a static exchange rate; others worried that the high value of the yen would price textiles out of overseas markets and that firms with large stocks of raw cotton would suffer a sharp drop in the value of their current inventories. Most producers of electrical machinery and goods believed that they could still match European rivals but feared a severe recession would drive prices down enough to erode profits. While avoiding active opposition to a gold standard, executives from this industry said they foresaw no gains from the policy. A dyestuffs manufacturer expected increased competition from German exports, but he remained confident that protective tariffs would enable the industry to grow.[79]

Some industries were preparing for a disaster. Executives from a shipbuilding firm and a company that produced spinning machines each argued that the stronger yen, despite reduced costs for imported steel, would hurt exports. In the developing chemical sector, a manufacturer of artificial fertilizer feared that his industry would face destruction. Iron and steel companies braced for shrinking production, because a flood of imports would bring lower prices and a squeeze on profits.[80]

Scholars have tried to categorize by industry the supporters and opponents of the gold standard in the late 1920s. Twenty-eight of the eighty-seven companies in the Industrial Club's study opposed removing the embargo on gold. Among the sixteen firms engaged in heavy industry, the newest and weakest sector in terms of cracking the world market, nine registered a protest; of twenty-seven in light industry, ten did.[81] To some writers these figures have suggested that resistance centered in the manufacturing sectors, which yielded nineteen of the twenty-eight opponents. Meanwhile, according to this scenario, the scions of the huge banks and trading companies pushed for the gold standard in order to create a fixed exchange rate that would ease overseas investments for excess capital.

One must note, though, the dissension within each sector and the qualified nature of many executives' support for the gold standard. Examples abounded even in the financial community, whose associations in 1928 began to champion restoring the gold standard at the old parity of two yen per dollar. Yano Tsuneta, the founder of the Daiichi Life Insurance Company and the Daiichi Mutual Savings Bank, argued that such a policy would destroy any hopes for a balanced foreign trade. Free trade in gold would work only at a much lower exchange rate, a new parity of three or four yen to the dollar.[82] As mentioned above, Sumitomo Bank's Yatsushiro gave only a grudging and belated endorsement of free trade in gold. In contrast, two representatives of the generally pessimistic steel industry, Kurimoto Yūnosuke and Iijima Hatamori, both advocated the immediate lifting of the gold embargo in June 1928. Inahata Katsutarō, president of the chamber of commerce in Osaka, the hub of the textile industry, embodied the ambivalence of that sector by first opposing the measure and then suddenly shifting his stand. His turnabout reflected more desperation than enthusiasm. The dwindling stores of overseas specie—by 1929 90 percent had been spent—and bleak prospects for an export surplus in the near future finally convinced him that Japan might as well try something new.[83] Although the predicted effects of the gold standard did not disturb the paper manufacturers surveyed by the Industrial Club, the industry's most prominent executive, Fujiwara Ginjirō of the Ōji Company, pleaded for special tax breaks and massive public works to blunt the impact on the economy. Yasukawa Yūnosuke of the Mitsui Trading Company offered support for a convertible currency only if the government took certain actions. The government, he wrote, had to restrict the import of luxuries or goods in which Japan was self-sufficient, check the outflow of gold, prevent a drastic constriction of currency, and foster export industries with tariffs and subsidies.[84] Thus, grave doubts remained about the side effects of the gold standard as economic medicine; many executives across the economy worried that the cure might be worse than the disease. Any consensus on the issue would have to allay their fears.

By 1929 most of the major business groups were campaigning for the gold standard. In June 1928 the Kōbe Chamber of Commerce passed a resolution complaining that the gyrations of the exchange rate hampered exports, as in the past six months the value of the yen had oscillated over a four-dollar range. The government had to peg the rate through the gold standard or some other means. Ten months later the chamber demanded an end to the embargo on gold. When Inoue Junnosuke visited Kōbe in August 1929, an impressive audience of three thousand people turned out to hear him lecture on the subject. To educate the public on the issue, the chamber published a series of pamphlets that discussed the benefits and challenges of returning to a convertible currency.[85]

The major banking organizations took up the cause. By the fall of 1928 the Tokyo and Osaka clearinghouses were both advocating the gold standard. Ikeda Seihin, the head of the Mitsui Bank and the Tokyo Clearinghouse, declared that the lower production costs that would accompany deflation and the "readjustment" of the *zaikai*—rationalization through mergers and cartels—would give a "new start" to the economy.[86]

Other organizations expressed cautious support. The Tokyo Chamber of Commerce in October 1928 called for lifting the embargo together with some measures to cushion the shock of increased imports and a flight of capital overseas. The government should at least postpone planned tariff cuts and discourage Japanese investment in foreign securities.[87] The Japan chamber had similar ideas. Observing that the major Western nations had all returned to a convertible currency, the chamber urged that Japan rapidly do the same to "make the base of the economy solid . . . by contributing to the stability of deals and eliminating a disadvantage in settling international loans and debts." To prepare, the government would have to slash the budget, trim national bonds, and somehow forestall a flood of imports.[88]

The Japan Trade Council, through the editorials of its monthly journal, *Bōeki* [Trade], lent its support. In early 1928 the council had urged an abrupt end to the embargo, because it hurt foreign trade. A year later the council found that the unpredictable exchange rate was still wreaking havoc with orderly international payments. The "ignominy of having an inconvertible paper currency" and the experience of seeing overseas stores of specie "disappear almost like smoke" were hard to bear. The Japanese had "indulged in idleness living off the profits of the world war." Now they would have to pay for "the crime of ten years of idleness." Nations like Italy, France, and Belgium had all practiced fiscal austerity to strengthen their currencies before restoring the gold standard; some had even restrained imports. Japan would have to swallow the same bitter pill. Some critics, such as the eminent economist Ishibashi Tanzan of the *Tōyō keizai shinpō* [Oriental Economic Review], presented a gold standard set at a lower parity as a panacea. They only raised false hopes of a quick fix. Creating a lower parity would cause less immediate damage to the balance of trade than a currency convertible at the old parity, but a halfhearted devaluation would contradict the "ultimate goal in international trade of importing cheap raw materials and exporting expensive manufactured goods."[89]

The Japan Economic Federation and the Japan Spinners Association each maintained neutrality by declining to issue a public declaration of support. This stance probably resulted from discord within each group. Some hints of disharmony appeared within the leadership of the Economic Federation. Inoue Junnosuke, Ikeda Seihin, and Gō Seinosuke avidly supported the gold standard; Dan Takuma had reservations.[90] Textile leaders, as the Japan Industrial Club's survey in 1928 revealed, split on the issue. Miyajima Seijirō of the Nisshin Spinning Company warned that a gold standard would cause a deep depression and send streams of unemployed workers into the streets. Abe Fusajirō, the head of the Spinners Association and the Tōyō Spinning Company, agreed with lifting the embargo but noted that he belonged to a "moderate faction" that urged careful timing in order to lessen the measure's impact. Some individuals vacillated. Mutō Sanji called for an immediate gold standard in June 1929; by November he had lost his nerve and cautioned that "in reforming the national economy after the end of the gold embargo the Japanese people will face bitter times."[91]

To settle the issue, the Seiyūkai cabinet of Tanaka Giichi organized the

Economic Council (Keizai Shingikai) in September 1928. Twenty major business leaders debated if, how, and when the government should adopt the gold standard. After three months only one participant, Ōkawa Heihachirō, remained defiant. His work in founding or managing many companies in a variety of industries made him one of the most prominent Japanese entrepreneurs of the late nineteenth and early twentieth centuries.[92] On the final day of deliberations he reiterated his stand in a desperate effort to disrupt the group's consensus. The timing, he said, could not be worse. Merely a year before, a financial panic had rattled the banking community and boycotts of Japanese goods in China threatened to strangle that important export market. Meanwhile, positive economic signs had just begun to appear, as the cheap yen was protecting new industries and helping exports. The nation should take advantage of this situation by developing sectors that had shown the most progress—the manufacture of chemicals and machines and the electrical industry. After these industries matured in five years or so, a gold standard would work. To prove his point, Ōkawa cited the plunge of the stock market when rumors of a return to a convertible currency had first spread. At the very least the government should prepare firm policies to block a tidal wave of imports. Ōkawa preferred tariffs that officials could alter quickly without waiting for the approval of the Diet as current laws required.[93]

Other discussants had evinced more hope, but they had also concurred that the government should try to offset the effects of lifting the embargo on gold. Arguing in a subcommittee that the cabinet could not delay a decision for long, Sumitomo Bank's Yukawa proposed that the Bank of Japan should keep foreign branches of Japanese banks from manipulating currencies to take undue advantage of a higher exchange rate. Inahata Katsutarō presented a list of policies to improve the trade balance when the nation moved to a convertible currency. The government should promote exports by creating an insurance system for them, providing ample capital at low interest rates to exchange banks, helping exports that showed great promise, and abolishing taxes on profits from overseas investments. The various ministries could stimulate industry through purchasing more domestic products, and higher tariffs that exempted food and raw materials could shelter products that had "future prospects." Despite some members' complaints about the vagueness of these provisions, the committee recommended most of them.[94]

Finally, the subcommittee approved a resolution composed by Dan Takuma. This short statement advocated ending the embargo on gold as soon as possible while "deciding on policies that must be established for planning a balance of international payments." The government had to "encourage banks to adopt some restraints so that drastic changes in the financial world will not occur." Officials should also extend the availability of credit abroad to prepare for an outflow of gold.[95]

Late in December Gō Seinosuke undertook the imposing task of drafting a detailed report for the entire council to accept. He was a good choice, because few in the business world could match his energy and wide-ranging experience. Seven years of study in Germany had earned him a doctorate in economics at the University of Heidelberg as well as a reputation as a heavy drinker and a strong arm wrestler.[96] Gō had returned in 1892 to work for the Ministry of Agriculture and Commerce. He entered the business world by managing the semigovernmental N.Y.K. Company. His success there led to opportunities to head other firms, including the huge Ōji Paper Company. He became famous for reorganizing and rescuing other enterprises, such as the Kawasaki Shipbuilding Company, and he directed the Tokyo Stock Exchange for twelve years. Meanwhile, his entry into the House of Peers in 1910 and role in organizing the Japan Industrial Club and the Economic Federation revealed a strong interest in public affairs.

Gō's final report fleshed out Dan's resolution and outlined the new consensus. Confident that a stable currency would prompt a boom in exports over the long term, the report admitted that severe problems could arise in the near future. Thus, the majority opinion favored enacting free trade in gold by the middle of 1929, along with several policies to aid Japanese industry. A special committee should have the power to increase and decrease tariffs to shelter companies that manufactured steel, iron, textiles, and chemicals. An export compensation system should encourage banks to grant loans to traders who would pioneer new markets. Small and medium-sized companies would need more loans to buy foreign currency to sell their products abroad. Removing the taxes on overseas offices of trading companies would make them more competitive in arranging trade between third parties. Finally, a new national committee should guide the movement to rationalize industrial production in order to "aid industrial development." Along this line, Gō endorsed the principle of export planning—selecting products that might sell well abroad and fostering their growth.[97]

Although the Economic Council did not specify that industries should organize into cartels, the emphasis on industrial rationalization pointed in that direction. Nine months later a new minister of commerce, Tawara Magoichi, followed the council's advice and formed a committee to investigate policies of rationalization as a means to counteract the effects of the gold standard. The committee soon issued a report calling for mergers and cartels.[98]

This development contained some irony, because supporters of the gold standard, such as Inoue and Mutō, had long protested government interference in the economy. They argued repeatedly that the economy had to become self-regulating so that the balance of trade could determine prices and the value of currency. Yet, the consensus within the *zaikai* to accept a gold standard depended upon the prospect of more intervention. It became a crucial ingredient in the business community's comprehensive prescription for prosperity.

In the late spring of 1929, Inoue, Gō, and Dan visited Finance Minister Mitsuchi Chūzō. Struck by their plea not to act hastily, Mitsuchi promised not to end the gold embargo until the economic situation improved. This conference convinced some observers that Inoue wavered in his convictions,[99] but he must have realized that the policy had no chance to succeed without the firm support of the *zaikai*. Switching to a convertible currency without progress toward some of the policies recommended by the Economic Council would have been foolhardy. Subsequent events would prove that Inoue's resolve to institute a gold standard had not diminished.

He soon had an opportunity to show the strength of his beliefs. In July 1929 the new premier, Hamaguchi Osachi of the Minseitō, asked Inoue to take the portfolio of finance, and the cabinet quickly announced its intention to restore the gold standard. True to his previous advice, Inoue began to reduce both the budget and the issuance of bonds while waiting for the balance of trade to improve. The government distributed thirteen million leaflets explaining the need to lift the embargo.[100] After five months, though, the mood of economic uncertainty stirred the impatience of business leaders. When Inoue visited Osaka in August, they vented their frustrations with the cabinet's inaction. Iijima Hatamori, Itō Takenosuke, and Nihon Cotton's Kita Matazō all implored Inoue to order an immediate end to the embargo, if only to dissipate the fog of confusion over future economic policies. Hirao Hachisaburō, Kodama Ichizō, and Iwai Katsujirō, a trader, each complained about the government's lack of aggressive initiatives for limiting imports and overseas investment. Even policies toward indigenous rice wine (*sake*) came under attack, as one participant soberly asserted that its prohibition should anchor a badly needed campaign to reduce wasteful consumption.[101]

Inoue offered a nonchalant response. The advent of free trade in gold, he claimed, would not present an "unusually difficult problem." Because few foreign stocks paid high dividends, he did not expect much capital to flee Japan. The current paring of government expenditures would restrain imports. A massive campaign to limit civilian consumption was not yet necessary; citizens could drink as much *sake* as they wished. Japan had to "wait and see" until foreign trade gradually attained an equilibrium and the exchange rate approached parity.[102]

That moment arrived late in the fall of 1929. Dismissing the stock market collapse on Wall Street as a temporary fluke, Inoue emphasized two other positive trends. Japan had registered a sizable trade surplus from July to October, and the exchange rate at $48.00/100 yen had come close to the old parity.[103] In November, he declared that Japan would return to the gold standard on the first day of the new year.

With one-half of the Economic Council's program in place, attention now turned even more to the other half: policies to aid export industries. Aware of the strong backing that business groups and leaders had expressed for export insurance, the Ministry of Commerce and Industry had started work on an Export Compensation Act in May 1929. By September the ministry had presented a draft to the joint business-government Council on Improving International Debits and Credits. This would commit the government to repay designated banks for 80 percent of losses incurred through purchasing promissory notes for exports to new markets. The Finance Ministry, with its eye always on the budget, then suggested limits. The guarantees should cover 70 to 80 percent of notes only for exports of miscellaneous goods to unindustrialized areas. Council members haggled for two months over details, such as the fees charged to banks to help fund the program. Chairing a special committee on the issue, Inoue Junnosuke helped the council reach a compromise: a proposal to insure 70 percent of notes for any exports to areas designated by the government. In January 1930 the Council on Commerce and Industry gave its hearty endorsement. On May 1 the cabinet submitted the bill, which sped through the Lower House of the Diet in eight days and became law by the end of the month. Initially the act applied to Central America, Africa, the Balkan nations, "central Asia minor" [chū shō Ajia], and the Soviet Union. As the scope expanded to include the whole world except for Europe, the United States, India, and the Dutch East Indies, the banks' extension of credit to exporters increased rapidly.[104]

In 1931 a major revision of the Export Association Law enhanced the powers of the individual associations. The right to purchase members' goods and to sell them meant that the groups could coordinate sales of a product and control the flow of goods to a particular market. The associations could also serve as sources of capital, as they could accept deposits and advance funds. The Ministry of Finance made low-interest loans available for this purpose. In addition, another law permitted industrial associations to form in all sectors, not just those geared toward exports. The government could now provide subsidies to these groups to assist the construction of joint production facilities.[105]

The campaign for industrial reorganization culminated in the Important Industries Control Law of 1931. The result of intensive deliberations between business leaders and government officials during 1930 and 1931, this law fulfilled the zaikai's aim of sanctioning cartels for firms of any size. The provisions permitted considerable autonomy for the cartels, while the Ministry of Commerce and Industry retained a general authority to supervise their formation and activities. A "control committee" composed of officials and executives would designate crucial industries in which cartels should form to regulate production and prices. If one-half of the companies in such an industry applied to create a cartel, the head of the ministry would then grant final approval. Under certain conditions—if members representing two-thirds of the firms in an industry agreed and the control committee consented—a cartel could ask the commerce minister to force even nonmembers to comply with its policies. With the approval of the control committee, however, the minister could rescind actions of a cartel that "opposed the public interest."[106] The lack of provision for the minister to impose any policies on the cartels mirrored a deep concern for a balance of power between the public and private sectors.

Of all the proposals of the Economic Council, tariff protection for selected industries had the least success. As the next chapter will discuss more fully, the Japanese perceived in the 1920s a disturbing trend toward high tariffs in most overseas markets. Because the government had already raised levies in

1926 for products in budding industries, further hikes would weaken its stance in favor of free trade. Aware of Inoue's philosophical aversion to protectionism and the opposition from foreign trading partners, the Council on Tariffs appointed by the government refused to recommend major increases.[107]

By 1931 the government had adopted much of the comprehensive program to revive foreign trade that business leaders had proposed in the Economic Council of 1928. Scholars have accorded too much credit for these policies, especially the measures relating to industrial rationalization, to officials of the Ministry of Commerce and Industry. By the late 1920s some may have promoted the movement, but it did not sprout suddenly from their brains. In 1928 Mutō Sanji boasted about the progress of the spinning industry in achieving rationalization. Two years later the economist Takahashi Kamekichi noted that the business community had advocated and practiced industrial rationalization for some time. Indeed, some industries, such as the spinning sector, had made great strides.[108] Furthermore, business groups and leaders had constantly demanded increased productivity through mergers, cartels, and techniques of mass production throughout the previous decade. The economic legislation of the early 1930s took effect rapidly, because both officials and executives acknowledged the potential benefits.

The enactment of laws relating to trade reflected important aspects of how economic policies evolved. Business leaders and groups set forth proposals; executives then discussed them at length with government officials in formal conferences. Broad support for a proposal would prompt the Ministry of Commerce and Industry to draft legislation and begin negotiating with other ministries. Sometimes this process could be arduous; the penny-pinching Finance Ministry proved most troublesome. Once a law had cleared the bureaucratic hurdles, the consent of the Diet followed easily. Although the Minseitō and Seiyūkai had gained power during this era of party cabinets, they each received the bulk of their financing from the *zaikai*. Many eminent politicians came from the top ranks of the civil service.[109] When officials and business leaders agreed on an economic issue, the political parties showed little inclination to resist.

In the case of the gold standard, the government waited for a decision by the business community. One sector did not impose its will on others. Proponents and skeptics existed in all industries, and the former had to make concessions to mollify the latter. Perhaps Inoue Junnosuke did believe that the policy would aid the nation's banks more than some manufacturing sectors. Depicting his policies as a victory for bankers, traders, and monopoly control,[110] however, has diverted attention from the important achievement of a consensus on the urgency of closer collaboration between companies and the government on trade matters. Business leaders thought that exports could expand only with the government's aid.[111] Significantly, the steps toward this new partnership—the Export Compensation Act, the revised export and industrial association laws, and the Important Industries Control Law—proved more durable than the gold standard.

THREE
DISCOVERING THE LIMITS OF INFLUENCE,
1931–1934

I n the early 1930s a series of economic and political shocks jolted the business community. The worldwide depression, rapid deflation, the imperial army's sudden thrust into Manchuria, and the profusion of trade barriers abroad posed unprecedented challenges. The *zaikai*'s struggles to cope with this bewildering international environment yielded three results.

Acrimonious disputes with trading partners and the utter failure of the London Economic Conference of 1933 generated profound pessimism about the future of international trade. The extension of economic and military influence in China begat new concerns about how to maintain that position and to turn it to the nation's economic advantage. Finally, accomplishments of the Industrial Rationalization Bureau proved that the public and private sectors could work together and pointed the way toward new strategies for trade.

Meanwhile, executives also learned the limits of their influence over national policies. Daring officers of the imperial army presented a *fait accompli* to which the business community had to adjust. Unilateral decisions by foreign nations changed the rules of foreign trade and made inevitable the government's mediation in solving bilateral trade frictions.

ENDING THE GOLD STANDARD

Problems with the gold standard dismayed the *zaikai*. Regardless of the theoretical merits of the policy, unforeseen external events had undermined it. Contrary to Inoue Junnosuke's judgment, the Wall Street crash of 1929 ushered in an extended depression in the United States. Japan suffered directly, as American demand for raw silk, Japan's most important export, tumbled. The collapse of the large American market cut the purchasing power of farmers, many of whom depended upon sericulture for secondary income. As domestic demand fell, so did industrial production and employment. The worldwide nature of the economic depression created one more problem: ubiquitous deflation caused prices everywhere to drop. Hence the prices of Japanese goods and services declined, as proponents of lifting the embargo on gold had promised, but the nation's products did not become more competitive, because comparable goods in major markets became cheaper too. Japan's industrial production shrank greatly in value in most major industries, while the value of foreign trade also withered.

Despite these dismal results, support for the gold standard remained remarkably strong during its first year. Leaders of the Seiyūkai, the party out of power, did their best to shake public confidence in the policies of the Minseitō cabinet. The former finance minister, Mitsuchi Chūzō, for example, ridiculed the basic assumptions behind the gold standard—that deflation and reliance on the natural forces of the international market could assure the nation's long-term economic health. The government's emphasis on reducing domestic demand would, he explained to the Japan Trade Council, force a decline in overall industrial production. Free trade, an idea that England devised when it had dominated the world's economy, had become obsolete. Without special protection, Japan's industry could not grow.[1] Mitsuchi implied that he favored more pump priming through public works and the aggressive use of tariffs.

Some business leaders agreed. Mutō Sanji contended that the lack of intervention by the government could court disaster; the depression could continue indefinitely and become a "catastrophe beyond the Kantō earthquake."[2] In October he advocated reimposing the embargo with the goal of setting a new parity. The presidents of two trading firms, the Kurokawa and Kimata companies, wanted to foresake the gold standard. Among zaibatsu executives, one from the Mitsubishi Trading Company admitted that a convertible currency had not worked, because the political parties had trouble "enacting thorough policies against the depression." Tōzawa Yoshiki of the Yasuda Trust Company desired a new parity. Even several bankers faltered in their loyalty to the old one. Claiming that he still favored the gold standard, Mori Kōzō of the Yasuda Bank said he would reconsider if the situation worsened. Ishii Kengo of the Daiichi Bank opposed a new parity in principle but vowed to study the idea. Kurokawa Fukusaburō, who headed his own trading company, cynically but presciently urged that the government abandon a convertible currency abruptly with no advance warning. This approach would prevent speculation by Japanese businessmen in foreign currencies.[3]

Most business leaders rallied to the support of the current policy. Their arguments stressed a desire to avoid more woes: a new parity or an end to the gold standard would not help much and might even make things worse. Ono Ichitarō of the Meiji Spinning and Weaving Company remarked candidly that, although the gold standard at the old parity had not brought the expected results, "there is no gain in rebuking this [policy] today." He agreed with Imai Takuo of the Sumitomo Bank that deserting the old parity would harm the "trust" of the nation abroad. Noguchi Kōki of the Daiichi Bank warned against "changing directions in the middle of a stormy voyage across the sea." An unpredictable exchange rate for the yen would damage international trade. Ōkura Hatsumi thought that those who wanted a reimposition of the embargo on gold had forgotten the problems it had caused during the previous decade. Imai voiced a common sentiment when he pointed out that the worldwide depression, which obviously had not resulted from domestic policies, could take the blame for many of the nation's problems. Suzuki Ryōsaku of the Ashikaga Bank believed that Japan had "no choice but to wait for a favorable turn in world trends."[4]

Many viewed the issue as a test of national character. Itō Takenosuke, a critic of the gold standard in the early 1920s, now argued that opponents suffered from a weak will. Ōkura Hatsumi believed that the Japanese had to sacrifice to rebuild their currency just as they had done in resurrecting Tokyo after the earthquake in 1923. Imai Takuo suggested that instead of a new parity the economy needed a "fresh start (denaoshi) for industrial management."[5] The head of the Kōbe Chamber of Commerce, Kagoshima Fusajirō, and Sumitomo Bank's Yatsushiro Norihiko both underlined the urgency of rationalizing management. Unless "business leaders" (zaikaijin) recognized the need for change, nothing would happen. Yatsushiro exclaimed, "Clearly a hundred policies will ultimately end up worthless if [businessmen] lack this consideration, realization, and effort [toward rationalization]."[6]

By early 1931 a survey of executives' opinions about solutions to the nation's economic troubles found solid backing for the gold standard. The Japan Trade Council, like many respondents, recognized that measures to reduce domestic spending and the hemorrhage of specie had drained the lifeblood of capital from industry. Refusing to consider an embargo on gold, the council recommended expanding the new export compensation system, restraining unnecessary imports, using tariffs to protect promising industries, promoting the rationalization of production, and employing export controls. Japan could then "progress from the era of crude manufactures at cheap prices

to one of fine goods at cheap prices." Yamazaki Ichihō of the Tōyō Cotton
Company and Shiraishi Motojirō of the Nihon Steel Tube Company both
affirmed the need for lower production costs. Tanahashi Toragorō from the Nihon Smelting Company urged drastic action by the government. Noting that
officials and executives on the Council on Tariffs had proposed giving the
government the authority to set such levies swiftly without Diet approval,
Tanahashi argued that many companies, especially in the chemical sector,
needed a refuge from foreign competition. The government should also close
inefficient factories and allow only efficient ones to grow. All plans for new
facilities should receive governmental approval based on careful studies of
future supply and demand. Hara Yasusaburō, an executive from a chemical
manufacturer, was one of the few respondents to argue that free trade in gold
should stop. This act would, he wrote, require "unprecedented resolution by
the *zaikai* and the authorities."[7]

In the autumn, international events made the debate over the gold standard even more acute. The clash between Chinese and Japanese forces in
Manchuria on September 18 upset the business community. Three days later it
received another blow: England decided to quit the gold standard. This action
vitiated one of the most powerful arguments for a convertible currency—the
need to conform to the policies of the other industrial nations. Moreover,
devaluation in England and her colonies put Japanese exports at an immediate
disadvantage in those markets.

Critics of the gold standard took heart. Complaining that the recent
embargo would aid England's exports, Mutō Sanji urged that Japan help its
industries by following this example. Tsuda Shingo of the Kanegafuchi Spinning Company characterized England's move as a sly effort to erect a de facto
tariff against Japanese exports. Because "Japan's power to expand [had] been
checked," the government had to reinstate the embargo on gold. An executive
from the fertilizer industry, Futagami Shunkichi, saw no end to the flow of
specie out of Japan and the further contraction of currency. He thought that an
immediate devaluation would lift the nation out of its economic misery by
upping prices for agricultural goods and boosting citizens' purchasing power.
The government should no longer "sacrifice the national economy to protect
the currency system." Fujiwara Ginjirō panicked. A flood of imports from
Europe combined with the fighting in China and the general exhaustion of
Japanese industry presented the "economic world" with an unprecedented

crisis. Japan, he wrote, must "enact an appropriate and positive policy of protection and carry out measures to respond to the decline in the exchange market or fight against devaluation with the same weapon."[8] In early November the Seiyūkai passed a resolution demanding an end to the gold standard.

Major business leaders and organizations fought hard to maintain the status quo. In early October and November, Finance Minister Inoue staunchly defended his policies. He twice raised the Bank of Japan's discount rate to entice more investment in domestic bonds and to limit the flight of specie.[9] The situation, he said, warranted little concern. England's betrayal of the gold standard had no direct effect on Japanese finance; high costs for raw materials would negate any advantage that British exports gained from a weaker pound. Having erased its surplus of imports, Japan would register a surplus of international receipts for the year. The depletion of stocks of gold would soon stop.[10]

On November 6, Inoue and major business leaders met to issue a proclamation of total faith in the government's economic policies. The list of participants read like a "who's who" of the business world: Dan Takuma, Gō Seinosuke, Kimura Kusuyata, Kushida Manzō, Ikeda Seihin, Kagami Kankichi, Inahata Katsutarō, Isaka Takashi, and Yatsushiro Norihiko. They resolved that despite England's embargo on gold, "international payments [had] become orderly." A switch by Japan to an inconvertible currency would only bring "drastic changes to the exchange rate" and "a change to the basis of our economy." The day before, the Fifth Day Society (Itsukakai)—a monthly gathering of leaders from the finance industry—had decided that in spite of the "unease" caused by recent events, the government should not alter its policies relating to currency.[11] A few days later the Japan Chamber of Commerce took a similar stand.[12]

The actions of some major companies soon aroused strong public skepticism about the sincerity of such forceful declarations. After September several banks, especially Mitsui, purchased large amounts of dollars, an act which the newspapers promptly dubbed the "dollar buying" incident. Bankers quickly justified this decision as essential to cover huge losses that investments in England incurred after the pound's devaluation. Critics suspected that the denizens of the zaibatsu were plotting to profit from the imminent end of the gold standard. Economist Takahashi Kamekichi spoke for many when he surmised later that "in their hearts" these executives knew that the yen's devaluation was inevitable.[13]

The Minseitō's political position collapsed in 1931. Along with Inoue's stubborn insistence on maintaining a deflationary policy, the inability of Premier Wakatsuki Reijirō and Foreign Minister Shidehara Kijūrō to curb the fighting in Manchuria or to resolve disunity within the party proved fatal. When the minister of home affairs, Adachi Kenzō, boycotted cabinet meetings in the hope of forcing an alliance with the rival Seiyūkai, the entire cabinet resigned in December. The new Seiyūkai cabinet of Premier Inukai Tsuyoshi stopped free trade in gold within one day of assuming office.

This rude dismissal of the gold standard embarrassed the business community. The failure of the policy, which had attracted broad support in 1929, brought into question the judgment of top business leaders in regard to national economic policy. The banks' alleged speculation in foreign currency during the autumn of 1931 also convinced many citizens that executives valued their companies' balance sheet more than the national welfare. Finally, the Seiyūkai's decision demonstrated that a cabinet could defy a strong public position taken by prominent business leaders.

One could argue that the *zaikai*'s vocal defense of the gold standard in recent months contained more show than substance. For example, although the Japan Trade Council did not call for a change in policy, the group's journal, *Bōeki*, published articles by critics, such as Mitsuchi and Mutō. The Japan Economic Federation and the Japan Spinners Association each remained silent on the issue. Bankers' purchases of huge amounts of foreign currency seemed to contradict their public pleas for a convertible currency. One scholar speculates that executives, such as Mitsui's Ikeda Seihin, rallied to Inoue's support only because of an obligation to maintain a semblance of government-business unity on the issue. One official in the Finance Ministry, Aoki Kazuo, has surmised that even Inoue remained steadfast only because he thought an admission of failure would ruin his political career.[14]

Still, the dogged faith of important business leaders suggested that the business community and the Minseitō intended to keep a convertible currency in the foreseeable future. Inoue never vacillated in his public stands. Continuing to defend his policies, he made restoration of the gold standard a major issue in the general election of February 1932.[15] Such persistence in the face of public outrage against the "dollar-buying" incident showed great courage. Inoue paid for his beliefs with his life when, in February 1932, a right-wing fanatic murdered the former finance minister as a symbolic protest against the

corrupt and selfish zaibatsu. Two weeks later, an assassin cut down Dan Takuma, the president of the Japan Industrial Club and the Japan Economic Federation. Undisturbed by these events, Gō Seinosuke, the new president of the
federation, did not hesitate to take up the cause of restoring free trade in gold!
A rapid devaluation, he claimed, would only brew a dangerous inflation that
would diminish Japanese exports. An international conference, Gō advised,
should reinstate the gold standard and bring stability to international trade.[16]
Substantial support for free trade in gold continued to exist in the business
community, but it could not overcome the harsh effects of the world depression, the unexpected switch in Britain's policy, and the debilitating discord
within the Minseitō.

THE CHINA CHALLENGE

Relations with China posed other problems for the *zaikai*. As Sino-Japanese
ties in trade and investment became closer and more extensive, the business
community began to realize a new restraint on its influence: the difficulty of
adjusting to Chinese nationalism. In the 1920s China had emerged as a large
market for exports and a supplier of some raw materials—raw cotton, coal,
mineral ores, and agricultural products, such as wheat and oil cake. Moreover,
Japanese textile firms invested heavily. Lured by low labor costs and flush
with profits from the boom during the world war, Japanese companies nearly
quadrupled their textile production in China and came to own about one-third
of China's total textile facilities. Prior to 1914 Japanese exports of cotton cloth
and production in China had provided about 8 percent of total consumption; by
the mid-1920s exports and production reached almost 28 percent.[17]

These gains made the Japanese a fat target for nationalistic sentiment.
Japan's single-minded determination to keep the province of Shantung, cap-
tured from the Germans during the world war, had already sparked mass
demonstrations in several cities in 1919. After this issue was settled, protests
against the Japanese presence turned to economic matters. Although China
became divided in the midst of constant and bloody fighting among various
warlords, a bitter anger against foreign privileges energized workers, students,
and intellectuals. They particularly resented the degrading commercial treaties
that dated from the nineteenth century. These curbed the tariffs that China
could levy on imports, excused foreign residents from trial by Chinese courts,

and permitted self-governing international settlements in major cities. When the Nationalist party finally managed to bring a nominal unity to the nation in 1927, the party promised the restoration of full sovereignty.

Indifferent to Chinese aspirations, the *zaikai* desired to preserve its economic privileges and to extend its influence in China. In 1923, for example, the National Federation of Chambers of Commerce bemoaned the prospect that the Chinese government would raise tariffs to the maximum level of 5 percent allowed under the commercial treaties. The federation preferred a gradual implementation over "many years." Far from encouraging Chinese self-determination, the group sought to share England's venerable monopoly on managing China's Maritime Customs Service.[18] In the same year Chinese businessmen, led by textile executives who wanted to shield their fledgling enterprises from Japanese exports and investment, organized boycotts against purchases of Japanese goods and exports of raw cotton to Japan. The movement had only mixed success but drew a sharp Japanese response. The federation advised that restraining exports of cotton would sabotage both nations' "coprosperity." The Japan Trade Council urged that if necessary the cabinet should take strong action against the boycotts.[19]

The stance of business groups changed little for the rest of the decade. Those whose members held large investments in China—the Japan Spinners Association, the Japan-China Business Council (Nikka Jitsugyō Kyōkai), and the Trade Association of Spinners in China (Zaika Bōseki Dōgyōkai)—lodged strident objections to treaty reforms. The textile industry took a paternalistic perspective. Japan was granting China a great favor by purchasing cotton and creating jobs. To keep these advantages, China should preserve "free economic activity." In November 1926 the Osaka, Kyōto, and Kōbe chambers of commerce, all deep in textile country, decided together that a new commercial treaty should allow China to set its own rates after five years, but Japan would have to approve levies for important goods. Two months later, the march of the Nationalist army north to defeat its warlord rivals made members nervous. When the army approached the major port and industrial center of Shanghai, the chambers declared that as the "lives and property of Japanese face[d] danger" from the fighting, the government must force China to respect past treaties. By the end of the year the Osaka chamber had organized a Federation to Protect Commercial Rights in China. Twenty-eight other groups, including

other major chambers, joined. In August, this federation stated that if cooperation proved impossible, "the imperial government must consider the special
political and economic relationship between Japan and China and resolutely
create a policy of unilateral self-defense and protect our commercial rights
which are being destroyed."[20]

As anxiety over the safety of Japanese investments and property grew, so
did Chinese indignation. Following specific requests by the Japan Spinners
Association to defend textile factories during battles between Nationalist and
warlord forces, the government twice sent troops to the province of Shantung.
In 1927 several thousand soldiers landed, and in 1928 a division clashed with
Nationalist troops in the city of Tsinan. These military maneuvers aggravated
Chinese hostility to the extent that anti-Japanese boycotts flared all over the
nation. In some cities activists erected wooden cages to punish merchants who
continued to handle Japanese goods.[21]

Mounting popular fury in China moved Japan's business groups to soften
their stand only a bit. They stoutly defended military intervention as "self-
defense."[22] The Japan Chamber of Commerce denounced boycotts as anti-
Japanese acts instigated by the Nationalist party for political reasons. Western
nations' recognition of China's sovereignty over its tariffs, however, forced the
chamber to do likewise. Still, the chamber insisted on the right to sanction
rates on twenty-seven crucial items, such as cotton cloth. As for the issue of
extraterritoriality, the widespread corruption of officials and inadequate legal
codes rendered reform unthinkable. General disorder made dismantling the
major international settlements impossible.[23]

Despite the consensus on preserving past privileges, business groups
differed in the intensity of their activities and the boldness of their statements
about the Japanese position in China. The Japan Chamber of Commerce, the
Spinners Association, and the Osaka chamber became outspoken champions
of Japanese prerogatives. The latter helped form in 1928 the Japan-China
Economic Council (Nikka Keizai Kyōkai) for the explicit purpose of influenc-
ing the government's policy on the Asian mainland.[24] The Economic Federation, on the other hand, pursued a more circumspect policy. Reluctantly, it
joined the Spinners Association and the Japan chamber in sponsoring a business conference on China in May 1928. The meeting's vague resolution
expressing sympathy for China's aspirations, deploring political chaos there,

and calling for consistency in Japanese policy suggested disagreement on specific actions.[25] The federation reversed a decision to defend the government's China policy before the International Chamber of Commerce in 1929, because the issue promised to stir up so much controversy.[26] Concern for the federation's role as the international representative of Japanese business, sensitivity to external criticism of Japanese policies, and a desire to maintain smooth relations with the Western powers contributed to the group's passive public stance on this issue.

Even those advocating a staunch defense of Japanese commercial rights did not call for political or military dominance over China. Pleas for military intervention in particular crises did not mean that textile executives expected a sustained military presence.[27] Far from proposing to reinforce the army for subjugating the continent, the *zaikai* continued to favor disarmament for budgetary purposes. As discussed in Chapter 2, business groups had backed cuts in military spending since the end of the world war. The most vociferous proponent had been the head of the giant Kanegafuchi mills, Mutō Sanji. He complained that a huge standing army could sap a nation's economic power and increase the chances of wasteful misuse of forces. He cited as the most recent example Japan's dispatch of 70,000 troops to Siberia between 1918 and 1922 in a futile attempt to thwart the Bolshevik revolution. Mutō wanted to slash the size of the army by almost one-half, do away with the general staffs of the army and navy, and merge the two service ministries into a national defense ministry.[28] Belief in the inviolability of Japanese privileges in China did not keep the Japan Chamber of Commerce from applauding the savings to come from the reductions in armaments achieved at the London Naval Conference of 1930. This would create a wonderful opportunity for the government to grant tax relief to spur economic revival.[29]

The onset of fighting between Japanese and Chinese forces in Manchuria in September 1931 took the business community by surprise. The nation held an important stake there—control over the South Manchurian Railway and the 1,312 square miles of the Kwantung Leased Territory, both gained in the peace settlement for the Russo-Japanese War. Charged with the defense of these interests, the imperial army had for several years perceived a threat from rising nationalism in China and the growing hostility of the local warlord. Without the knowledge or approval of civilian leaders in the cabinet, officers had plotted the conquest of Manchuria. On September 18 the field army blew up a small section of track near the city of Mukden, blamed the act on Chinese forces, and launched a full offensive.

To be sure, business groups had repeatedly emphasized the economic importance of Manchuria, which comprised the northern three provinces of China. The Japan Chamber of Commerce had portrayed the area as a vital export market in the future. In July 1931 the Kōbe chamber, whose members had extensive dealings with China, warned that the nation had to retain special privileges in Manchuria. Not only did it play a strategic role—as Nicaragua did to the United States and Egypt to England—but the region constituted an "economic lifeline." The chamber took offense at what it dubbed "illegal acts" of harassment by the Nationalist government since it had gained tariff autonomy in 1930. If the previous boycotts had represented a type of covert guerrilla tactics in economic warfare, the Chinese government was now making frontal assaults. A double tariff on goods entering and leaving the Japanese-controlled port of Dairen threatened to cripple the city. A hefty hike of the export levy on raw materials shipped from various parts of China to Japan's Kwantung Leased Territory would suffocate Japanese industry there. Japan had to "turn from its disadvantageous position" to a more vigorous policy. Still, Kōbe business leaders conceded the eclipse of the era of "scream[ing] for a strong foreign policy or a positive policy" every time the Chinese proved irksome. The Japanese must now "coolly investigate each real and immediate problem and move from screaming to real actions" to find solutions. As the political situation in parts of China stabilized, Japan might even consider a "gradual policy" to phase out extraterritoriality.[30] In 1931 executives in Kōbe and elsewhere anticipated no radical changes in the status quo. In fact, as the boycotts of Japanese products tapered off after 1929, these executives felt even less pressure to advocate military action.

The aggressive strategy of the Kwantung Army in Manchuria at first elicited support from the *zaikai*, because it thought that a brief, victorious conflict might make the Chinese more amenable in commercial negotiations. Almost immediately the Osaka Chamber of Commerce sent a telegram to the cabinet censuring the Chinese for causing the conflict. They had "neglect[ed] Japan's fair rights every time, ridicul[ed] Japan, and pursu[ed] anti-Japanese boycotts that contradict[ed] the basic principles of world peace." Confronting the violent actions of the Chinese army, the imperial forces had to resort to "temporary means of proper self-defense." "The Japanese hope[d] that the

Chinese government and people [would] change their previous provocative attitude and reflect suddenly upon realizing coprosperity between China and Japan and peace in East Asia."[31]

Eleven major business groups in the Kansai region near Osaka formed the China Economic Federation in order to recommend policies toward Manchuria and Mongolia. Members wanted the government to seek a basic revision of Sino-Japanese relations. As explained by Murata Shōzō, the president of the Osaka Shipping Company, Japan could no longer tolerate anti-Japanese boycotts because China was so important to the nation's economic development. A "strong foreign policy" must "sweep away past problems of plots between Japan and China" and take advantage of the current "good opportunity" to establish a permanent China policy.[32]

The president of the Japan Spinners Association, Abe Fusajirō, traveled to Tokyo to deliver this message to colleagues and officials there. The warm reception from "Tokyo business groups" pleased him; the cold caution of Foreign Minister Shidehara Kijūrō and Premier Wakatsuki Reijirō did not. According to Abe, these officials feared that "movements to arouse Japan's popular opinion might cause misunderstanding in the League of Nations [and] they can, on the contrary, retard negotiations between Japan and China and bring misfortune to the nation." This response discouraged federation members. Murata regretted the attempt of the government to "trample our movement." Takayanagi Matsuichirō objected to the assumption that the "unity of public opinion" would complicate efforts for peace. Sakata Kanda wondered "what the true intention of the government was."[33]

The Tokyo Chamber of Commerce deplored the "illegal, inappropriate, and arrogant" attitudes of the Chinese and urged a basic solution to "guarantee everlasting peace in East Asia." With the Western powers perturbed anyway, the Japan Economic Federation now did not hesitate to justify the nation's policies. The federation told the International Chamber of Commerce that Japanese troops acted in "self-defense" against Chinese provocations. Later the federation helped host Lord Lytton's commission, which the League of Nations appointed to study the crisis in Manchuria. The federation characterized Japanese trade with Manchuria and investment there as a "gift of Japanese development." The fifteen-fold increase in trade and the outlay of two billion yen since 1907 had brought prosperity to the region, not exploitation as charged by the Chinese government. Peace required direct negotiations based on guarantees of Japanese rights and Chinese leaders' abandonment of "mistaken policies."[34]

The eagerness of the business community waned as the conflict dragged on and anti-Japanese protests broke out once more. A "Resist Japan and Save the Nation Movement" prodded Chinese residents of Shanghai not only to avoid Japanese products but to stop working in Japanese factories. By early October domestic textile managers decided that their companies would have to curtail production because exports to the southern regions of China had suffered a sharp decline of 70 percent.[35] Some executives voiced fears that the resolve of the imperial army to conquer all of Manchuria would lead to "international war" and the "end of international trade."[36] In desperation they appealed to the League of Nations to marshal international opinion on Japan's side. Business leaders portrayed the boycotts as "acts of war without military arms" and "amazing barbaric acts without parallel in other nations of the twentieth century." Thus "China [was] without the real quality (*jisshitsu*) of a nation of laws." Surely the Western nations would concur that China had "trampled on international treaties" and pressure China into negotiations with Japan.[37]

The rising chorus of Western criticism against Japan precipitated a quarrel over Japan's status in the League of Nations. Some in the textile industry believed that because withdrawal might well incite a destructive world war, Japan had to "manipulate the league through skillful diplomacy." They complained that brutal actions by the army, such as the bombing of civilians at Chinchow, needlessly inflamed world opinion against Japan. Others insisted that Japan should leave the league if it would not accept Japan's "righteous" stand.[38] Nakayama Taichi declared at one meeting of business leaders in Osaka that, because America and Britain were fomenting the boycotts in China, abandoning the league was a good idea; a war would "bring the nation everlasting good fortune." Confident that the Japanese should not "fear the future," Takayanagi Matsuichirō of the Osaka Chamber of Commerce said at the same meeting that the time had come to "risk the fate of the nation." Shimada Ichirō, on the other hand, reminded the gathering that stopping trade would "cut off the road of life in today's society." Mori Heibei and others counseled caution. Neither this gathering nor the China Economic Federation could take a clear stand on whether Japan should seek dominance over Manchuria at the risk of permanently antagonizing the Western powers.[39]

As the imperial army swept across the plains of Manchuria, the attention of the business community gradually shifted to economic planning for the area. In January 1932 the Kwantung Army sponsored a conference on economic policy attended by delegates from the Japan Chamber of Commerce and chambers in Manchuria. The meeting concluded that Manchuria would prove most useful as a market for manufactured goods and a source of raw materials. Japan should allow only "special industries that would not threaten Japanese industry" to locate there. The Kwantung Army soon adopted these principles.[40] A few months later the Tokyo chamber proposed its own plan for the region. A special cabinet council, composed of officials and private citizens, would "plan appropriate facilities based on consistent [and] basic national policies." Existing financial organs would combine into one central bank and encourage the rise of "primitive" (genshi) industries. One could anticipate loud complaints from the Western powers that these policies would shatter the hallowed principle of the "open door" adopted by the Washington Conference of 1922—that all nations should enjoy equality of commercial opportunity in China. The chamber claimed that despite the tighter regulation of Manchuria's economy Japan would somehow adhere to the "open door."[41]

Toward the end of 1932 the minister of development, Nagai Ryūtarō, convened a conference of business leaders to discuss the economic development of Manchuria.[42] Japan had just bestowed official recognition to the region as the independent state of Manchukuo; Japanese troops, of course, blanketed the area, and the army dominated its government. Gō Seinosuke chaired the first session. The question of how seriously to take Manchukuo's alleged independence split the members. Some argued that accepting Manchuria as a sovereign nation meant that Japan must help industries there without asking for special privileges. Others sympathized with one participant who confessed that "considering Manchukuo as a foreign nation is strange (hen)." In frustration the conference deferred a solution to the deliberations of a smaller committee.

After several more meetings, Miyajima Seijirō finally offered a compromise in the form of two vague principles: "Japan and Manchuria, both [being] nations, must in the future cooperate and complement each other," and "Japan must avoid emphasizing special benefits (rieki) and rejecting [the rights of] third nations." Discussion then turned to the nature of such collaboration. Speaking on behalf of the Japan Spinners Association and the Trade Association of Cotton Cloth Exporters, Itō Chūbei recommended a cut in tariffs levied on cotton goods entering Manchuria from Japan. Lower tariffs would aid both consumers in Manchukuo and producers of textiles in Japan. This policy would, however, hamper the growth of a textile industry in the region. The group decided to propose tariff reductions for cotton products and other items that Manchukuo did not already make in great quantities. Eight months later, on July 23, 1933, Manchukuo's government reduced tariffs on "daily necessities" and tariffs "which are so high as to be in the nature of protection in spite of the fact that there exist no industries in this country requiring such protection."

The crises in China during the late 1920s and the early 1930s revealed the *zaikai*'s narrow focus, lack of imagination, and limited ambition in regard to foreign policy issues. Throughout the 1920s business leaders and groups had pressed for steep cuts in the military budget. Even when executives felt victimized by Chinese boycotts or double tariffs, they saw no need to call for conquest. Responding to the rise of Chinese nationalism, they wanted to keep existing privileges. Unaware of the Kwantung Army's aim to subjugate Manchuria, business leaders first cheered the outbreak of hostilities in 1931 as a way to intimidate China into dropping demands to alter the old commercial treaties. Presented with the *fait accompli* of Manchukuo, executives favored keeping the region's colonial economic role intact. They neither elaborated any ideals of assisting Chinese national development nor did they dream of a grand empire. Buffeted by events apparently beyond control, the business community focused on maintaining as much of the status quo as possible. If executives were insensitive to Chinese aspirations and blind to their implications, neither did they seek to propel the nation toward military imperialism. They still held faith in the virtues of peaceful foreign trade.

CONFRONTING INDIA

In 1933 a trade war with the British colony of India sparked another foreign policy crisis. This trauma portended future difficulties that quickly became all too common. It also called into question both the prospects for free trade and the ability of international commerce to bring prosperity to the nation.

Indian anxiety over Japanese exports of cotton yarn and cloth first surfaced in the early 1920s, when native textile industrialists agitated for increased tariffs on imports. In 1921 and 1926 these protests were virulent enough to prompt the Japan Spinners Association to petition the Indian government to reject the demands. The complaints puzzled the spinners, because Japanese exports to India then comprised less than 4 percent of that nation's cotton cloth production and less than 3 percent of yarn production. The steady increase in Indian output proved that these exports were not squashing native mills. Moreover, the overall balance of trade favored the British colony, thanks to Japan's voracious appetite for Indian raw cotton and pig iron; the value of these items often reached a value two or three times greater than the worth of the goods that India received. Riled by charges that they engaged in unfair competition, the spinners issued a detailed and spirited defense of their labor practices and wages. The cartel also threatened that a tariff hike could incite retaliation against Indian exports.[43]

The government of India refrained then from taking any action. Still, Japanese executives should have perceived that as their exports grew, tensions over trade would too. Appeals to overall economic justice and threats of retribution would not suffice to defuse crises in the future. This early dispute should have served as a warning that only sensitive and adroit diplomacy could prevent more severe problems.

The steady increase of Japanese textile exports over the next five years came at the expense of British exports. Statistics for two years, 1929 and 1930, showed that Japanese exports soared by over one-half to enlarge their share of the Indian market from 8.4 percent to 30 percent. England's slice of that pie shrank from 75 percent to 65 percent.[44] When the Indian government considered upping the tariff on cotton imports to 31.25 percent in early 1930, the Japan Economic Federation fired off protests to every major chamber of commerce in the colony.[45] The rapid enactment of the new levy in March reflected the panic that the perceived tidal wave of Japanese exports induced among the Indians and British.

The trade situation for India deteriorated quickly. In 1932 the precipitous devaluation of the yen by almost 50 percent helped spur a huge surge in Japanese exports that produced for the first time a favorable balance of payments with India. Japan now supplied one-half of all cotton textile exports to India. By 1933 British textile executives could see that in the past six years their total exports to all markets had dropped by 66 percent, whereas Japan's had grown by 50 percent. Meanwhile, the British share of the world market in textiles had fallen from 52 percent to 38 percent, while Japan's share had risen from 17 percent to 39 percent.[46] Japan's new success fanned the resentment of both native Indian industrialists who strived to raise their textile production and the mill owners of Lancashire who wanted to preserve their dominance of world markets.

Misjudging the situation, the Spinners Association failed to slacken exports to India. Textile executives perhaps imagined that gratitude for their huge purchases of raw cotton—fully one-half the total that India exported—would deter further protectionism. Also, as boycotts helped diminish exports to China, the spinners needed alternative markets.[47]

The Japanese strategy for extending textile exports soon met a dramatic response. The Ottawa conference in the summer of 1932 first imposed a system of preferential tariffs for trade among members of the British empire. Then India boosted its tariff on non-British imports to a hefty 50 percent, twice the rate for British goods. Japanese exports to India continued to grow, because they still enjoyed a price advantage. In April 1933 India abruptly declared that the government would renounce its commercial treaty with Japan, which dated from 1904, in order to gain more freedom of action in trade matters.

Stunned, the Japanese textile industry cried foul and vowed revenge. The head of the Spinners Association, Abe Fusajirō, taunted British textile executives by saying that they did not dare to compete on the world market. Tsuda Shingo of the Kanegafuchi Company prepared for battle: "conciliatory measures [were] useless . . ." because the other side was "unreasonable." Two trade groups, the Cotton Textile Association and the Japan Export Cotton Textile Traders Association, disdained the thought of any concessions; the Indian side might interpret them as an admission of weakness. These groups urged a boycott of Indian cotton, an increased tariff on raw cotton, and the promotion of cotton cultivation in Manchuria and Mongolia.[48]

The Japanese government tried to minimize the crisis. Nakajima Kumakichi, a leader of the Japan Economic Federation and minister of commerce and industry in the cabinet of Admiral Saitō Makoto that took office in May 1932, professed optimism about negotiations. He explained that the government had intended to restrict exports to India, but some urgent internal issues, especially the merger of major steel companies into one huge firm, had deflected attention from this goal. Nakajima believed that both sides had much to lose. Kurusu Saburō, the head of the Commerce Bureau of the Ministry of Foreign Affairs, told British diplomats that the government was "using every effort to diffuse a calm view" despite "great difficulty with the textile industry."[49] When Walter Runciman, the president of the British Board of Trade, proposed a British-Japanese conference to plan the sharing of all colonial markets, the Japanese government eagerly entered into serious discussions. By late May both sides had agreed to talks in India.[50]

Officials then faced the daunting task of persuading textile leaders to participate in these talks. The Economic Federation, as the primary representative of large companies, helped by attuning its proposals to the government's policies. Before Nakajima's attitude became clear, the group refused to reply to a plea from the Manchester Chamber of Commerce for textile talks between the two nations. Once the government backed negotiations, the federation stressed the importance of overall economic ties between Britain and Japan: "regarding problems between India and Japan, [and] concerning the economic relations of Japan and England revolving around the Indian problem, not simply the cotton industry but [also] the effects on other export goods to India must enter into consideration; and, taking a comprehensive viewpoint, [we] must proceed with a spirit of cooperation between Japan and England." To the *Daily Mail* in London the federation wrote that the two nations "had to moderate and correct the current competitive situation." The message explained: "We feel the need for both nations together to reflect on continuing the uncontrolled competition in commercial goods between the two nations as something that will ultimately lead their economic exchange to destruction."[51]

British and Indian officials rebuffed these conciliatory gestures. On June 6 the Indian government raised the import levy to a prohibitive 75 percent. The Japan Spinners Association retaliated immediately. Complaining that the Indian government "lacked sincerity," the spinners ceased purchases of Indian cotton. The next day the Japan Cotton Trade Association (Nihon Menka Dōgyōkai) agreed.[52]

The government and other business groups struggled to contain the dispute. Commenting that the government could not interfere in the spinners' "natural" reaction to India's policies, the head of the Commerce Ministry's Trade Bureau, Terao Susumu, reiterated Japan's willingness to negotiate. Warning of the spinners' "angry and excited mood," Kurusu Saburō, head of the Foreign Ministry's Commerce Bureau, told British Commercial Attaché

George Sansom that the Japanese government would discuss restraints on exports. Ambassador Matsudaira Tsuneo informed British officials in London that Japan desired to finish any talks by October 10, when the commercial treaty would officially expire.[53] The Economic Federation dispatched a telegram to the Federation of British Industries and other major business organizations in England admitting that the spinners had acted "through an excess of excitement." Lamenting the current tensions and pleading for negotiations to begin, the federation also criticized India's arbitrary actions. All trade sanctions violated the spirit of the London International Economic Conference, which would soon tackle the awesome challenge of resuscitating world trade. Labelling the boycott of Indian cotton an "inevitable" reaction to the new tariffs, both the Kōbe and Tokyo chambers of commerce advocated the start of negotiations.[54]

Nakajima knew that textile executives would have to participate, because they would have to carry out any agreements. When he met with textile leaders in late June, Abe consented to have two members of the Spinners Association join talks with Indian businessmen. The Export Cotton Textile Traders Association (Yushutsu Menshifu Dōgyōkai) agreed to do the same. The Commerce Ministry's announcement that Yoshino Shinji would travel to Osaka to confer on policy toward India suggested that Nakajima promised close consultation with the textile industry.[55]

Over the summer both nations devised strategies for the talks. The Commerce Ministry conferred with the Ministries of Finance and Foreign Affairs and with businessmen to outline an initial position that everyone could support. Officials and business leaders managed to concur on two principles: Japan would ask India to cut the 75 percent duty in return for curbs on textile exports. In addition, if India ended discriminatory levies on sundry goods, Japan would restrain those exports.[56] Meanwhile, the Indian government confronted conflicting interest groups. While warning the Spinners Association that indignation against Japan could inspire a total boycott of Japanese goods, the East India Cotton Association, which represented cotton growers, asked its government to resolve the trade dispute quickly. Industrial groups, however, lobbied for more protection. India's elected assembly considered legislation that would tie quotas of imports to monthly changes in prices and the exchange rate.[57]

The two governments finally agreed to commence negotiations in late

September. The soothing climate and pleasant scenery of Simla, a mountain resort town in India, provided the setting. Discussions between business delegations from Britain, India, and Japan would supplement the efforts of their nations' diplomats. Ideally, the business leaders' talks would iron out the details of a general pact sketched by the official talks.

These began ominously. The initial positions of the Japanese and Indian delegates clashed. The Japanese representative, Sawada Setsuzō, proposed to hold exports of cotton goods to 578,529,000 square yards, the level reached in the fiscal year 1932–33, if India slashed its textile tariff to 50 percent. Claiming that the level of exports for 1932–33 had been abnormally high, the chief Indian negotiator, Sir Joseph Bhore, dismissed the offer. He suggested the novel solution of linking export quotas for Japan to its purchases of Indian cotton. Sawada responded that Japanese textile leaders would never accept such a system. As if to prove this point, the Spinners Association in early October repudiated the government's initial offer, because the quota was too low and the tariff too high.[58]

The conferences of private businessmen yielded equally dismal results. The delegates from India and Japan met only twice. Japanese and British businessmen got together more frequently, but did little more than insult each other.[59] Sir William Clare Lees opened these talks with an indictment of Japan's "competitive attack" as proceeding "at a pace which could only be regarded as abnormal." He continued, "We cannot be reproached for proposing to cope with it by measures which must necessarily be equally unprecedented." The Japanese countered that the efficiency of their industries was due neither to "deliberate national policy nor to concerted action on the part of industrialists" but resulted from "patriotic efforts to stimulate production as a measure of self-preservation." While complaining about the weak yen, the British should remember that they had devalued the pound. Lees then candidly identified the nub of the British view: "If [a nation's] policy imperils the well-being of the people of other nations, it is natural that they should act vigorously in their own defense." He added that, "in a world consuming less, Japan was producing more; this had to stop." Subsequent discussions proved unproductive.

In the diplomatic arena, the Indian government unveiled a detailed proposal on October 17. It would impose on Japan an export quota of 300 million square yards, the average level of exports for the period from 1924 to 1931; in return for this magnanimity Japan would pledge to buy 1.25 million bales of cotton per year. The Japanese would have to spread their exports evenly over the four quarters of the year and stay within prearranged quotas for each of six categories of textiles. Japanese businessmen would thus lose the flexibility to shift exports from one product to another and to compensate for slack exports in one period by funneling them into another one. Finally, although the tariff would decrease to 50 percent, it would climb if the yen continued to depreciate.[60]

The talks then recessed so that the Japanese could scrutinize the proposal. Claiming that the "Japanese government cannot withstand the pressure of Osaka," Sawada privately implored the Indian representatives to make a concession. They told him that because Indian mill owners adamantly demanded an export quota of 250 million square yards, 375 million was tops. Kurusu then promised British diplomats in Tokyo that if the Indian government would grant a quota exceeding 300 million yards, he could convince the cotton industry to accept a system of tying exports to imports.[61]

Yoshino Shinji and Kurusu went to Osaka in late October. Meeting with industrialists on the thirtieth, these officials stressed that the talks at Simla had to end soon. The India-Japan commercial treaty had officially run out and was operating on a shaky ad hoc basis. Textile leaders continued their tenacious opposition to the whole Indian proposal. They refused to contemplate any limit on exports to India, the division of the quota into four installment periods, the assignment of quotas for six categories of products, and special duties to balance any changes in the exchange rate. They also took exception to the preferential tariffs for British goods. The Spinners Association then disclosed what it considered a compromise plan. If India would forgo maximum limits on exports, installment periods, categories of products, special duties, and preferential tariffs, the textile industry would pledge to purchase one million bales of cotton for each 500 million square yards of textiles that Japanese companies exported. Knowing that this plan would infuriate the Indian government, Yoshino and Kurusu spurned the proposal on the spot. Another day of discussions brought the two sides no closer together.[62]

To show they meant business, Yoshino and Kurusu scheduled the next meeting for November 8 in the official residence of the vice-minister of foreign affairs in Tokyo. Just one day remained until the Simla negotiations would resume. Facing a possible rupture of these talks, the six textile delegates met beforehand at the Japan Industrial Club and set a new strategy. They would tolerate the division of exports into two instead of four annual install-ment periods and the assignment of quotas to three categories of goods instead of six. The executives continued to balk at linking levies to the exchange rate and at approving any preferential tariffs. Later, government officials and textile leaders agreed on a ratio of 400 million yards of exports in return for the purchase of one million bales of cotton. "Regarding other practical conditions, [the government pledged] to stress totally the emphasis of the civilian side in the Japan-India commercial talks on the ninth [of November] and to expect their enactment."[63]

The dickering over details between the Japanese and Indian negotiators then began. They quickly decided to institute two annual installment periods, four categories of exports to be governed by quotas, and a ratio of 400 million square yards of textile exports for 1.5 million bales of cotton imports. The major disputes raged over the low percentage of the quota assigned to bleached cottons—8 percent with a variation of 10 percent—and Indian insistence on the right to impose additional duties if the yen fell further. The Japanese wanted a 20 percent share for bleached goods and, of course, no additional tariffs.[64]

Indian intransigence on these minor issues almost destroyed the tenuous coalition on the Japanese side. Lambasting the Indians for their "insincerity," textile executives in late November swore to continue the boycott of cotton and to withdraw their representatives from Simla. Upset that Japan had sacrificed too much already, Tsuda Shingo decided to make the first move; he had Kane-gafuchi's emissary sent home immediately. Miyajima Seijirō told Kurusu that India's rejection of a "10 percent allowance," which would permit a category's share of the quota to vary by an amount equal to 10 percent of the whole quota, could doom the entire agreement.[65] Japanese officials in the Indian capital of Delhi tried to maintain an air of confidence. They reassured their Indian counterparts that "as for the negotiations, up to 99 percent were progressing satisfactorily" and that a settlement would come soon. In private, Kurusu apologized to British diplomats for the obstreperous behavior of his nation's textile leaders.[66]

The government at last decided to bring the spinners into line. Yoshino Shinji was ordered to Osaka. The message he conveyed remains undocu-mented, but within a week major textile industrialists along with managers of smaller firms had declared total confidence in the government's negotiators. On December 9 Commerce Minister Nakajima held another meeting with leaders of the most powerful textile groups. He proclaimed that an "amicable settlement . . . was necessary for Japanese commerce as a whole and indeed for Japan politically." He asked for and received industry consent to accept the anticipated pact with India.[67]

Straightening out details took another month. The Indians allowed a slight variation in the quota of bleached goods. A Japanese suggestion to limit new duties to situations in which the yen's exchange rate plummeted 20 percent or more over three consecutive months evoked only a vague promise of moderation. The Indian government would keep increases "to what is necessary to correct [the] effect of such depreciation on [the] duty paid value of Japanese goods imported into India." The two sides also squabbled over the amount of the export quota for 1934–35.[68] When the negotiators managed to sign a provisional pact in January 1934, the spinners promptly terminated the boycott of raw cotton.

The resolution of this trade dispute exposed the delicate balance of power in Japanese government-business relations. Neither side could dictate to the other. The Spinners Association first opted to act on its own with little regard for the government's wishes. Other business groups proved more amenable. They either stayed aloof or, like the Japan Economic Federation, advocated a quick start of negotiations to contain the spread of protectionist sentiment abroad. Officials, in effect, found themselves mediating between the spinners and the government of India.

The government could not force the spinners to back down. It listened to and accommodated their views; after all, they represented the nation's most successful and largest industry. Frequent meetings sought to combine textile leaders' demands with terms that the Indian side might accept. As Sawada constantly told his counterparts at Simla, the government could not compel industrialists to cease their boycott or to purchase set amounts of cotton each year. Any arrangement for a so-called link system would depend upon industrialists' goodwill, because they would have to carry out any controls.[69] The stubbornness of the textile leaders made life miserable for Yoshino, Kurusu, Sawada, and other officials. However, they could accomplish little of what the Spinners Association wanted, and yet made it comply with the pact that resulted.

The government then had to referee a dispute between domestic textile groups, which immediately began wrangling over the control of exports to India. A group of textile exporters put forward a plan for a special export association to monitor the flow of goods. The Spinners Association preferred that a federation of exporters, importers, and producers supervise the trade. The spinners aimed to guarantee that established producers would retain their current share of the market, whereas the exporters wanted to open up at least 30 percent of the Indian quota to competitive bids. The Ministry of Commerce and Industry devised a compromise within a week. A special council to guide general policies would embrace delegates from the three major textile groups: the Spinners Association, the Japan Federation of Industrial Associations for Cotton Woven Goods (Menkōren), and the Export Association for India. The latter would assign specific quotas to various exporters. The Spinners Association and Menkōren, which represented manufacturers of woven cotton products, would do the same for producers. This council later decided to reserve 20 percent of the total quota for competitive bids; the spinners and weavers agreed on a formal division of the production quota.[70]

A cynical analyst of the negotiations between India and Japan might suspect that the government secretly encouraged the bluster of the textile leaders in order to gain an advantage in the talks. Without the boycott of cotton purchases, the government of India would have had no reason to make concessions. The boycott, though, came as a knee-jerk response to a sudden shock, the 75 percent tariff enacted on June 6. The speed with which the Spinners Association acted precluded extensive discussions with government officials. Moreover, the move countered the fervent wish of Commerce Minister Nakajima for an amicable settlement of the trade crisis. Abhorring the prospect of a formal rift with the British empire, the government insisted that an official extension of the commercial treaty become the first item of negotiation in October.[71] If the government and the spinners had collaborated, Tsuda and others would not have tried to scuttle the talks toward the end. If Tsuda felt any gratitude toward the Japanese negotiators, he kept it well hidden. Long afterwards he berated the government for its abject surrender to Indian demands.[72]

The trade crisis exasperated both the Spinners Association and the government. The efforts of the latter to mediate between the association and the harsh reality of the outside world won few thanks. Although officials wanted to aid the textile industry, they also had the unwelcome task of educating the spinners about the volatile force of trading partners' resentment.

THE FAILURE OF AN IDEAL

Major business groups repeatedly advocated international agreements to abolish trade barriers. As early as 1928 the journal of the Japan Trade Council had defined rising tariffs as a major obstacle for Japanese trade and had discerned the difficulty of halting the trend. Only "seeking some radical changes in the present economic structure" could solve the problem. An economic "new liberalism" would have to transcend a "narrow view of the nation" and progress toward a "large view of the world and of humanity." The situation required that "the economic, public finance, and trade promotion policies of the new Japan [had to] decide its path with this new liberalism as its beacon and reject completely the old thought of [selfish] utilitarianism."[73] While the council fretted about whether international meetings could inspire real cooperation among nations, the Tokyo Chamber of Commerce took a hopeful stance. The government should attend the international economic conference sponsored by the League of Nations at Geneva in 1930, because the agenda featured discussion of a "pact for a truce on tariffs." The failure of that conference to produce an agreement did not prove discouraging. Believing that tariff wars would "prevent the recovery of industry and trade for each nation," the chamber gamely proposed another gathering. Sessions of the International Chamber of Commerce gave delegates from the Japan Economic Federation opportunities to underline the need for international collaboration as a solution to the world depression.[74]

Another International Economic Conference, scheduled to start in London during June 1933, aroused the expectations of Japanese businessmen. Again sponsored by the League of Nations, the meeting planned to assemble delegates from sixty-six nations in order to focus on issues relating to currency and trade. That the minister of foreign affairs for Britain, Sir John Simon, took charge of the organizing committee signified the importance of the meeting. It would have the authority to produce formal treaties, because each government would send an official delegation. Many governments expressed hopes that the conference might revive multilateral economic cooperation.[75] The officers of the Japan Industrial Club, the Japan Economic Federation, and the Tokyo Chamber of Commerce drafted a resolution in April and issued it in May. These groups desired a "spirit of cooperation" to end retaliatory tariffs, a "spirit of mutual compromise" to reduce ordinary tariffs, and an "international treaty to sweep away limits and embargoes on exports and imports." Mirroring the sentiments of many colleagues, Suzuki Shimakichi, a director of the Economic Federation, pleaded for resurrecting a stable exchange rate and lowering tariffs all over the world. "For Japan," he wrote, "this conference is a problem of life and death."[76]

Preparations for the conference heartened Japanese business groups. The United States recommended to the organizing committee that in order to ease tensions all participants should promise not to boost any tariffs until the conference ended. After the committee adopted the proposal, forty-two nations pledged to abide by it. The Tokyo chamber applauded this development and added that, rather than settle for the American goal of a uniform decrease of 10 percent in levies, the conference should strive to restore the tariff levels that existed before 1930.[77] Commerce Minister Nakajima explained the lofty aspirations of the business community at a special gathering held in honor of the Japanese emissary, Ishii Kikujirō. Highlighting tariffs as Japan's major concern, Nakajima said that "the great causes of the current economic collapse could be eliminated only through the means of international cooperation, but now it seems that we cannot expect effective or remarkable results from international activity. Therefore we cannot help turning to this economic conference and hoping for the creation of some new political philosophy concerning internationalism and economic nationalism."[78]

Ishii, the distinguished former ambassador to the United States, France, and the League of Nations, did his best in London to further the cause of free trade. Soon after the conference began he branded economic boycotts as the main impediments to freedom of commerce and world peace and proposed a treaty to end all such actions. Later he advocated a pact to uphold the sanctity of the "most favored nation" clauses in commercial treaties. Proper respect for this principle would forestall trade barriers aimed at specific nations.[79]

Unfortunately for the Japanese delegation, the conference collapsed without confronting these issues.[80] Inviting officials from eleven major nations for preliminary talks in Washington, the United States had tried mightily throughout the spring to persuade participants to concentrate on trade issues in London. Despite promises to do so, British Prime Minister Ramsay MacDonald derailed the proceedings in his opening address. He declared that the United States' refusal to forgive loans made to its allies during World War I throttled any hope of European recovery from the depression. As the American delegation, led by Secretary of State Cordell Hull, battled to avoid discussion of that issue, currency matters ignited new debates. American delegates angered their British and French counterparts by an offhanded rejection of a pact that would stabilize exchange rates, a goal of many participants. Having just abandoned gold two months before, President Franklin D. Roosevelt wanted the freedom to devalue the dollar in order to raise domestic prices as a counter to the deflationary effects of the depression. American officials seemed callous in refusing to sympathize with problems in foreign trade that the weakening of the dollar and other currencies posed for European nations with a gold standard—France, Italy, Belgium, Holland, and Sweden. Frustrated, these nations gave up and forced adjournment of the conference in early July.

This fiasco darkened Japanese attitudes toward the future of international trade. A special edition of the *Tokyo asahi* announced the news with the headline: "Now the Destruction of Cooperation-ism." The *Asahi Economic Yearbook* viewed the London Conference as verifying the strength of nationalism as a worldwide force, because no nation stepped forward to sacrifice its interests in order to save the world economy.[81] Within the business community, the failure of the conference became a common symbol of a basic change in the world economy. To Fujiyama Raita the fate of the conference marked the passing of the age of economic "liberalism," and to Kadono Chokyūrō it forebode more restrictions on free trade and the rapid growth of economic nationalism. The executive director of the Mitsui Bank, Kikumoto Naojirō, characterized the failure of the conference to his branch managers as an "epoch-making event," because it would bring unstable exchange rates and rampant protectionism. The semiannual report of the Mitsubishi Bank emphasized the gloomy aftermath of the meeting, as America pursued an inflationary policy, France adopted new import barriers, and England declared the sterling bloc. "Thus the economic wars between each nation [could] get worse, and one [had to] think that the recovery of the world economy based on international cooperation seem[ed] full of difficulties in the future." To Nakajima Kumakichi, the conference had raised high hopes and its collapse had underscored how, in foreign trade, "various unfavorable things [were] piling up like a mountain."[82] Executives and officials had to join forces to create new forms of controls to bolster the trade sector.

A NEW PARTNERSHIP

To cope with these bewildering international difficulties, many executives sought a closer relationship with the government. The impressive progress of the industrial rationalization movement showed that business leaders and civil servants could work well together. The Temporary Industrial Rationalization Bureau (Rinji Sangyō Gōrikyoku), which the Ministry of Commerce and Industry formed in June 1930, embodied this cooperation. One of the ministry's ablest officials, Yoshino Shinji, directed the office; Nakajima Kumakichi, then a top officer of the Japan Economic Federation, represented the business community. Comprising officials and executives, six standing committees supplemented the permanent staff and studied general policies to raise industrial efficiency. Ad hoc committees discussed solutions to problems in specific industries.[83]

Nakajima lauded the bureau as a truly joint venture between government and business, because the former aided the latter without dictating policy. The bureau, he said, appeared like a "bureaucratic organ" located in a government ministry. But, "when one observe[d] its real work, it [was] totally the same as a private self-governing body; there [were] specialized committees that [were] under the Rationalization Bureau and spread across every industry and which conduct[ed] research on rationalization. There [were] committees mainly for enacting control of related enterprises based on discussions between businessmen; entrusting everything to voluntary (*jihatsuteki*) research and self-governing control [was] the reality of our Industrial Rationalization Bureau."[84]

Business, however, could not succeed alone. Nakajima predicted that when "welfare-ism" replaced "greed-ism" as the dominant economic ethic, industry would have to "recognize the meaningful intervention of the state in the public and private economy." The state must make sure that the rationalization movement fulfilled its role of "service to society" and its mission of "open[ing] a new age." Nakajima cited the German economist and industrialist, Walter Rathenau, who had argued that industrial rationalization meant "planning the reform of industry and regulation of production based on unifying all organs in one industry and guiding them toward one goal through an independent central administrative organ." By insuring the fair distribution of profits to stockholders, to the "nation," to those "related to production," and to consumers through lower prices, the state could prevent the usual evil effects of cartels. In return, the state had to "recognize industrial monopoly in the economic system." Working together on the basis of a "group spirit," the state and industry could "produce a [new] form of the nation's economic life" in response to the "stagnation of material civilization."[85]

Among the various joint government-business committees in the Rationalization Bureau, the Control Committee had the greatest effect on legislation. Members included the fastest-rising stars in the Commerce Ministry, Yoshino Shinji and Kishi Nobusuke. Eminent executives graced the list of business participants: Mitsubishi's Matsuoka Kinpei; bankers Hōrai Ichimatsu, Yamamuro Sōbun, and Kikumoto Naojirō; the Japan Spinners Association's Takayanagi Matsuichirō; and Zen Keinosuke from the Japan Industrial Club.[86] By February 1931 the group's discussions had produced a draft for a new "industrial control law." Although some Diet members worried about potential abuses by new cartels, the bill passed easily in March.[87] The Important Industries Control Law allowed cartels to form in designated sectors. Whatever influence Kishi and Yoshino wielded, the committee ratified a proposal long advanced by business groups. Many years later, Yoshino still remembered the eagerness of executives on the committee for the law.[88]

When the original Control Committee disbanded upon completing its mission of drafting a cartel law, a new committee formed to advise the commerce minister. This body assumed significant powers both in selecting industries for cartels and in approving requests to have the government compel firms not in a cartel—so-called outsiders—to follow its policies. At first, eighteen sectors received designation as major industries, and the number soon grew to twenty-six. The committee, though, showed little interest in supervising the cartels' routine activities.

The Control Committee took its boldest action in 1934. Disturbed by an expansion of cement factories while unused capacity remained high, government authorities tried to persuade executives of different firms to plan together for the future. Finally, a dozen companies agreed to coordinate production, prices, and planning. When the companies petitioned the committee to make all other firms comply with these guidelines, it consented to do so.[89] To prevent future crises, it also suggested that a special committee of business-

men and government officials in the Industrial Rationalization Bureau probe
the basic problems of the cement industry and forge a consensus on solutions.
In two other cases, when prices for paper products and then sugar jumped, the
committee settled for publicizing warnings against further increases.[90]

The ad hoc committees of the Rationalization Bureau furnished many
examples of effective cooperation between government and business. Nakajima took special pride in the groups created in 1930 to help the striped cloth
and the cotton crepe industries.[91] The striped cloth industry, for example, had
fallen on hard times. In the 1920s production had risen steadily to meet a
surging demand in Asian nations, where the material was often used to make
shirts. By 1930 the competition for sales among the 370 small manufacturers
had devastated prices. Slim profit margins tempted manufacturers to cut cor-
ners on quality; as overseas consumers realized this, orders dwindled. After
preliminary talks between producers reached a standstill, Commerce Ministry
officials convinced industry leaders to create an "improvement committee" in
the Rationalization Bureau. A businessman, Yamada Atsushi of the Nihon
Cotton Company, served as chairman; most members represented industrial
associations from the four areas where most of the cloth was made.[92]

Two weeks of discussion in July 1930 brought progress—a plan to supervise production, prices, and quality. A national federation of local industrial
associations for striped cloth would regulate the industry. All of the companies
would have to arrange their sales through the federation, which would open a
cooperative sales office in Osaka. A special committee of producers, the Shō
Giinkai, in the federation would determine the quotas on production and
minimum prices.

Developments in the cotton crepe industry followed a similar pattern.
Embracing many small firms that sold most of their products to other Asian
markets, this sector had suffered from cutthroat internal competition. In October 1930 a council of executives agreed on the urgency to apply national
controls; a committee soon formed in the Rationalization Bureau. Only one
official from the Commerce Ministry participated. This group proposed the
national regulation of production, sales, and prices through a national federation of industrial associations.[93]

The changes helped both textile sectors. During the first year of these new
controls, production and profits rose. Neither industry escaped the economic
turmoil of late 1931, when the shrinkage of markets all over the world caused a

massive drop in the volume of all exports. Each sector, however, recovered well after that.[94]

The ease of creating these solutions and their early success inspired glowing words of praise. *Sangyō gōrika* (Industrial Rationalization), which the Japan Chamber of Commerce published as the official organ of the rationalization movement, boasted that the reform of the striped cloth industry constituted the "spearhead of rationalization" and the "first [example of] industrial control for the whole nation." The industry's revival could help reinvigorate the entire economy, proving that rationalization was not just a negative program to cut costs by forcing workers off the payroll but a positive contribution to prosperity. The improvement committees provided a model of how businessmen and officials could profitably pull together and advance the nation's economic success.[95]

Yoshino Shinji concurred. Impressed by the results of the policies toward the striped cloth industry, he took pride in the special provisions that encouraged efficiency. Every year part of the annual production quota was reserved for new or current manufacturers who could surpass the present level of productivity. Viewing the evolution of cartels as natural, Yoshino believed that in an ideal world executives in an industry would voluntarily collaborate to lower costs, improve the quality of products, and work for the benefit of their sector as a whole. At least for the near future, Yoshino thought, the government should aid cartels by curbing any tendencies to abuse their powers and supply funds for investment in more productive facilities.[96]

Other industries were quick to copy the policies of the striped cloth industry. In 1931 a committee gathered in the Rationalization Bureau to discuss the pottery industry, whose exports had slipped over 25 percent during the previous year. Again a national federation of industrial associations assumed the task of adjusting production to meet demand in certain categories of products.[97] The recommendation of another ad hoc committee in 1930 persuaded the government to declare phosphoric fertilizer an important export so that producers of it could form a national industrial association.[98] A farsighted concern for future problems rather than an immediate crisis compelled the Rationalization Bureau to help organize the Federation of Industrial Associations for Cotton Dyed Woven Goods, which comprised about one-third of Japanese cotton exports. This body too aimed at the coordination of production and sales within the industry.[99]

In some industries, joining forces was hard. Settling on a production agreement in the match industry required almost two years of negotiation. In 1934 a committee to reshape the citrus fruit sector faltered, because producers and exporters fought so viciously over allotting profits from the lucrative North American market. When a plan for regulating exports failed to emerge, the government had to impose a strict system of licensing.[100]

Beyond specific successes or failures, the Industrial Rationalization Bureau gave businessmen and government officials a chance to experiment with a new cooperative relationship, one that approached the ideal of "reciprocal consent."[101] The Control Committee permitted businessmen to draft an important law and to implement it. The government encouraged executives in the ad hoc committees to solve their own problems. Still, officials played a crucial role because they could arbitrate disputes and coerce recalcitrants into complying with the decisions of a cartel or industrial federation.

In trade matters, executives wanted officials to help blunt the ruinous effects of wasteful competition in addition to giving various kinds of financial aid and ensuring access to markets. In turn, civil servants, such as Yoshino and Kishi, seemed comfortable in this mediating and supporting role. The strategy of combining state power and private initiative within each major industry held great promise, as long as trading partners did not retreat entirely behind their castle walls of tariffs and quotas.

FOUR
WAGING A TRADE WAR,
1934–1937

I n mid-decade dramatic political and economic changes fomented tensions with Japan's trading partners. They watched with alarm the rising power of the military and the strengthening of the nationalistic mood within Japan. On May 15, 1932, naval cadets sauntered into the residence of Premier Inukai Tsuyoshi and murdered him in cold blood. Fearing that party politicians could not maintain law and order, the emperor proceeded to entrust military officers with leadership of the cabinet. The military's share of the budget began to climb. The thought police rounded up thousands of suspected dissidents and launched a systematic and effective program to have them expunge all alien thoughts and to pledge allegiance to the throne. Reservist associations and right-wing groups hounded the nation's most eminent legal scholar, Minobe Tatsukichi, into resigning his imperial appointment to the House of Peers. He had committed the crime of deemphasizing the emperor's divine origins as the source of his supreme constitutional authority. Commerce Minister Nakajima Kumakichi also came under fire, because fourteen years before he had dared to publish an essay about a fourteenth-century warrior, Ashikaga Takauji, who had betrayed an emperor to seize political power. Advised by the premier to resign, Nakajima did so in 1934.[1] These events made outside observers worry about where this virulent chauvinism would lead.

The brash acts of the military provided scant reassurance. The navy pressured the cabinet to quit the strictures of the Washington naval pact, while the army began to pry loose the provinces of North China from the control of the Nationalist government. In February 1936 the first division in Tokyo revolted, seized the center of the capital, and assassinated several cabinet ministers and advisers to the emperor. The leaders hoped to create a government of direct imperial rule that would proclaim martial law. After several days the rebellion petered out, but by unsheathing the threat of rebellion the military garnered more political power into its hands. Later that year the cabinet asked for a huge boost in military spending; in 1930 about one-quarter of the national budget had been allocated to the military, but now it consumed fully one-half of expenditures. The growth of the military and its actions in

China generated suspicions abroad about the ultimate aims of Japan's foreign policy. When trade disputes broke out, the Japanese had few reserves of trust or goodwill left to draw on. In this context, the surge in the nation's exports seemed particularly sinister.

The business community responded effectively to the challenge of dealing with a constant series of disputes over trade barriers. Discussions with officials resulted in machinery to invoke sanctions that made trade partners dismantle the most unfair obstacles to Japanese exports. Executives worked hard to fashion a national trade structure that would embody the principles evident in the success of the Industrial Rationalization Bureau. Civil servants and business leaders would together set general policies and delegate implementation to private groups. Deciding on issues of foreign policy proved more vexing. Although dark clouds hung over the horizon of international trade, the zaikai did not view dependence on a regional Asian bloc as an adequate haven from stormy disputes over trade. Businessmen decided to take advantage of Japan's position in China while preserving as much trade as possible with the Western powers and their colonies.

Japan's goods appeared to flood world markets. Total exports more than doubled between 1932 and 1937. Increases in shipments of cotton yarn, woven goods, chinaware, toys, iron, and steel led the advance. As this trend obsessed trade partners, they overlooked Japan's chronic trade deficit caused by the need to import more and more raw materials for expanding industries. The nation registered a trade surplus in only one year, 1935.[2] By then Japanese exports still constituted only 3 percent of the world's total, less than a third of the United States' 10 percent share. At the time one American economist, Miriam Farley, observed with unusual objectivity that the rise in Japan's share of world exports had been "very moderate" and well "balanced" by imports. The Japanese had reason to take offense at new attempts to limit their exports everywhere. Farley speculated that Japan, as what scholars would later call a "late developer," had merely "picked the wrong century in which to industrialize."[3] At least Japan's export surge was ill-timed, because it occurred when most nations' industrial production had plummeted and world trade had shrunk by 25 percent. Governments were hard pressed to ignore the widespread cries for protection from foreign competition. By 1932 the unemployment rate in the United States had soared to 32 percent, in Germany to 18, and in Britain to

12. Shortening the long lines of workers seeking jobs took priority over concerns for not offending Japanese sensibilities.

By 1936 every major nation had curtailed the influx of Japanese exports. After the link agreement with British India, the Dutch East Indies followed suit. Upset by Japan's seizing an 83 percent portion of the cotton textile market in their colony, the Dutch demanded negotiations to begin in 1934. When these stalled, the Dutch imposed strict quotas on many goods. France in 1932 placed quotas on imports into its colonies from all other nations. After talks between Japanese and British businessmen failed because of the former's refusal to discuss worldwide quotas for textile exports, Britain applied quotas in all its colonies and protectorates. The Nationalist government in China effected new tariffs in 1933. The United States protested Japan's emergence as the major supplier of cotton textiles to the Philippines and forced the Japanese to accept a share of less than 50 percent of that market. American textile concerns then lobbied for restraints on exports to the United States despite a massive trade surplus with Japan. Even relatively new markets, such as Cuba, Iraq, and Egypt, swiftly enacted high tariffs or quotas as Japanese goods began arriving in force. Farley concluded with scholarly understatement: few nations could boast that in trade "conventional equality of opportunity prevail[ed]."[4]

ENTERING THE TARIFF WAR

Retaliation provided one tempting response to the wave of trade barriers. In the wake of the boycott of Indian raw cotton by the Japan Spinners Association in 1933, business leaders began to consider using import restrictions as part of a planned national strategy. The long period of time required to get the Diet's approval of new tariffs made this tactic difficult. For reprisals to work, the government would have to change tariffs quickly to counter hostile acts by other nations.

This idea had emerged already in the business-government Council on Tariffs in 1929. Anticipating a return to the gold standard, the council proposed that government officials be able to alter tariffs within a given range to protect industries from an expected flood of imports.[5] The Japan Economic Federation elaborated on the council's proposal. In July 1931 a special committee began to study tariff policies and six months later issued a major report.

It affirmed the need for protective tariffs for some industries: those necessary for national defense and those central to the economy, as well as promising new ones, such as the manufacture of aluminum and automobiles. Some other goods might need sheltering in special circumstances, such as sudden swings in exchange rates that would depress the prices of imports, or attempts by competitors to dump surplus production on Japanese markets. Noting the popularity of discriminatory tariffs abroad, the federation favored a multiple-tariff system. The government would apply the highest rates to imports from nations that refused to sign a commercial treaty with Japan or that "gave our exports a disadvantageous reception compared to [that given to exports from] other nations."[6]

Business leaders sought a structure to encourage equal cooperation between government and the business community. The Economic Federation believed that such a tariff system should not come under the purview of a single government ministry. Because tariffs affected the entire economy, a "broad general viewpoint" must guide their enactment. Only a new tariff council in which private citizens would constitute at least one-half of the members could overcome sectional bureaucratic interests. The members would include businessmen, citizens knowledgeable about the economy, politicians, and officials from related ministries. Attached to the cabinet, this group would have access to all economic data and could solicit testimony from government officials, individuals, and corporations. This council would make the final decisions on all levies.[7]

In late 1933 high-level talks between officials and executives focused on the strategy of wielding tariffs as a weapon in trade crises. The collapse of the London Economic Conference induced the Ministry of Foreign Affairs to establish a group to consider the ramifications. Embracing top business leaders, this Commercial Council (Tsūshō Shingi Iinkai) began meeting in September. The ministry explained the council's purpose as coping with rampant economic nationalism, which was bound to intensify; a special report that listed the protective measures taken by twenty-two major trading partners in recent years provided ample proof.[8] In the group's first two meetings Foreign Minister Hirota Kōki and Commerce Bureau chief Kurusu Saburō set the tone by stating that the failure of the London Conference had wiped out any hope of eradicating protectionism in the near future.[9]

Council members at once seized on the tactic of retaliatory tariffs to bludgeon trade partners into a more reasonable frame of mind. The president of the Mitsui Trading Company, Yasukawa Yūnosuke, clamored for flexible tariffs and the capability to alter tariffs rapidly without the Diet's approval. At the next session Inahata Katsutarō of the Osaka Chamber of Commerce made a formal proposal that set forth the case clearly: if other nations were going to wage a tariff war, Japan needed a system that would permit retaliatory levies to respond to the "maneuvres of partner nations."[10]

A special subcommittee mulled over the tariff issue. Kawashima Shintarō of the Foreign Affairs Ministry favored the active use of retaliatory tariffs to aid negotiations and preserve existing commercial treaties. Some members harbored doubts. An official from the Finance Ministry, Nakajima Teppei, wondered whether restraining imports might cause more harm than good. Japan had, for example, eliminated all tariffs on 60 percent of its imports, because the nation's industries could not operate without these raw materials. Hirao Hachisaburō, an insurance and shipbuilding executive and an official of the Free Trade Association, phrased the problem more bluntly: "levying taxes on absolutely necessary goods can be an act of suicide." Foreign Affairs officials replied that the government would have to act with caution and added that the lack of retaliatory duties left Japan defenseless in trade wars.[11]

A consensus had already crystalized by the end of the first session. Yasukawa voiced his support for Kawashima's proposal, and Nakajima concurred. Tsurumi Sakio, representing the Tokyo Chamber of Commerce, recalled that some chambers and the Economic Federation had already endorsed the idea. On February 23, 1934, the subcommittee passed a unanimous resolution that "there is a need to enact promptly a law to enable the government to create appropriate measures for protecting the trade of Japan." Immediately afterwards, the full Commercial Council adopted the same resolution. Only the means for enacting the tariffs provoked debate. Inahata backed the plan that the Economic Federation had drafted in 1931 for a council of businessmen and officials to administer tariffs. Kurusu responded that members of the subcommittee had discussed the idea and that officials would consider it as they composed appropriate legislation.[12]

In fact, as early as December the Ministry of Commerce and Industry had begun preparing a law to enhance the control of foreign trade. The bill would empower the commerce minister to regulate exports and imports and to use retaliatory duties. By February officials had completed a draft, but objections from the Finance Ministry caused substantial revisions. It believed strongly that the government should rarely resort to such reprisals because the economy depended so heavily on imports such as cotton, wool, fertilizer, and machines. The final version of the bill in early March contained a five-year limit and restricted the levying of retaliatory tariffs to cases of extreme provocation by trading partners. As another concession, the Commerce Ministry agreed that the minister of finance would chair the Tariff Investigation Committee that would decide when to take action.[13]

When the Lower House of the Diet debated the legislation in March 1934, two issues drew fire. Some members feared the Diet's loss of authority over setting tariffs as a dangerous precedent. Others wanted to make sure that the Tariff Investigation Committee would have sufficient power to make important decisions on trade matters. Consequently, the Diet reduced the time-limit to three years, and the House of Peers urged reinforcing the Tariff Committee by having it "embrace authoritative figures from every area."[14]

The final version of the Law to Protect and Regulate Trade bestowed upon the government the authority to modulate exports and/or imports in emergencies.[15] An obscure body called the Tariff Investigation Committee gained the power to approve or veto all proposed actions. Created in 1926, the committee previously could just advise on policy and could accept as members only business leaders whose enterprises would not be directly affected by changes in any tariffs. Now, with twenty additional representatives from the business community, the fifty members of the committee became the command center for plotting counterattacks in trade conflicts.[16]

The new legislation met the concerns that business leaders expressed in the Commercial Council. Two pieces of evidence suggested the direct influence of the group's deliberations. Inahata Katsutarō's testimony before the Commerce Ministry's Important Industries Control Committee in December 1933 repeated many ideas that pervaded the deliberations of the council. Also, Ashida Hitoshi and other colleagues in the Diet revealed a detailed knowledge of the council's proposal when they questioned Finance Minister Takahashi Korekiyo about the phrasing of the government's bill. In particular, these politicians wanted to know why the government had added the idea of "regulating" trade to that of "protecting" trade. Takahashi answered that the law had the modest aim of preserving a balance of trade with specific nations.[17]

Canada provided the law's first target. Benefiting from enormous exports of raw materials, that nation maintained a huge surplus in its trade with Japan that reached 45 million yen [U.S. $13,274,336] in 1934. Still, Japanese exports encountered especially high duties there. In a Commercial Council meeting of May 1934, Miyajima Seijirō first suggested reprisals. After Kurusu counseled caution, no one else took up the cause. A year later, trading company executives Miyakegawa Momotarō and Yasukawa Yūnosuke joined Fukai Eigo, the vice-president of the Bank of Japan, in demanding immediate action. The council voted to create two subcommittees, one to "carry out practical research" on the wisdom of imposing sanctions against Canada and one to investigate utilizing the trade law as a general policy. Within three months the government placed an extra 50 percent levy on eight major Canadian imports, such as wood, pulp, and wheat. The two nations reached a new trade agreement before the end of the year.[18]

Australia became the next victim. Here too, a healthy export surplus did not prevent a major trading partner from placing heavy duties on Japanese textiles. A sharp rise in these tariffs in May 1936 prompted appeals for retribution from many Japanese business groups, including the Japan Economic Federation and the Japan Spinners Association. The Tariff Investigation Committee decided that a 50 percent tax on Australian imports and a licensing system for major items, such as wool, wheat, and flour, might gain more sympathy for the Japanese perspective. Within a few months a new trade pact tied Japanese exports of cloth with purchases of Australian wool. Pleased at these initial successes in commercial negotiations, the government amended the Trade Protection Law to extend it for another three years.[19]

The law presented a clear example of efficient cooperation between officials and executives. If the former had not been disposed toward such a measure, they would not have convened the Commercial Council. The latter seized the chance to bolster the nation's bargaining position with unruly trade partners. Both sides deliberated together about the timing and targets of economic reprisals. Politicians in the Diet had fretted about the expansion of the bureaucracy's role in foreign trade;[20] executives, though, felt comfortable sharing power with the government for the sake of effective national trade policies.

THE BLOC ECONOMY

The vision of building an East Asian bloc economy commanded attention as another strategy to cope with deteriorating international trade. The Foreign Ministry's stark announcement in 1934—the so-called Amau Doctrine—that Japan alone could determine the fate of China stimulated thoughts to move in this direction. Within the imperial army, officers in charge of long-range economic planning assumed Japanese dominance of the continent. The changing attitudes of the Mitsui Trading Company demonstrated the appeal of trade with Asia. As the largest trading company, Mitsui had a huge stake in international commerce. By 1933, however, the directors judged that the bleak future of international trade mandated more emphasis on neighboring nations. Goaded by the imperial army, the firm made substantial investments in Manchukuo.[21] In 1932 Mitsui had already collaborated with the Ōkura Trading Company to build the Mukden Arsenal. Over the next two years the company acceded to requests from the army to create the Japan-Manchuria Flour Company and the Japan-Manchuria Linen Weaving Company. Mitsui helped form the Manchurian Petroleum Company and in 1937 contributed funds to the Manchurian Synthetic Fuel Company that planned to produce oil from coal.[22] Most investments in other parts of Asia concentrated on gaining sources of raw materials, such as wood from the Philippines and rubber from the Malay Peninsula and Sumatra. The three largest zaibatsu—Mitsui, Mitsubishi, and Sumitomo—joined forces to organize the Kyōwa Mining Company. Designated as a national policy firm, it guided all overseas oil exploration and production in the region.[23]

North China offered another field of opportunity. The army's activities in the provinces south of Manchukuo led to the creation of sympathetic local governments that sanctioned smuggling. Japanese goods flowed into China through these northern provinces without the payment of proper customs to the Nationalist government. By 1936 major trading companies, such as Mitsui, were taking full advantage of this illegal trade. Meanwhile, Japanese textile companies snapped up Chinese factories in northern cities, such as Tientsin and Tsingtao.[24]

Some business leaders placed a top priority on closer economic ties with China. The inconsistency of the government's policies deeply disturbed steel executive Kurimoto Yūnosuke. Diplomats wanted to return to the principles of free trade, but the army aimed at a regional bloc. Kurimoto's reading of world trends sided with the army. "Shifts in the world economy" had brought the "age of the 'bloc economy.' " Like Britain, nations would "form self-sufficient blocs of commerce within their domains." Germany was already organizing a commercial union in Eastern Europe, and an "autonomous trade policy led by strong politics" had gained access to important raw materials in the Near East through bilateral trade pacts.[25]

Even if a major nation like Japan could not hope to become totally self-sufficient, it needed a "group of nations [as] an economic community." Officials had to adjust to world trends and devise a single national policy that confronted both economic woes and concerns of national security. The government must "form a close, indivisible chain of important policies, preserving sufficient harmony with regard to Japan's policy on the continent for structuring a special bloc economy for Japan, Manchuria, and China; the demands of public finance for an increase in bonds and increased taxes; social policy toward small and medium businesses; and national policies for raw materials and fuels."

Tsuda Shingo became a fiesty proponent of commercial expansionism in Asia. A graduate of Keiō University who had worked his way up through the ranks of the Kanegafuchi Company, he had succeeded Abe Fusajirō as head of the Spinners Association. A forty-day trip on the continent convinced him that Japan had entered a life-or-death competition with Western nations for the control of China. "While Japan loudly debate[d] at the front door of China . . . Russia and England from the back gobble[d] up China's economic territory without making a sound." In the interior, the Soviet Union was seizing control of Mongolia; on the coast, England was pouring investment into the city of Tientsin; and the Germans were constructing railroads in their old sphere of influence, the province of Shantung. Tsuda worried that Japan, because of its irrational "fear of white people," could become isolated from China, the "tip of the nation's nose." The Japanese should respond by pursuing the "great hundred-year plan" of developing regional self-sufficiency. For example, purchasing wool from Mongolia would balance Soviet economic influence and reduce Japan's reliance on Australia. Similar tactics could help resolve problems with the United States, which was supplying over one-half of the nation's raw cotton and demanding restraints on Japanese exports. Cultivating raw cotton in North China would bind the economies of the two neighbors closer together and hand Japan a bargaining chip for trade negotiations with America.[26] The Japanese should purchase raw materials only from nations that bought Japanese goods.

Tsuda hailed the Manchurian Incident as launching a new assertive policy toward China. Even the Chinese would welcome this. The peasants of North China, crushed by the exactions of the Nationalist government, yearned for liberation. Japanese investment could provide better jobs and more income for the Chinese, and the area would become a better market for exports. "Raising the level of the people [had to] be the basis of industrial policy." Manchurian resources could help insure that "the future of Japan [would] be secure." To lead the way, Tsuda's own company, Kanegafuchi Spinning, built a factory in Manchukuo to manufacture pulp for rayon. Tsuda wrote: "By all means, [we] must abandon the illusion of seeing the continent as a distant shore and use discretion in the creation of a new era."[27]

No executive argued more stridently for increased military and economic expansion in Asia. But even Tsuda was not so narrow-minded as to think that a bloc economy could fulfill Japan's needs. While decrying foreign trade barriers, he strained to profess optimism about the general prospects for textile exports. Clothes made of artificial materials—rayon and staple fiber—were catching on and had excellent potential as exports. Companies had to penetrate new markets. Even in the old ones, he predicted, high tariffs would backfire, because they would prompt smugglers to create black markets for Japanese goods.[28]

Textile executives like Tsuda knew well the difficulties of rapidly boosting the production of cotton or wool on the Asian mainland and the dangers of relying on a single source. As Abe Fusajirō explained to the Commercial Council in 1935, the textile industry needed freedom to purchase raw materials from a wide variety of nations. If one source failed, companies had to switch, and, as the demand for products changed, companies had to adjust their purchases of materials.[29] Tsuda's evocation of a "*hundred-year* policy" [italics mine] reflected a clear awareness that achieving self-sufficiency, if at all possible, might well take that long.

Veteran trading company executives Yasukawa Yūnosuke and Itō Takenosuke wanted to have their cake and eat it too. Yasukawa had just completed a controversial reign as president of Mitsui Trading. His ploys of selling supplies to Chinese commanders during the Manchurian Incident and of squeezing out small enterprises by intruding into the domestic poultry business had earned him a reputation as a ruthless opportunist.[30] Having become president of the Oriental Development Company (Tōyō Takushoku Kaisha), Yasukawa envisioned a positive role for Japan in China. Constant strife between regional warlords had exhausted the Chinese people. The nation's chaos and turmoil reminded him of Korea in the late nineteenth century before it received the benevolence of Japanese rule. Subjugating China may have seemed unlikely, but he thought that economic cooperation could accomplish a lot: if China "completely eliminates previous feelings [toward Japan], bares her heart, and thrusts herself into Japan's feelings, . . . this will bring a good influence to both nations politically and economically." Yasukawa continued: "Japan faces China and Manchuria with strong points. And, as these [nations] help each other's good points and bad points, a real bloc economy can arise."[31] Itō, the executive director of the Itō Chū Trading Company, offered the obtuse suggestion that Japan split control of China's territory with England. Ideally, North China would secede from the central government and share a common currency with Japan and Manchuria.[32]

The vision of an East Asian bloc, though, did not blind these men to the imperative of international trade. Itō emphasized the opportunities available in new markets and the steady growth of textile exports in spite of barriers. He recommended changes in the composition of exports to avoid formidable tariffs.[33] Yasukawa cited the technological and managerial strengths of Japanese industry as evidence of its capacity to outdo all rivals.[34] Japan had to focus much more on the Orient, and China presented the "most hopeful market." Still, he accented the need to maintain friendly ties with every trading partner. This meant restraining exports to prevent reckless competition and helping other nations develop products or raw materials to sell to Japan. Sensitivity to others' economic woes and a greater variety of exports would help too.[35]

The idea of a bloc economy did not please most business groups. The threat of competition bothered some, as shown in one report by an observation team that the Japan Chamber of Commerce sent to Manchuria and Mongolia. The authors feared that building new industries in North China to take advantage of cheap labor and nearby raw materials could harm domestic companies in Japan. Industrial development in Manchuria needed strict controls. The government should "adopt a policy of dividing industry between the nations of

Japan and Manchukuo as a single economic unit." This would "avoid the evils of duplicating investment and competition in markets." The report recommended: "Thus we must plan effective industrial control [in Manchuria], consider the appropriateness of an industry under a licensing system, and establish a strong investigation organ based on cooperation between government and business."[36]

Other problems lurked ahead. Manchuria and Mongolia might become too successful as suppliers of raw materials. For example, too many imports of Manchuria's "inexhaustible" coal reserves could damage domestic mining. The report suggested that a single firm, such as the South Manchurian Railway Company, should supervise the gradual development of coal reserves to avoid competition with Japan's mines.[37] Moreover, the railway should continue to finance and implement economic projects through subsidiaries as it had done since its creation in 1906. The government could then preserve its precious resources for helping domestic enterprises.[38]

These conclusions exposed a basic ambivalence about the benefits of empire. Laced with the rhetoric of lauding Manchuria as a "lifeline of Japan" and forging a "hundred-year" plan to transform the area into a "paradise," the report assumed perpetual Japanese domination. A common currency and lower mutual tariffs would integrate the two economies. Spreading Japanese language instruction in Manchuria would further this cause, and efforts to improve sanitation in urban areas would publicize Japan's goodwill.[39] Yet the focus on the potential harm to domestic industries conveyed strong doubts about the ability of a bloc economy to solve Japan's economic ills.

A report that the Tokyo Chamber of Commerce issued a year later echoed this skepticism. The Tokyo chamber recognized Manchuria as a vital market for Japan's new industries but wondered how much capital Japan could afford to invest on the continent. Burgeoning military budgets and the drain of funds to Manchuria had produced awesome government deficits that threatened to deplete capital within Japan, especially because stagnating profit levels had yielded only a slight increase in domestic savings. The report contended that the government had to balance the need for investment in Manchuria with the demands of domestic companies for financing. Japan also had to "plan enough harmony with the types of industry that we must develop in Manchuria so that they do not harm established domestic industries."[40]

While willing to exploit opportunities in China, the business community did not display much enthusiasm toward autarky. The growth of the nation's industries mandated trade with the West. Moreover, a larger empire might lead to unwanted competition for domestic producers. The business community adjusted to the government's foreign policy rather than act forcefully to affect it.

PREPARING FOR ECONOMIC WAR

Instead of retreating into a regional economy, many business leaders sought to define a new national strategy for maintaining or expanding overseas trade beyond East Asia. This attitude rested on the perception that a new era of economic diplomacy had begun. Nations were no longer just stumbling toward the pit of protectionism, as business leaders had argued in the 1920s; the world was now engulfed in it. Commerce Minister Nakajima Kumakichi wrote that "the road of free competition [was] blocked." The recent spread of tariffs and the near-universal flight from the gold standard had destroyed the old principle of the "natural regulation [of production] based on price changes" in the world market.[41] Miyake Gōta of Kanegafuchi Spinning and Fujiyama Raita, the former head of the Tokyo Chamber of Commerce, agreed that the age of trade liberalism had begun to ebb a decade before, when Western governments had started to intervene in their nations' economies to spur recovery from the world war.[42] Mukai Tadaharu, who replaced Yasukawa as the new executive director of Mitsui Trading, remarked that Japan "could not advance through free trade." In the past Japanese policies had encouraged exports and the sale of "superior goods at low cost," but "confronting today's new situation with just that [policy] is completely no good."[43] The Japanese had to define what policies could meet the challenges of the new age.

Many business leaders thought that they and government officials would have to tighten the national regulation of trade. Having backed such controls since the mid-1920s, Nakajima pointed out in 1933 the advantages of industries that exercised some form of national supervision as compared to those that allowed unlimited competition. The latter endured reduced profits and invited accusations of dumping in foreign markets. The former, he said, "still protect production quotas within associations, make strict inspections of manufactured goods, submit to the regulations of cooperative sales, and strictly warn each other about planning the expansion of factories and production based on temporary prosperity; at the same time, turning to foreign markets they continue exports by making advance sales at the highest price . . . while collecting sufficient profits and causing no suffering [among customers]."[44] As good examples, Nakajima might have had in mind the striped cloth and cotton crepe industries, both of which had implemented national controls through the Industrial Rationalization Bureau. Admitting that unfettered competition could most directly stimulate the low-cost production of goods, Nakajima countered that the era of the laissez-faire economy had passed. Now the times demanded national economic controls that could regulate supply and demand.[45]

The cause of national controls found an even more fervent spokesman in Kawai Yoshinari. He had a broad range of experience as an executive in the life insurance, construction, and wool yarn spinning industries and in the management of the Tokyo Stock Exchange. Citing the example of German policies after the world war, Kawai called for "creativity" in Japan's economic policies. "What the government [had to] do [was] lead and control [the economy] skillfully, standing on a peak with a fair and comprehensive perspective." Fairness would mean accurately discriminating between productive and unproductive industries, those that made essential goods and helped secure the future of the nation and those that did not. Through the exercise of "national power," the government would permit investment only to the former. If necessary the government would even guarantee dividends to attract funds to favored sectors.[46] Kuhara Fusanosuke, a founder of the new industrial giant, the Nissan Company, and a leader of the Seiyūkai, pleaded for more state controls over the economy. To upgrade the international competitive position of industries, the government should coerce firms into donating one-half of their profits to the government. It would plow the funds into industries best able to crack foreign markets.[47]

Kuhara and other executives insisted that exports would flourish if companies adjusted their strategies. Fujiwara Ginjirō of Ōji Paper saw great opportunities in emerging Pacific markets as well as Latin America and Africa. The Japanese could not lose heart. England's resort to trade barriers signaled its economic demise. Japan must continue to be "aggressive in economic matters, penetrating and attacking the gaps of opponents."[48] The government's dominance of trade policy in Germany and effective government-business cooperation in England caught the attention of Miyake Gōta. He deplored Japan's pitiful efforts to deal with trade problems: "it is necessary to organize a strong structure to respond" with a "central organ for [trade] control" that would include both government officials and business leaders. Export associations would then carry out the decisions of this council.[49]

Mukai Tadaharu of Mitsui outlined the goals for a national trade strategy. Japan had to diversify sources of raw materials, as only three nations—the United States, India, and Australia—provided 54 percent of all imports. Bridling excessive competition would prevent charges of dumping. Japan, Mukai wrote, must "control trade and rationally plan an [export] advance."[50]

More detailed proposals came from Katō Kyōhei of the Mitsubishi Trading Company. Protesting vainly that "I am not completely abandoning economic liberalism," Katō urged that Japanese must "add some controlism" to the economy. He defined "controlism" as special measures to solve trade crises, "means appropriate to the era." First, the nation should circumvent potential crises with trading partners: "We are facing the need to build a united policy between civilians and the government and to use [various] means to avoid diplomatic and political problems in order to advance Japan's trade." Executives and officials would have to learn to examine the effects of Japanese commerce on each trading partner and export only products that the other nation did not produce. Japan should also shun trade that might displace exports from a Western power to its colony. Even with these constraints, exports of at least sixty-two products could expand into eight markets to create additional trade worth more than 400 million yen per year, an increase of almost 20 percent. Such fine-tuning would entail close coordination between producers, traders, and officials. The government would grant funds not only for research to discover new markets, but also to foster industries to meet that demand.[51]

Some executives nominated industries for special treatment. Doubting the possibilities for great quantities of new exports, Itō Takenosuke wanted an emphasis on more sophisticated items, such as elaborate textile products, that would fetch higher prices and encounter fewer tariffs.[52] Mori Nobuteru, the head of the Shōwa Electrical Engineering Company, advocated "one clear emergency national policy for industry." Because textiles were reaching the "saturation point" in worldwide sales, he thought that the nation had to concentrate on new sectors, such as the chemical industry. Japan would enjoy a rare advantage because its many swiftly flowing rivers could produce the electricity needed for manufacturing many important chemicals.[53]

The imperative to maintain good trade relations commanded much attention. Fujiyama Raita hoped for a spirit of compromise in trade negotiations. Japan had to "inch along and strengthen its [trade] bases gradually."[54] Yasukawa observed that Japanese firms could no longer "say with a challenging attitude toward foreign industry that they would lay waste to international markets"; Japanese businessmen had to "keep in mind [the ideal] of coexistence and coprosperity."[55] Katō suggested that the Japanese had to take care not to aggravate trade frictions. On a trip to the United States, Europe, and Asia he had noticed that everyone was "saying selfish things" regarding trade policies. "If Japan too says selfish things," he queried, "won't we have to dread the future?"[56]

Kadono Chokyūrō of Ōkura Trading argued passionately that self-interest dictated Japan's pursuit of international cooperation. Bemoaning retaliatory "controlism" in trade policy, he described the current trampling of the spirit of free trade as a "temporary trend." Facing Western hostility engendered by the Manchurian Incident and the withdrawal from the League of Nations, Japan must follow a "cautious attitude" to prevent total economic isolation. Businessmen from various nations should meet to solve trade problems, presumably by agreeing to a multilateral sharing of markets. Japan's success in trade mandated that she take the lead in this process. He wrote: "That Japan has fortunately risen most successfully above today's world depression and has received relatively few shocks from it means that Japan is in a leading position facing present difficulties; and I hope Japan realizes that she has a responsibility to spark a spirit of international cooperation and plan the establishment of correct trade policies with foreign nations."[57]

Others did not share this enthusiasm for national or international controls on trade. Tanaka Kanzō, the executive director of Mitsubishi Trading, snapped in a group discussion (*zadankai*), "if [you] intend to promote trade, don't interfere with it." Moves to limit so-called excessive competition within Japan would only weaken Japanese companies for the economic battle in the world arena.[58] Tsuda Shingo despised government controls. He believed that if the Japanese government had held firm and allowed the boycott of Indian raw cotton to continue into 1934, the Japan Spinners Association could have brought the Indian government to its knees; the spectacle would have deterred other nations' protectionist measures. He added that the current regulation of textile exports to India that divided quotas mostly among existing firms destroyed all incentives for entrepreneurs to devise new export strategies and to create new firms.[59]

The business community, though, readily adopted Kadono's strategy in many cases. For example, both the government and businessmen came to tolerate bilateral agreements that amounted to barter trade. In 1934 negotiations with the Dutch East Indies resulted in formal quotas for Japanese exports of cotton and rayon goods. The next year saw the acceptance of voluntary restrictions to divide the Philippine market for cotton goods with American companies.[60] Even the obstinate Spinners Association relented to sign a two-year pact with a special delegation from American textile groups in early 1937. The spinners consented to lower exports of cotton piece goods and create a committee to discuss restrictions on other products.[61] Later complaints indicated that Japanese textile executives agreed to these voluntary controls with great reluctance. The industrialists failed to see the justice in limiting cotton exports when the United States ran an annual trade surplus with Japan of some 200–300 million yen.[62] Still, the spinners kept their gripes to themselves. At least they had lessened the danger of sudden unilateral barriers by gaining an American commitment to negotiate on other products. Furthermore, many textile executives probably felt the resignation expressed by a leading textile exporter, Abe Tōzō of Mataichi Shōten, when he characterized a trade dispute with Egypt in 1935 as an event that had become commonplace.[63]

Energetic efforts to augment channels of liaison and to improve relations with other nations' business communities accompanied the acceptance of bilateral agreements. In June 1934 the Japan Economic Federation sponsored the creation of the Japan-America Trade Council as a forum for executives from both nations to discuss economic issues. A few months later a Japan-England Trade Council formed for the same purpose.[64] Economic missions became popular. Lord Barnby led one from the Federation of British Industries to Japan in 1934, and a delegation of American businessmen headed by the former ambassador to Japan, Cameron Forbes, followed the next year. In return, a group of Japanese businessmen led by Kadono Chokyūrō visited the United States and Britain in the spring of 1937. Although no startling breakthroughs on economic disputes emerged from the trade councils or the missions, they held symbolic importance as attempts by the *zaikai* to ease economic tensions and to demonstrate friendly intentions toward the Western powers.

Meanwhile, business groups campaigned for increased national control of foreign trade. Although some scholars have contended that the imperial army in the late 1930s first championed a powerful ministry of trade that would centralize the regulation of trade,[65] proposals for such an organ had appeared in the business community in the early 1920s. By 1929 one government-business council appointed by the premier, the Council for Improving International Debits and Credits, had formally recommended a single agency to coordinate the administration of trade policy.[66] As discussed above, Inahata Katsutarō underlined the need for a unified trade structure when he explained the need for comprehensive controls to the Commercial Council in 1933. The government, he said, should have the authority to restrain exports of any items after consultations with appropriate chambers of commerce, presumably those whose members would be most affected. Major industries dominated by large firms could police themselves, but the government and chambers of commerce would have to demonstrate "ways of control" for smaller businesses. The government would aim at achieving a balance of trade with each nation.[67]

By the mid-1930s business groups were demanding a full-fledged ministry of trade. The Kōbe Chamber of Commerce, citing the need to make policy more rapidly and accurately in "today's delicate foreign negotiations," called for a trade ministry.[68] The Japan chamber backed the unification of trade policy to overcome the lack of coordination between the Commerce Bureau of the Foreign Affairs Ministry and the Trade Bureau of the Commerce Ministry.[69] The Japan Trade Federation (Nihon Bōeki Renmei), which comprised the Japan Trade Council and five regional trade councils, favored "official and civilian cooperation to control exports as a policy to revive trade." "Regarding trade with nations [that used] a managed exchange [rate], the establishment of a permanent official-civilian organ [was] encouraged."[70] The first National Conference of Export Associations in March 1935 declared the need for the "unity and strengthening of administrative organs for trade by creating a bureau to blend the operations of the Finance Ministry's Tariff Section, the Foreign Ministry's Commerce Bureau, and the Commerce Ministry's Trade Bureau."[71]

A major report by the Japan Economic Federation in 1935 recommended broader controls over the nation's industry.[72] After soliciting opinions from twenty-eight different business groups, the federation found that rivalries between industrial associations, export associations, and cartels most bothered executives. For example, the Japan Spinners Association, which was then governed by the Important Industries Control Law, determined policies relating to the spinning of cotton yarn, while industrial associations of small companies set policies regarding the production and sales of cotton woven goods. The absence of a mechanism for joint planning between the cartel and the industrial associations hindered the smooth development of the manufacturing of cotton goods. Friction also arose between producers and exporters. The Spinners Association, for example, lodged bitter protests about the bid system administered by the export association that controlled access to the Indian market. Textile makers charged that the system, which forced companies to submit bids to gain licenses for exports beyond assigned quotas, served only to line the pockets of the exporters at the expense of producers.[73]

To provide liaison between these different types of groups, the Economic Federation recommended a national committee for industrial control. Attached to the cabinet and headed by the premier, the committee would set fundamental industrial policies. Having civilians occupy one-half of the membership would guarantee the cooperation of the private sector. Associations of businessmen familiar with each particular industry would decide specific tactics and ensure effective responses to changing world conditions. In order to supervise this new structure, government offices dealing with trade matters would have to centralize their operations.

Supplementing this plan, the federation proposed in July 1936 the creation of a new trade council. Embracing officials from each ministry that handled trade matters and delegates from civilian industrial groups, this body would determine general trade policies. A new central "organ" would administer them.[74]

By August the Tokyo, Yokohama, Moji, and Japan chambers of commerce had all issued position papers supporting these basic ideas and adding suggestions on details. The Tokyo chamber wanted the premier to head the trade council with the finance and foreign affairs ministers as vice-presidents. The council itself should contain government officials and executives from various sectors of the economy.[75] The Yokohama chamber envisioned an investigation section that would collect data on economic problems from existing business groups. A separate trade bureau would take charge of the domestic side of trade policy, while the Foreign Ministry's Commerce Bureau would continue to handle trade matters overseas. These would probably include the supervision of commercial officials stationed abroad, the management of exhibition halls in foreign nations, and the negotiation of treaties. Both bureaus, however, would have the same director.[76] The Japan chamber made a terse request for a joint civilian-government trade council to set policies and a central trade organ to carry them out.[77] The chamber from Moji, a small port city in northern Kyūshū, favored a ministry of trade and new associations to regulate both exports and imports under government direction. The chamber explained: "In order to advance further Japan's trade that has achieved great gains in recent years, [we] must make a unified government-civilian policy a basis, add some limits to the free activity of all, keep always a close relationship between imported and exported goods, and assist the development of the business world in a manner of mutual aid." In a similar spirit, the Yokohama chamber advocated legislation to force traders to participate in appropriate export associations and to create an integrated control structure. This would coordinate the production of goods and their shipment abroad in order to balance exports and imports according to the principles of "compensationism" between trading partners.[78]

The Ministry of Commerce and Industry felt the pressure of these mounting demands. In July 1936 the ministry asked the Japan Economic Federation to collect executives' opinions on ways to improve current legislation. Even though officials hesitated to surrender their jurisdiction over trade to a new agency, they were willing to consider amendments to the Export Association Law and the creation of import associations. The export associations had become vital to the nation's trade. By 1936 eighty-five of them handled fully one-half of all exports. Financed mostly by fees for their various services, the groups arranged cooperative purchases of supplies, stored and packed goods, exported them on consignment, set their prices, inspected their quality, and publicized them through overseas offices. Because the associations commanded access to foreign markets, their power rivaled that of producers' cartels and groups.[79]

The responses to the federation's survey revealed a broad consensus on several points, particularly the idea that special committees should coordinate the activities of industrial and export associations in each sector.[80] Many groups and companies concurred on the need for curbing exports to satisfy other nations' demands for "compensatory trade." The Japan Federation of Industrial Associations for Cotton Woven Goods (Menkōren) preferred that export associations direct all exports to each major market. The Japan Federation of Industrial Associations for Rayon Woven Goods favored the creation of new trade groups that would fuse export and industrial associations in each market. These new groups could then calculate the amount of goods to be exported and allocate production quotas. The Iron and Steel Council wanted a national organ to determine export strategy for its members. The Mitsui Trading Company recommended granting the Commerce Ministry the right, subject to the approval of a consultative council, to order the formation of export associations and to compel companies to join. Mitsubishi Trading warily abided increased powers for export associations as long as members could exert real influence on national policies that affected them. The associations should "take as their premise [the expectation] that unending mutual understanding of desires and liaison and cooperation between the government and appropriate civilian businessmen will occur."[81]

Mitsubishi's fear that export associations might lose their autonomous character reflected an acute awareness of the government's disposition to use them to satisfy the terms of new commercial treaties. For example, the government had in recent years empowered associations to determine how Japan would fill its quota of textile exports to India and to the Philippines. The prospect that the associations would become mere agents of bureaucratic decisions frightened executives.

The control of imports proved the most contentious issue. Most respondents tolerated this measure as a necessary evil to help obtain a balanced trade with each nation. The Spinners Association, however, made strenuous complaints. It claimed that much of its members' success had originated in the freedom to buy raw cotton freely from several different regions of the world and to adjust purchases to changes in season and shifts in the balance of supply and demand. If manufacturers lost the capability to make swift decisions on purchases of raw cotton, sellers could take advantage of Japanese companies and raise prices. The spinners would concede only that if a dire emergency arose, a committee dominated by producers, and certainly not importers, should impose such controls.[82]

During the fall of 1936, a special committee of the Economic Federation labored to reconcile the different recommendations. That several members from Osaka initially backed the Spinners Association's denunciation of import controls complicated the process. By October, however, these members and the federation had worked out a compromise that would give producers a voice in setting import policies.[83]

The federation unveiled its proposal in October 1936. Takashima Seiichi, a top officer of the group, and Kadono Chokyūrō delivered it to Commerce Minister Ogawa Gōtarō.[84] The report advocated a centralized structure for trade controls. A council composed of producers, traders, and officials would decide overall guidelines for regulating imports and entrust the enactment to new import associations. Another council of executives and officials would determine general export policy. For both exports and imports a government-business arbitration agency would judge disputes that arose between different business groups. Export and industrial associations would jointly manage "investigation organs" that would enforce strict rules regarding the quality and prices of goods shipped abroad.

The Commerce Ministry responded promptly. Minister Ogawa had already drafted a trade association law to create import associations and special control committees to mediate between manufacturers and exporters. After considering the federation's ideas, the ministry framed additional legislation: a trade control law that mandated a council to set general policy and granted the government extensive powers to limit exports and imports far beyond the provisions of the Trade Protection Law of 1934.[85] Gōdō Takuo, the new commerce minister in February 1937, became a fervent supporter. A retired admiral and former head of the Tokyo Chamber of Commerce, he aspired to create a ministry of trade. He submitted the new legislation twice to the Diet, in March and July.[86]

The Diet passed the laws in early August. When one delegate complained about the negative tone of restricting trade, the government replied that the acts would enhance the growth of exports. The vagueness of the role of the trade council and the control committees in the policy-making process bothered some members, because the legislation did not specify whether these bodies would report to the premier or the minister of commerce and industry. Others worried about whether the control committees would have sufficient authority to solve disputes and whether the profusion of new associations might exacerbate the existing confusion in managing the nation's trade. One prominent politician, Ashida Hitoshi, harbored serious doubts, but he believed that the times demanded that Japan follow the German economic model of intensifying the control of foreign trade.[87]

The Trade Association Law permitted the formation of import associations and encouraged the organization of national federations to encompass both these and export associations. The Trade Regulation Law enabled the Commerce Ministry to set levels of exports and imports after compulsory consultation with a newly formed trade council. Consisting of civilians and officials, the council would decide basic trade policy. When friction between producers and exporters occurred, the ministry could help organize special control committees in those industries to find solutions.[88]

These new laws embodied several basic ideas advanced by the business community in the mid-1930s and prominent in the Economic Federation's report of 1936. Those had included the need for import associations, a mechanism for resolving disputes between producers and exporters, better liaison between the various types of associations, and a joint government-business organ to set trade policy. The central principle of having officials and executives decide general policies and entrusting their operation to business groups resembled procedures used before in the Industrial Rationalization Bureau to help export industries and in the implementation of the Trade Protection Law. One newspaper report even referred to government-business cooperation in the Rationalization Bureau as a model for the new control committees.[89] This approach had become familiar to both civil servants and business leaders and had worked well.

During the mid-1930s the *zaikai* presented a strong front on trade policy, with the Japan Economic Federation clearly taking charge. Many prominent executives had spoken out in favor of national trade controls. Support came from a broad spectrum, not only large companies but also chambers of commerce which embraced many small enterprises. Only the maverick Spinners Association remained unenthusiastic. Finally, even it modified its stand, allowing the federation's report to serve as a summary statement representing all business groups among the membership and hence each major industry. In this way the unity of the business community was even stronger than in 1928 when the Economic Council resolved to end the embargo on gold. Aided by the increasingly assertive role of the Economic Federation, the business community could achieve more cohesion on trade issues and maximize its influence on officials.

THE BUSINESS COMMUNITY AND THE MILITARY

Influence on the nation's military proved much more difficult. During the 1930s security concerns began to influence economic policy, as the political power of both the army and navy intensified. As discussed previously, military expenditures ballooned, and military leaders started to dominate the premiership. Although the government managed to suppress the February 1936 rebellion by the first army division in Tokyo, that mutiny reminded civilians of the army's ability to disrupt national politics and it thus became a tool of intimidation.

A special pamphlet issued by the Ministry of the Army in 1934 baldly presented its economic aims. Simply put, it wanted to replace the inefficient capitalist system with centralized planning geared toward the total mobilization of resources for war. Asserting that "cooperative diplomacy" with the West and "makeshift" policies would fail to settle the current diplomatic crisis in Asia, the pamphlet implied the inevitability of an East Asian bloc. Japan had to accept its destiny and nurture the courage to establish a grand hundred-year plan for the nation to attain an "autonomous national defense."[90]

The business community adapted readily to the political ascendance of the military, although close ties with the two main political parties caused some regret about the abrupt end of party cabinets. A few executives had become important party politicians, and companies provided crucial financial backing for election campaigns.[91] At a meeting of the Osaka Chamber of Commerce in May 1932, for example, both Abe Fusajirō and Nakayama Taichi denounced the recent assassination of Premier Inukai Tsuyoshi as a shocking crime. Members decided to consult with their counterparts in Tokyo to reach a common stand. The emissaries soon returned with cautious advice. Abe reported that business leaders in the capital counseled retreating into a safe neutrality by supporting any cabinet that emerged and assuming "a leading role in policies to promote industry."[92] Although some executives, such as Nakajima Kumakichi, strived to revive the parties' power through a merger between the Minseitō and Seiyūkai,[93] the pragmatic attitude of Gō Seinosuke as head of the Japan Economic Federation prevailed. Predicting that the two major parties could not bury their fierce rivalry and declaring that "we must plan the cleansing of the political world," he wrote in 1934 that the nation needed a strong nonparty cabinet under the current premier, Admiral Saitō Makoto.[94] Political stability had to become the paramount concern.

Meanwhile, the growing military expenditures began to cause concern. Business leaders and groups recognized the benefits of munitions production; Gō admitted that it had stimulated economic recovery. The Tokyo Chamber of Commerce credited the huge rise in munitions produced by civilian plants as the main force in Japan's new prosperity. From a different perspective, Fujiwara Ginjirō advocated more military spending as an essential "background" to abet the nation's industrial advance in Asia. Textile leaders Abe Tōzō and Nangō Saburō joined Tsuda Shingo in praising the opportunities for trade and investment created by the army's growing dominance over North China.[95]

This reliance on military spending made some business leaders uneasy. Doubting that unprecedented levels of deficit financing could continue for long, Gō saw the military's boost to the economy as fleeting. Although Katō Kyōhei's firm, the Mitsubishi Trading Company, served the zaibatsu that invested most heavily in munitions production, he too argued that the economy could not rely for long on military spending in order to achieve prosperity. One year later a report of the Tokyo chamber argued that the government should trim military spending, because the economy's capacity to absorb bonds would soon decrease.[96] Viewing the profits accruing from munitions as a temporary windfall, executives wanted to design national controls to expand foreign trade as a more permanent method of securing the nation's economic future.

At least one observer noted intriguing parallels between the *zaikai*'s demands for centralized trade controls and the army's call for a planned economy. Writing a pamphlet for the Tokyo Chamber of Commerce, economist Takeuchi Kenji discerned a basic affinity in the aims of the Ministry of the Army and Gō Seinosuke, the president of the Japan Economic Federation. They both sought to reform laissez-faire capitalism through a controlled economy. Takeuchi thought that rather than fear the army, capitalists should "agree on the legal reform of capitalism. In this case, [we] will learn that there is no basic difference between the thinking of the military and our thinking." The demand by the army in its notorious 1934 pamphlets for "unified national control" over the economy was no more radical than Gō's advocacy of a "comprehensive industrial policy."[97] Gō, after all, advocated regulation by business groups over most aspects of the economy and conceded that in areas "where autonomous control is not sufficient for the public welfare, the government must advance and strengthen this control."[98] Everyone, Takeuchi argued provocatively, had to recognize that domination by national monopolies had become a "necessary evil," just like prostitution.[99]

Takeuchi perceived correctly that demands for national economic controls emanated from the private sector as well as the military and the government's economic bureaucracy. In basic ways, though, the goals of the army and the business community differed. The army saw increasing foreign trade as just one part of war mobilization, of getting more raw materials to produce as many arms as possible. Executives did not anticipate war. Faced by a difficult international situation, they campaigned for what one might call trade mobilization, the direction of the nation's resources as much as possible toward expanding foreign trade in order to improve economic growth.

The influence of the *zaikai* on Japan's actions in China has become the focus of much scholarly debate. Citing large firms' increased investment in China and rising profits during mid-decade, some historians have argued that the zaibatsu guided Japanese imperialism. Others paint a more innocent picture by underlining executives' efforts to show goodwill toward Western businessmen. In fact, the business community displayed both caution and opportunism.[100] Companies leaped to exploit opportunities that arose from the gradual conquest of the continent, but no business group promoted the cause of all-out war. The outbreak of the China Incident in July 1937 surprised the *zaikai* as much as anyone else.

In contrast, the business community actively shaped trade policies. Proposals brought an increasingly swift reaction from officials. Whereas earlier campaigns for trade measures—the creation of industrial and export associations and export insurance—had taken from five to ten years, the Diet passed the Trade Protection Law soon after the Commercial Council proposed it. Concerted efforts to form a trade council succeeded in less than two years.

A relationship of "reciprocity" seemed firmly established. Executives and officials acknowledged that each had to play a crucial role in trade strategy. Dissatisfied with the previous patchwork of ad hoc conferences, the *zaikai* aimed to consolidate this partnership by creating a permanent government-business council to determine trade policies. Businessmen, and not officials, would carry out its decisions through cartels and associations. In this way business leaders aspired to a corporatist partnership in which they would become an official and equal part of the policy-making process.

The new legislation of July 1937, even if it omitted a ministry of trade, represented a triumph of the business community's concept of trade mobilization. This new system, unfortunately, did not receive a fair trial. Within two months a new conflict in China recast the economic situation and posed a new set of opportunities and challenges to the business community.

FIVE
ATTEMPTS TO BLEND
MOBILIZATION FOR WAR
AND FOR TRADE, 1937–1942

The all-out offensive launched by the imperial army against Chinese forces during the summer of 1937 brought sharp changes to Japan's political and diplomatic context. At home the military demanded a marshaling of the nation's resources for war; a buildup ensued at breathtaking speed. Within a few years calls for a "national defense state" by civilians and officers alike became commonplace; only its character would remain open for debate. The bloodletting in China disturbed the British and American governments. When Premier Konoe Fumimaro in 1938 issued his belligerent vow to oust Western imperialism and to create a new order in East Asia, he doomed prospects for a climate of international trust so essential to reviving free trade.

The business community decided to further its interests within the framework of war mobilization. Executives emphasized the importance of trade for acquiring vital raw materials. They devised a link system that would spur both exports and imports while conceding some restrictions on the latter. Eliciting support from the army, business groups crusaded first for a special ministry and then for a national association that would embody the principle of reciprocal bargaining between officials and the private sector on trade matters. As the gates on overseas markets began to swing shut, interest in a regional sphere of prosperity heightened.

The fragmentation of the government presented the main obstacle to the *zaikai*'s strategy. The Ministry of Commerce and Industry proved sympathetic to proposals, but other ministries fought doggedly to torpedo, delay, or alter the initiatives. Business leaders managed to ward off the most obnoxious bureaucratic controls and to preserve a strong sense of autonomy. Still, the victories were partial.

The war in China rendered obsolete the trade laws that the Diet passed in July 1937. No sooner had Commerce Minister Yoshino Shinji announced detailed plans for implementing the Trade Regulation Law in August than

Army Minister General Sugiyama Hajime instructed the cabinet that the economy must be "reorganized under a war system." Yoshino promised to submit emergency legislation to the Diet.[1]

Within a few days he offered a package of direct controls on imports and exports. The hand of the government would reach as well into the domestic distribution and consumption of goods that restrictions on trade might affect. On September 10 the Diet approved the Law for Temporary Measures for Imports and Exports. It empowered the commerce minister to regulate trade. He could even direct the allocation and consumption of goods to prevent steep price rises and hoarding and he could list goods that required his permission to sell or purchase overseas.[2] Because the law required no consultation with business leaders, the ministry gained dictatorial control over the nation's trade.

State supervision of the economy spread in other ways. In October Konoe endorsed the merger of the cabinet's Resources Bureau and the Planning Office (Kikakuchō) into the Cabinet Planning Board (Kikakuin) to compose national economic plans. The agency immediately set to work drafting a National Mobilization Law. Its broad sweep stunned Diet members. This enabling act permitted specific decrees for directing the use of the labor force, raw materials, manufactured products, capital, enterprises, and factories. Control could extend to regulating prices, restricting profits, prohibiting labor disputes, and banning newspapers and other publications. The Diet passed the measure only after the premier craftily vowed not to invoke it during the current conflict, a pledge that he soon broke.[3]

The electric power industry provided another arena for proponents of state planning to further their cause. Since mid-decade the Army Ministry and officials in the Ministry of Communications had wanted to reorganize the industry to promote faster growth, because the supply of electric power determined how fast chemical manufacturing and other important sectors could expand. Early in 1937 Communications Minister Tanomogi Keikichi proposed a law based on the principle of "private ownership and national management." Power companies would donate their facilities to a new national stock company and receive a fee for their use. Viewing this as a thinly veiled expropriation of private property and as a menacing precedent for other industries, the business community issued vehement protests. After the bill stalled in the Diet, Konoe's minister of communications, Nagai Ryūtarō, submitted a revised bill. It aimed to create a private national electric power company that would operate "according to the will of the nation." The Japan Economic Federation and the Tokyo and Osaka chambers of commerce opposed the proposal.[4] They stressed the adequacy of electric power production and the economic disruption that would arise from such unpopular legislation. Two years after the bill's passage the new company had formed, but much of the electrical power industry remained free from direct national control.[5]

Just as executives dreaded any prospect of nationalization, they abhorred the thought of restrictions on profits. The most serious threat came in 1938, when the military services campaigned to limit companies' gains through article eleven of the Mobilization Law. Fortunately for the private sector Mitsui executive Ikeda Seihin had entered the cabinet as minister of both commerce and finance. A graduate of Keiō and Harvard Universities, he had proved a tough-minded executive while forcing through reforms of his zaibatsu to blunt public criticism of its greed. He had banned Mitsui family members from executive posts and had released some stock of the combine's various companies for public sale. He barely succeeded in fending off the military's attack on private profits.[6]

Other controls granted by the new trade legislation and the Mobilization Law found easier acceptance. Because the latter took the form of a general enabling act, executives realized that they could influence specific decrees based on it. As for the new trade laws, they were supposed to expire soon, when Japanese forces achieved the expected easy victory over China.[7] Business leaders had every intention of continuing to develop a close and equal partnership with the government in order to promote trade.

Doing this required a more unified and effective business lobby. If the government was going to centralize its economic planning, the business community had to do the same. In September 1937 the Japan Economic Federation forged the Federation of Economic Organizations (Keizai Dantai Renmei). Headed by Gō Seinosuke, this body included the federation, the Japan Chamber of Commerce, the Tokyo and Osaka clearinghouses, the National Council of Provincial Banks, the Association of Trust Companies, and the Council of Life Insurance Companies. The group aimed to study national economic policies and to "plan appropriate and effective implementation through cooperation with the government." Business leaders quickly cited the new federation as evidence of their willingness to work with the government to create effective economic controls.[8]

As one might expect, the Japan Spinners Association most jealously guarded its independence and hurled the harshest criticism at the government. Shortly before the war in China began, this cartel had delivered a scathing attack on exchange controls, because they destroyed the industry's freedom to import raw cotton as cheaply as possible. Instead of hampering the nation's largest export industry, the government should ease the import of materials. Only positive measures to aid exports could correct the growing imbalance of trade.[9] This stand received only scattered support from other business groups, however. The Kōbe Trade Conference (Kōbe Bōeki Dōshikai) provided one exception, resolving in August to resist new trade legislation because the current laws sufficed and stricter controls might damage export industries.[10]

The validity of these fears rapidly became clear. The government immediately targeted the textile industry as the primary casualty of war mobilization. On October 1 the Commerce Ministry employed the new trade law to shave imports of raw cotton by 10 percent and imports of wool by 27 percent. The cabinet approved huge supplementary military expenditures equal in size to the entire regular budget! With raw materials for producing munitions receiving top priority, a special committee began to determine more extensive cuts in imports for the manufacture of civilian products. Newspapers reported that only a "drop in the bucket" would remain for use in the so-called peace industries.[11]

GROPING FOR NEW TRADE CONTROLS: THE LINK SYSTEM

The swift extension of these controls on imported wool and raw cotton placed the textile industry in a dilemma. Challenging them would seem unpatriotic in the middle of a crusade for a new Asian order; acquiescence would harm manufacturers' efficiency and lead to a smaller share of the world market. Executives had to find some way to modify bureaucratic interference without hindering the production of munitions.

Textile executives began to advocate a new program of economic controls to encourage exports. Nangō Saburō of the Nihon Cotton Company emphasized the need for foreign raw materials to make products for export. Only a new government-civilian agency could transcend vested interests to decide fairly the distribution of such imports.[12] Abe Tōzō, who also traded in cotton, urged that its import be tied to the export of cotton products and that currency controls should not apply to the purchase and sale of these items. Executives of the two major trading companies agreed. Hasegawa Sakuji of Mitsui believed that export industries should have free access to crucial raw materials. Tanaka Kanzō of Mitsubishi pointed out that in the long run the current policy of restraining imported raw materials would destroy the export trade and Japan's ability to obtain foreign exchange. Without the latter, the government could not purchase materials essential for munitions. Tanaka recommended a system that would coerce companies to export goods in order to earn access to imports.[13]

By the early spring of 1938 the campaign for a link system had attracted wide interest. The Economic Federation suggested that the government should assign import quotas to each industry that relied on raw materials from abroad. In return, it would have to export a certain amount of goods. When an industry exceeded its goals, it could receive a larger amount of raw materials. To boost the manufacture of goods that used only domestic raw materials, firms that made pottery, raw silk, silk manufactures, and glass products should receive the right to import raw materials, presumably for sale to other companies. About a month later the Tokyo Chamber of Commerce called for the grant of import rights to individual companies based on their exports. Furthermore, companies could trade their import rights among themselves.[14]

Combining for strength, five major economic groups merged into a Trade Conference (Bōeki Kondankai). The participants were the recently formed Federation of Economic Organizations, the Central Council of Export Associations, the Central Council of Agricultural Associations [Sangyō Kumiai], the Central Council of Industrial Associations [Kōgyō Kumiai], and the Japan Trade Federation. After several weeks of deliberations, this organization recommended to the Commerce Ministry a system that would reward the most successful exporters by directly linking a company's imports and exports.[15] This system would induce companies to increase exports without diminishing the supply of materials for munitions and would wrest control of crucial imports away from government officials.

The struggle to achieve consensus then shifted to the Japan Chamber of Commerce. Two proposals dominated debate. One would create a national council to make trade policy, and the other would form a national trade company to spur exports and modulate imports. The council would comprise all major economic organizations. The new company would purchase all imported raw materials and allocate them according to the export performances of individual firms. As an agent of the council, the company would pay a maximum dividend of 6 percent. Both the Trade Conference, which had consulted closely with Commerce Ministry officials, and the Tokyo Chamber of Commerce lent a strong endorsement to these measures.[16]

Sharp criticism from the Osaka and Kōbe branches, however, threw the Japan Chamber of Commerce into turmoil. The Osaka chamber feared that the proposed national company would "deliver a fatal shock to [established] traders." A system that benefited individual companies would probably favor large firms too much. Hence the government should compensate industrial associations according to the overall export performance of their members and delegate the proper distribution of raw materials to the associations. Agreeing that a new national organ should oversee trade policy, both chambers wanted to utilize the existing trade and industrial associations in order to keep the control mechanisms as simple as possible.[17]

In deference to this criticism, the final draft of the Japan chamber's proposals dropped plans for a national trade regulation company. Existing trade and industrial associations would implement controls that a new trade organ would devise. This body would encompass delegates from chambers of commerce, various business groups, and government officials.[18]

The Ministry of Commerce and Industry responded swiftly to the business community's demands. By April a "group link system" served the cotton and wool textile industry. Trade or industrial associations in these sectors could apply for permission to import raw materials equal to 62.5 percent of the value of members' exports to nations outside of the Japanese empire, the so-called Yen Bloc, over the past two months.[19] The associations would then distribute the materials. Four months later the government switched to an "individual link system." A textile company could obtain materials equal to the actual volume used in the previous two months' exports. Spinners could gain such approval by either exporting yarn directly or proving that they had sold yarn to weavers who had then exported their products.[20]

Textile leaders voiced approval of the measures but suggested changes. Stating that "trade is like a war," Nangō Saburō urged a firmer government policy. To maintain the low prices of exports the government should forcibly reduce the domestic consumption of cotton textiles by one-third! Meanwhile, the individual link system should expand because it stimulated the dynamic of "individual free ambition."[21] The Spinners Association rejected some specific provisions of the system. For example, the practice of certifying imports according to the past two months' exports compelled firms to export as many products as possible within that short time. This pressure led to fierce competition to sell at any price, a rivalry that increased the volume of exports but diminished their value per unit. The spinners favored the elimination of all deadlines.[22]

The link system, which lifted arbitrary ceilings on exports and imports, helped the textile industry recover from the effects of the autocratic controls implemented in the fall of 1937. Exports in 1939, when the system was fully in place, reversed the steep decline of 1938. Shipments of cotton yarn soared, while those of cotton fabric rose in volume and held steady in total value.[23]

In the fall of 1938 the Commerce Ministry, already impressed by the benefits of the program, began to advocate a "comprehensive link system." It would govern every sector except for the production of munitions. The idea initially won enthusiastic backing from Ikeda Seihin; as head of the two economic ministries, he provided crucial support. Following the previously discussed proposals of major business groups, the comprehensive plan endeavored to simplify trade controls and reward as much as possible all effective exporters. They would automatically receive foreign exchange to buy imported raw materials according to a set percentage of the value of their exports. Individual companies could sell these purchase rights to other companies. Even exporters of goods that used only domestic materials would gain import rights.[24] As an extra incentive, exporters would receive from the Bank of Japan a premium equal to about 3 percent of the value of the goods that they shipped abroad.[25]

Prospects for adoption of the new system were bright, until the Commerce Ministry asked the Ministry of Finance to evaluate the proposal. The latter had to cooperate, because it supervised the Bank of Japan, which would have to arrange the automatic provision of foreign exchange to qualifying companies. By early September Finance Ministry officials had raised several objections, including the Bank of Japan's lack of expertise in overseeing foreign trade and the difficulty of calculating appropriate ratios of approved imports to exports. Opponents also warned that large companies would extend their dominance over foreign trade. Charging importers an extra fee to fund premiums for exporters would cause the prices of all goods, including exports, to climb. Finally, a comprehensive link system would lack a firm legal basis.[26]

Supporters could easily refute these arguments. Business leaders, for example, had continually cited the need to hold inflation in check and had no intention of letting their products become uncompetitive. As for the role of the Bank of Japan, its new duties were not supposed to be onerous. Complaints about the legality of creating a link system ignored the vast authority that recent legislation, such as the trade and mobilization laws, granted to the Commerce Ministry. The weakness of the Finance Ministry's arguments suggested that its stubborn resistance stemmed from resentment about losing control over foreign exchange matters.

Still, this defiance stymied the efforts of the Commerce Ministry and major business groups. After a month of haggling between subordinates in the two ministries that Ikeda headed, he finally decided to reject the comprehensive system. Threats from foreign ambassadors that their governments would adopt new protectionist measures if the system led to the dumping of Japanese goods abroad helped cool Ikeda's ardor for the project.[27]

Officials then devised a program that posed less danger to the Finance Ministry and foreign markets. This "special link system" would benefit companies by expanding the link principle to all export sectors, simplifying procedures for obtaining foreign exchange, and extending the deadline for exports made with licensed imports at least to six months and in some cases a year. Exporters, however, could only import materials in the amount used in recent exports; the Bank of Japan would pay no premiums for exports. Companies that exported goods made from domestic materials would not win import rights. Nor could companies sell these rights among themselves.[28]

These measures took effect in January 1939. They covered twenty-four products outside of the textile industry, which continued to operate under previous arrangements. The Commerce Ministry also created eight regional companies to distribute imported raw materials. Composed of businessmen in each major area of the nation and responsible to local officials of the ministry, these companies allocated materials to enterprises and guaranteed that they were used in manufacturing exports.[29]

The business community's efforts to create a link system demonstrated political strength and pragmatic flexibility. Overcoming disagreement over details for a comprehensive system, business groups convinced the Commerce

Ministry to assent to the dilution of its jurisdiction over trade. The obstreperous Finance Ministry forced a compromise, but business leaders remained unfazed. They next turned to the challenge of reshaping the entire economic bureaucracy.

THE FIRST CAMPAIGN FOR A TRADE HEADQUARTERS: THE MINISTRY OF TRADE

The business community became even more determined to effect dramatic changes in trade policy. To exert maximum pressure on the government, a new group, the Japan Trade Promotion Council (Nihon Bōeki Shinkō Kyōgikai), aimed at embracing every group related to trade. The initial sponsors in November 1938 were the Japan Economic Federation, the Tokyo Chamber of Commerce, the Japan Trade Council, and the Central Committee of Trade Associations. The organizers—Gō Seinosuke, Gōdō Takuo, Kodama Kenji, and Morimura Ichizaemon—proselytized for the new body by arguing that it would enhance cooperation between officials and executives. Headed by the energetic Gō, the council aspired to become a type of "trade headquarters" or, as one report remarked, the equivalent of a cabinet planning board for the private sector.[30]

Almost immediately the council designated a ministry of trade as its top priority.[31] Major groups, such as the Japan Trade Federation and the chambers of commerce in Tokyo and Osaka, reiterated their long-standing support for a new ministry.[32] On orders from the Ministries of the Army and Navy, the Cabinet Planning Board began to sketch plans.[33] The military hoped that mobilization for trade would enhance mobilization for war; the nation somehow had to boost exports to obtain more materials for munitions production. At a conference of executives and government officials in January 1939, Aoki Kazuo, assistant director of the board, and Gōdō Takuo, head of the Tokyo Chamber of Commerce, each stressed that molding a successful bloc economy in Asia required a ministry of trade.[34] By June, Aoki had taken charge of the planning board, and the Trade Promotion Council promptly decided to force the issue with cabinet officials.[35]

While proclaiming patriotic loyalty to the war aim of building a new Asian order, the business community pointed to the urgency of paring the bewildering complexity of trade controls. They had become a bureaucratic maze involving six different ministries. According to newspaper reports, a company had to fill out thirty pages of forms for each transaction to import a product. To purchase a load of raw cotton abroad, manufacture a product from it, export the items, and import another load required 160 separate approval procedures.[36] This inefficient system cried out for reform.

Within the business community, textile executives voiced the most serious doubts about a ministry of trade. In June Tsuda Shingo, always on guard to protect the autonomy of the Spinners Association, complained that the proposals for a ministry brushed aside the concerns of manufacturers. A director of the association, Shiraishi Kōzaburō, wondered whether the industry could afford to wait three or four years for a new ministry to function efficiently.[37] Still, the lack of a strong public stand by the association suggested a division of opinion.

The economic ministries that stood to lose jurisdiction over trade matters put up a ferocious resistance. Commerce Minister Hatta Yoshiaki and Finance Minister Ishiwata Shotarō enlisted the support of Premier Hiranuma Kiichirō by contending that the demands of the China conflict made a rapid and "radical unification [of trade administration] in wartime" difficult. Far from calming bureaucratic rivalries, combining sections of different ministries might aggravate tensions, disrupt foreign trade, and constrict the supply of vital goods.[38] In a desperate move to deflect the campaign for a new ministry, Hatta recommended instead a trade committee of business leaders and officials from major ministries. Under the watchful eye of the Commerce Ministry, the committee would recommend policies to the cabinet. By the end of June Hatta had persuaded Premier Hiranuma to accept the idea.[39]

Advocates of a ministry of trade remained adamant; they suspected that Hatta's committee would deteriorate into a consultative organ with no power at all. The Trade Promotion Council pledged to continue its campaign. A disgruntled Army Ministry accepted the committee only as a temporary measure and stipulated that it must have the legal authority to coordinate trade policy.[40]

When Hatta presented his plan to the whole cabinet on June 21, he received a rude shock. Aoki, as director of the Cabinet Planning Board, brushed aside the proposal for a trade committee and demanded more drastic changes for the sake of national mobilization. General Koiso Kuniaki, the minister of development, accused Hatta of trying to pull a "childish trick," and the minister of agriculture, Sakurauchi Yukio, called for the simplification of trade administration.[41] An astonished Hiranuma instructed the Planning Board to complete blueprints for a trade ministry. Hatta later told reporters that he would not oppose a good plan.[42]

Meanwhile, the Trade Promotion Council escalated its efforts. Gō Seinosuke issued a public plea to the Commerce Ministry for a ministry of trade. Within several weeks both the council and the Planning Board released similar outlines. Each envisioned that the new ministry would handle commercial negotiations with foreign nations, determine tariffs, and regulate trade-related industries. It would absorb the Commerce Bureau of the Ministry of Foreign Affairs, the Trade Bureau of the Commerce Ministry, and the Exchange Bureau and Customs Section of the Finance Ministry. The Ministry of Agriculture and the Commerce Ministry would cede their rights to supervise certain imports. The Ministry of Communications would lose its control of marine transport, and the Ministry of Development would surrender its direction of economic development projects outside of China and Manchuria.[43]

The United States' sudden renunciation of its commercial treaty with Japan on July 26 startled the cabinet. Aoki issued dire warnings on the need to increase munitions production and pursue creation of a self-sufficient economic bloc. The ministry of trade would become a crucial part of the "structural arrangements for a war economy."[44] Within a week Hiranuma summoned Aoki and the ministers of foreign affairs, finance, commerce, agriculture, and development for a conference. They resolved to carry through drastic trade reforms, but disagreed on how to proceed. In contrast to Gō and Aoki's proposals, some officials favored a merger of Commerce and Agriculture into a new ministry of industry and a transfer of all trade matters to the Ministry of Development. When the talks deadlocked, the exasperated premier asked the Cabinet Planning Board to continue working on this project.[45]

The Hiranuma cabinet resigned at the end of the month, before taking any action. Discontent with the cabinet's indecision on trade policies had helped weaken Hiranuma's political position; however, his failure to conclude a pact with Nazi Germany contributed most to his downfall. The army had long desired an alliance to fortify Japan's strategic position against the Anglo-American powers, and the resignation followed the declaration of a Neutrality Pact between Germany and the Soviet Union, which the army viewed as its archenemy.

The composition of the next cabinet boded well for the creation of a new ministry. An army officer, General Abe Nobuyuki, became premier. A military man, first Abe and then Admiral Nomura Kichisaburō, held the post of foreign minister. Aoki Kazuo became finance minister, and Gōdō Takuo headed the Commerce Ministry. Gōdō immediately repeated his enthusiastic and long-standing support for a ministry of trade.[46]

The three cabinet secretaries—Aoki Kazuo as head of the Planning Board, Endō Ryūsaku as cabinet secretary, and Karasawa Toshiki as secretary for legal affairs—began drafting a plan. Building on the earlier work of the board and the Trade Promotion Council, they completed their work by September 26. The new ministry would encompass parts of five separate ministries. The cabinet passed the plan unanimously.[47]

The business community claimed a victory. The Japan Trade Council's journal, *Bōeki*, eagerly anticipated the creation of the ministry within two months.[48] Even the textile industry, whose leaders had voiced skepticism, promised cooperation. When the cabinet made its decision in late September, newspapers reported that the spinners planned to create a special organ to advise the trade ministry on their special needs.[49]

While business groups celebrated their triumph, career civil servants in the Foreign Affairs Ministry schemed to sabotage the cabinet's decision. They argued that they should retain their authority over negotiating commercial treaties and collecting economic intelligence abroad. The final plan threatened to take away these powers. Stationing officials from the ministry of trade in foreign nations would preclude the need for the Foreign Ministry's commercial counselors and commercial consuls.[50] As Japanese companies turned to this network of overseas agents for help and information, the trade ministry would gain a dominant influence on matters of foreign commerce.

Foreign Affairs officials viewed the fate of the trade ministry as a matter of life and death. They had already suffered a major blow to their power in 1938, when Premier Konoe created the Board of Chinese Development (*Kōain*) to guide policy toward China. Detaching trade issues from their domain would mark the end of the venerable and prestigious ministry as a major force within the government. This fear gave rise to bold tactics.

Officials first offered a compromise. On October 9 they presented their minister, Admiral Nomura, with a request for the cabinet to let the ministry retain control over trade negotiations and the appointment of commercial officers abroad. After the cabinet secretaries advised Nomura that these provisions too blatantly contradicted the cabinet's decision, he dropped the matter and told the petitioners to stop complaining. He later admitted that he had underestimated the depth of their resolve. They then met and decided to resign; over 110 officials, everyone who held the rank of section head or above, quit.[51]

Raising the threat of grave dissension within the cabinet, this unprecedented action spurred Premier Abe to immediate action. After several days of fruitless discussions, he succeeded in receiving from the cabinet its blanket approval of any solution that he could effect. As the various ministries and cabinet members feuded, Foreign Affairs officials remained on the job. To the disgust of business groups, the prospects for a ministry of trade gradually vanished.[52] By the start of the new year the issue had evaporated.

The sequence of events exposed both the strength of the *zaikai* and the limits of its influence. The proposals for a trade ministry—a change heartily desired since at least mid-decade—were pragmatically and effectively couched in the language of furthering the goal of national mobilization for war. Business leaders approached officials with a unified position, and it won the consent of the cabinet. In the end, however, business leaders could not overcome the bureaucratic jealousies that scuttled the new ministry.

THE SECOND CAMPAIGN: THE TRADE CONTROL ASSOCIATION

The business community then focused on increasing foreign trade through more moderate reforms. These aimed at improving cooperation between the multitude of industrial, export, and import associations by amalgamating them into a national trade association. In January 1940 the Osaka Chamber of Commerce made two proposals.[53] Reciting the standard litany that government should tend to overall policy and entrust the details to civilian "creativity," the chamber advocated civilian-government control councils in each industry. A national-level civilian-government trade council would set general plans to expand exports. This body would "avoid the complications of procedures and the duplication of controls that have accompanied the profusion of trade associations and groups related to trade [by] rearranging and unifying these groups and creating a means of aiding them positively." National export promotion companies would help too.

The overabundance of trade associations had generated many complaints. A group of traders in Kōbe, the Bōeki Suiyōkai (Wednesday Foreign Trade Club), bemoaned the proliferation of such groups and the problems that they caused. Attempts of export associations to restrict goods heading for particular markets still infuriated industrial associations. The Kōbe executives preferred that all associations be organized by product and comprise both producers and traders. Delegates from different associations should form a separate national trade council to coordinate exports to all markets.[54]

The thinking of the Japan Economic Federation progressed along the same lines. A conference in the fall of 1938 provided a convenient opportunity to conduct a survey of business leaders from a broad spectrum of industries. Many disliked the large number of associations, because even a small entrepreneur might have to belong to several groups. These executives felt oppressed by the mandatory commitments of money and time that yielded little gain. Businessmen also looked forward to closer cooperation with the government through a central civilian trade organ. Small companies wanted national export and import companies that would keep larger firms from monopolizing foreign trade.[55]

Using data from this survey and other studies, the Economic Federation delivered a major report to the government in June 1940. Armed with extensive analyses of problems in each industry, the report accented the need for self-governing organs in each sector and a "civilian economic control organ that [would] have a legal base for control and unify the whole area of the national economy." This body would carry out national economic policy: "the government should stop at the determination and supervision of the outline of controls and entrust their operation to the responsibility and creativity of businessmen." Foreign trade would improve with more collaboration between the different government agencies that handled trade matters, a guarantee of sufficient personnel for the agencies, and a government-civilian organ to oversee trade policy.[56]

The head of the Commerce Ministry in June 1940, the prominent businessman Fujiwara Ginjirō, concurred with some of these ideas. Another Keiō alumnus who had reached the top of the business world, he had made the Mitsui-connected Ōji Paper Company into Japan's largest; it controlled 100 percent of newsprint supplies and 80 percent of the overall market for paper products. Earlier in the decade he had worked to defeat a labor union bill in the Diet. Persuaded to abandon a pleasant retirement from political concerns, he now charted a cautious course. Rejecting sweeping structural changes, he favored less ambitious "practical policies" and a "reform of operations." By the end of June he had convinced the cabinet to merge the eight regional export raw material companies into one national firm. It would handle the import of raw materials for all industries not covered by the link system and supervise their exports. Each industry with a link arrangement would have to clear its export plans through a single export company (Yushutsu Hin Kaitori Kaisha). Fujiwara hoped that this reform would induce a consolidation of the two hundred or so trade associations that existed and assist export industries.[57] Soon, however, the tempo of economic reforms accelerated.

In July Konoe Fumimaro again became premier and astonished the political and economic worlds by calling for radical reforms. He proclaimed that the nation had to unite as never before in order to build the New Order in Asia.[58] To become a "national defense state," the Japanese had to overcome the limitations of the existing political and economic systems. To expunge the chaos of parliamentary politics, Konoe dreamed of a totally revised political structure that would bypass the Diet and reach all citizens through a single "national organization." Inspired by the reform fever, the political parties obliged by dissolving themselves. Although protectors of the status quo ended up dashing Konoe's hopes, the government formed the Imperial Rule Assistance Association to coordinate the activities of groups aiding mobilization for the ongoing war in China.

Konoe also believed that the economy needed an overhaul. The cabinet solicited plans for drastic economic reforms. The Planning Board responded with an ambitious vision of bringing all industry under direct government supervision. Through the control of special cartels in each sector, the government would rein in profits to liberate management from the selfish demands of greedy stockholders and appoint a supreme economic council to design detailed plans for the whole economy. This approach evoked much sympathy from career civil servants in the Commerce Ministry and leaders of the imperial army. Konoe's minister of commerce, however, believed devoutly in the virtues of private enterprise. Yet another Keiō product, Kobayashi Ichizō had pioneered the construction of commuter railroads and adjoining suburban housing developments near Osaka; he also became a major force in the entertainment industry by building a chain of movie theaters. He loathed the prospect of bureaucratic controls.[59]

The Economic Federation cast its own version of a new economic order. In late August, Gō Seinosuke convened a Conference of Important Industry Control Groups. Gathering delegates from the coal, electric power, marine transport, shipbuilding, steel, and cement industries, this assembly studied blueprints for economic changes. Based on these discussions and consultations with the major chambers of commerce, the federation crafted a formal proposal by November. Executives would form an economic chamber to oversee each of the eight main economic sectors: fishing, agriculture and forestry, commerce, small and medium enterprises, trade, finance, transportation and freight, and industry and mining. Moreover, each major region would have a special chamber. United in a national economic federation, they would help create national economic plans for each economic sector.[60] Not surprisingly, the proposal skirted any reference to ideas championed by the Planning Board, such as limits on profits, the forced separation of management from capital, and the national control of individual enterprises.

As officials and executives pondered the future shape of the economy, new groups emerged to impress business views on the government. Gō transformed the Trade Promotion Council into a legal corporation and raised a large endowment for it. Starting with a personal contribution of 50,000 yen, he collected a total of one million yen from large corporations and industrial groups.[61] In September executives organized the Japan Trade Patriotic League (Nihon Bōeki Hōkoku Renmei), headed by Hatta Yoshiaki, former minister of commerce and president of the Japan Chamber of Commerce. Fujiyama Aiichirō and Kataoka Yasushi, from the Tokyo and Osaka chambers respectively, served as vice-presidents. Encompassing all private trade groups, the league pledged to "expect the advance of trade based on the priority of the nation and of the public good" and "to expect the creation of a healthy trade by responding to new world trends and assisting the reform and enhancement of the trade sector." Soon the league began to campaign for a trade cooperative council to make basic policy for the nation.[62]

The clash over the government's economic and trade policy culminated in early December. On the fourth, Gō summoned colleagues to a teahouse to discuss strategy. The recent secrecy surrounding plans for the new economic order, rumors of the radical aims of the Planning Board, and the strident calls of the army for curtailment of private profits made the *zaikai* uneasy. No transcripts of this meeting remain, but the decision soon became clear. On the next day delegates from the seven major economic groups, including the Economic Federation, the Japan Industrial Club, and the Japan Chamber of Commerce, drafted "An Opinion on the New Economic Order." Three days later Isaka Takashi, Miyajima Seijirō, and Gōdō Takuo delivered it in person to Premier Konoe.

The draft demanded a "recognition of fair profit," rejected the separation of management and capital, and balked at any direct government regulation of enterprises. This intense pressure brought results. In mid-month the cabinet affirmed the principle of civilian management and the concept of just profits based on increased productivity. As many business groups had proposed, control groups were to form in each major industrial sector to coordinate companies' activities with government plans.[63]

The cabinet's decision paved the way for the creation of a civilian national trade association in tandem with a complete revamping of the economy. Finally the consolidation of trade associations began. In December the eight regional export raw materials companies combined into the Japan Export Promotion Company with Nangō Saburō, the president of a cotton export firm, as president. Anticipating a new role as auxiliaries of a national trade control association, various export and import associations started to merge.[64]

Bureaucratic bickering, however, slowed the advance toward a national trade association. Officials argued over the most effective way to legislate the new control associations and debated the powers that each ministry would have over them.[65] Frustrated by the delay, the Japan Chamber of Commerce in June pleaded for a clarification of the government's trade policy. Recent years had witnessed the enactment of major innovations in trade policies with import associations, the link system, and special export companies. Businessmen were becoming confused: "Clarity is lacking in many areas of the concept of comprehensive consolidation that will pervade the structure of these [measures to promote trade], of the policies of practical implementation, and of the operation [of the system]. [This situation] makes businessmen apprehensive. Therefore [we] must at this time make clear the intent of the government and carry out quickly the necessary consolidation."[66]

Amid the uncertainty, business leaders held high hopes. In August

Matsuyama Fujirō, an executive director of the Japan Trade Promotion Council, predicted that a trade control association would have "direct and strong control and guidance over organizations and companies that belong." He also backed the formation of a "private central trade organ . . . that [could] represent the whole opinion of the trade sector as a cooperative organ of the control association" and help the government plan and implement trade policy.[67]

The government at last broke out of its inertia when the United States froze Japanese funds in July to counter the move of imperial troops into southern Indochina. This move portended the end to trade with the West. Shortly afterward the cabinet issued an Ordinance for Control of Important Industries that mandated control associations in each sector. In mid-September the government delegated responsibility for all trade to the Japan Trade Association. To assist the new organ, the Commerce Ministry proposed that export associations blend into one group per product; each would then match a government-supervised company being organized for each major export.[68]

Business groups praised the plans. The Japan Chamber of Commerce, for example, anticipated their rapid enactment. Members took a stoic stance toward the imminent loss of most trade with the West; they made the blunt suggestion that the government force unneeded traders to switch careers. The Kansai branch of the Trade Promotion Council had specific advice for the Japan Trade Association. Under it, the Japan Export Promotion Company should manage all trade in the Yen Bloc. Export associations should fuse into national units according to product categories and eventually combine with the government-sponsored export companies. The Trade Patriotic League made similar recommendations. The Kōbe and Osaka chambers of commerce supported a national trade association, because as an "axis for uniform trade control" it could reinforce the "positive planned character" of trade.[69]

Subsequent proposals by the Osaka chamber revealed some of the advantages that the business community hoped to derive from the association. The chamber insisted that business executives serve as the executive director and the main directors. A consultative organ should include delegates from the three major chambers of commerce, several prominent exporters and manufacturers, and officials from each of the major economic ministries. Not only would this body carve out a formal channel for business influence on national policy, but it would also tighten the coordination of trade administration and lay the foundation for a ministry of trade.[70] The *zaikai* could thus realize its long-term goal of simplifying trade administration and guaranteeing an equal voice in making policy.

The balance of power in making economic policy remained a delicate issue. Obata Tadayoshi, a Sumitomo executive working in the Cabinet Planning Board, explained that the government did not desire dictatorial power and preferred that private industrial groups "manage operations publicly and under their leadership make enterprises fit the planned economy." He cautioned, though, that business leaders had to learn to ignore selfish interests and to act as impartial "experts." Otherwise, the government might have to intervene.[71] Takashima Seiichi of the Japan Economic Federation underlined the crucial role of private initiative by drawing an analogy to sports: companies resembled players on a team. "In baseball," he wrote, "a batter should not be a robot of the coach. In other words, a true batter will get a hit on his own responsibility and with his own creativity, while paying attention to the coach. . . . One can say the same thing about the economy."[72] In other words, a coach could give advice, but the success of the team would depend on those playing the game. In the case of the national economy, private companies took the field.

The final order that created the Japan Trade Association on December 24, 1941, followed many of the suggestions of business groups.[73] All export, import, and trade associations, as well as major trading companies, would join. The export of each major product would come under the supervision of one export association that in turn would be governed by an export company. The Japan Trade Promotion Company would handle all sundry goods and all raw materials imported from East Asia for use in exports. A committee, consisting mostly of officials of trade associations and prominent traders, would decide the final details of the association's structure.

The Japan Trade Association began officially on January 27, 1942. A panel of business leaders selected Nangō Saburō as president.[74] The association's powers covered all aspects of foreign trade. These included helping to formulate the government's plans, exploring ways to encourage exports, and supervising the regulation and consolidation of the industry.

Japan's military successes in early 1942, however, altered the military and economic situation. The rapid conquest of Southeast Asia after the attack on Pearl Harbor in December 1941 brought the seizure of lands rich in raw materials. The nation also found itself with a broad front to defend against the

Anglo-American powers while the war in China continued. Anxious to attain maximum economic mobilization, the military insisted on direct supervision of trade with the recently seized territories and of trade involving raw materials vital for the production of munitions. Accordingly, the government deleted from the Trade Association's purview all dealings with occupied areas in the South Pacific. A special "corporation to supervise important goods (Jūyō Busshi Kanri Eidan)" would handle commerce in iron goods, non-ferrous metals, textiles, chemicals, and medical supplies.[75]

Events revealed a familiar pattern in the business-government relationship. The *zaikai* retained significant influence over specific trade policies but exercised little control over the general direction of foreign policy and military strategy. The business community stuck to its strategy of pursuing changes in trade policies while cooperating with the war effort. By 1941 the long-term goal of a national body composed of officials and businessmen to set trade policy had been achieved. Executives, however, had little direct influence over the decisions of military commanders. Their actions not only severed all trade with the Anglo-American powers, but the unexpected military successes also intensified the need for munitions production and undermined prospects for fruitful trade in Asia for consumer industries.

THE EAST ASIAN BLOC ECONOMY

After the start of the China war in 1937, business leaders still clung to the ideal of advancing Japan's trade on a worldwide scale. At the same time they faithfully supported the nation's policies in China. Few perceived that these two goals might conflict in any serious way.

Business groups and executives often expressed the dual nature of their goals. In July 1937 the Japan Economic Federation stressed its commitment to trade with the West by lauding the recent goodwill mission to the United States led by Kadono Chokyūrō. The federation welcomed the chance to hold a meeting of the International Chamber of Commerce in Tokyo in 1939. Yet four months later the group championed Japan's war against China. Although many Americans and British saw the conflict as unwarranted Japanese aggression, the federation published a defiant claim that the war constituted an act of Japanese self-defense against the "planned challenging attitudes of the Chinese side."[76]

Businessmen sought to increase trade with the Western nations through instituting the link system and campaigning for a ministry of trade, but they would not heed Western protests concerning the army's operations on the continent. For example, Tanaka Kanzō of Mitsubishi Trading wrote in 1938 that the United States had no moral or economic right to criticize Japanese policy in China. Tsuda Shingo explained to his employees that Japan must build a "permanent peace" and "protect the everlasting welfare of the Orient." The Japanese should prepare for a ten- or twenty-year struggle. The Chinese and Westerners deserved blame for the conflict. The former had provoked a crisis through anti-Japanese actions; as for the latter, he said, "Look at the history of the last few decades. Peace in the Orient has always come to be disturbed by white people." Britain, in particular, sought to check Japan's industrial threat by fomenting the war in China to sap Japan's economic strength. To Tsuda, the East Asian bloc held economic promise. For example, if the Japanese could tolerate products made with Chinese wool instead of the superior Australian variety, the nation's trade deficit would decline. Moreover, the demonstration of Japan's prowess through a victory might improve relations with the Western powers. "Going a step further, after the war Sino-Japanese relations [would] become close, and if the yen [came] to be used as currency in North China, the peoples of both China and Japan [would] prosper. . . . The Orient [would] become permanently stable. Making China wealthy, Japan too [could] live in comfort. If the nation [became] wealthy, then instances of [Japanese] being looked down upon by white people and receiving discriminatory treatment [would] fade. In front of money and power white people [would] show a fair attitude."[77]

Before a Western audience Tsuda took an equally strident tone. He lectured readers of an English language newspaper in Japan: "We sought a path of natural existence on the neighboring continent, but unhappily we found there not peace but a strong consciousness of resistance and hostile actions." A relationship of mutual aid with a free and friendly China would prove "the absolute path to the progressive existence of Japan." Because Westerners had no reason to fear a new order that produced peace and order in Asia, their complaints were irrational. Exclaiming that "East Asian peoples [were] exasperated by the selfish actions of the Americans and British," he warned against American intervention.[78]

Many business leaders favored an energetic development of East Asia.

Shortly after the China War began, Kobayashi Ichizō, the head of the Tokyo Electric Light Company, urged the formation of a North China development association to promote and regulate the local economy. Cautioning that Japan's inability to wipe out Western economic interests in North China would impede the nation's dominance of the area, Yasukawa Yūnosuke called attention to the tempting benefits of increased trade. The government should negotiate with "provincial self-governing organizations [separate from the Nationalist government]" and persuade them to "entrust the problem of national defense and security to Japan and make them bear the cost." In 1938 steel executive Shibusawa Masao boasted that access to Chinese coal and iron ore guaranteed the future success of his industry. He delighted in startling European colleagues by asking them to cede all markets east of the Suez Canal to Japan. Gō Seinosuke affirmed that Japan had to "cooperate in the building of a revived China and help its economic development." Issuing a sober warning that wars had become tests of national economic strength, he wrote that for businessmen an "awareness of bearing every sacrifice is necessary."[79]

Government efforts to enlist the *zaikai*'s help in China's development sparked eager collaboration. One extreme example was the Nissan Company, which specialized in mining, metal manufacturing, and relatively new industries, such as automobile production. Lured by the government's promise to guarantee profits, the firm moved its headquarters to Manchuria in order to unify and manage all of the "special" government companies there. Nissan even changed names to become the Manchuria Heavy Industry Development Company.[80]

The initial string of easy victories in China encouraged bold plans for economic projects there. Within six months the Nationalist government had abandoned its capital at Nanjing and fled far to the west. By the end of 1938 the army had seized many of the coastal provinces, the wealthiest part of China. After Konoe proclaimed his ambitious goal of devising a New Order in Asia to eradicate Western influence and attain coprosperity, the cabinet decided to form separate development companies for both North and Central China. The government would provide one-half of the capital for each enterprise, and the rest would come from private investors, including some from "third nations," that is, the Western powers. The two companies would promote and coordinate the efforts of mining and manufacturing firms in North China and revive existing factories to the south. Gō's appointment as head of the official committee to create the two companies symbolized business leaders' approval of the project. The committee included about fifty executives, vice-ministers from each cabinet ministry, and five representatives from each house of the Diet.[81]

The most serious conflict between the government and the business community erupted when the former tried to limit Japan's trade with China. By 1938 the nation had a huge export surplus with the Yen Bloc, including occupied China. Because these exports earned no foreign exchange, this trade did not help the nation in obtaining critical raw materials from Western nations or their colonies. Desperate for hard foreign currency, the government decided that the new link system for exports and imports would not apply to China. The regulation of exports to the Asian continent began.[82]

This policy dismayed the business community, which wanted lower tariffs for goods going into occupied China.[83] The Japan Spinners Association ranked among the most acerbic critics of the new controls. While arguing for the general expansion of the cotton trade during 1938 and 1939, the association prized East Asia as a growing market. Dazzled by the potential for increased raw cotton cultivation in China and awed by the market of 500 million people in East Asia as a whole, the association thought a central control organ should plan the development of the region's cotton textile trade. Such an agency could become the "cornerstone for a new economic bloc."[84] Dismissing Japanese intellectuals' theories of an East Asian cooperative body as too abstract, the spinners argued that a true bloc had to develop slowly through concrete programs. Moreover, as the fighting in Europe spread, Japan's trade would have to shift its focus to Asia. The overall export performance of the textile industry indicated its crucial value to the economy and the importance of its health. Deriding the common practice of labeling the textile sector as a peace industry, Tsuda Shingo called it a "war industry" and a "priceless jewel" for the nation because of the foreign exchange it earned.[85] By the end of the year, the association had helped organize an East Asian Cotton Industry Council that assembled delegates of five major textile groups in Japan and China to discuss issues of mutual concern.[86]

The Osaka Chamber of Commerce railed against the stupidity of restricting exports to China. This measure not only hurt the many producers of sundry goods around the city but also blocked the growth of a bloc economy in Asia. In addition, the resulting drop in Japanese exports presented opportunities for other nations' products to take over Chinese markets. If Japanese industries could ship more goods to China and receive raw materials in return, the purchasing power of Chinese citizens would increase and export industries would benefit. The chamber recommended a link system for East Asian trade and fewer restrictions on all exports.[87]

The Tokyo chamber concurred with these proposals. It suggested that the nation could overcome some trade barriers in the West by designing a triangular trade. China would send goods to the West to gain raw materials for Japan, which would then export manufactures to China. The chamber's concern for preventing industrial duplication and competition within the empire had not changed since the mid-1930s. Japan, Manchukuo, and China should merge into one economic unit that would combine "Japanese capital and technology with the resources of Manchuria and China" to achieve the ideal of a "chain of mutual aid." Industries that required high technology should locate in Japan, light industries in Manchuria, and beginning industries in China. Comprehensive industrial plans for the whole bloc and cooperative associations organized by industry should promote joint efforts among businessmen in the three nations.[88]

The most prominent national economic groups joined in the call for implementing the ideal of a bloc economy. The Japan Chamber of Commerce and the Japan Trade Promotion Council each supported extension of the link system to China.[89] In November and December 1938 the Japan Economic Federation organized a series of Economic Conferences for Japan, China, and Manchuria; delegates from all major business groups discussed policies toward the continent. This meeting led to the establishment in July 1939 of the East Asian Economic Conference as a permanent body. Headed by the peripatetic Gō Seinosuke, the conference opened offices in Japan, Manchukuo, and North and Central China. Here Chinese and Japanese businessmen could gather and consider ways of helping each other. A June 1939 report of the Industrial Control Committee of the federation recommended an East Asian Economic Council under the premier in order to minimize industrial "duplication and friction between Japan, China, and Manchuria."[90]

Comments in a committee meeting of the East Asian Economic Conference in the fall of 1939 revealed the zaikai's notion of appropriate regional economic development. After a Chinese delegate politely asked for help in developing industry in Hopei province, one Japanese executive after another explained the folly of such plans. Shiba Koshirō of Mitsubishi Heavy Industries advised that heavy industry could not succeed without a strong base of subcontractors. Kaneko Kiyota, the managing director of the Asano Portland Cement Company, argued that transplanting cement factories to China did not make economic sense; China could buy cement more cheaply from Japan. Noting that Japan imported only 3 percent of its raw cotton from China, Tsuda Shingo pointed out the great benefit to Chinese farmers in expanding those sales.[91] To these men mutual aid and coprosperity meant that China should provide raw materials and a market for Japanese manufactures. In the candid words of the Tokyo Chamber of Commerce, Japanese businessmen believed that "[We] must effect a policy similar to trade relations between Great Britain and its dominions."[92]

By 1939 even business leaders who began to voice doubts about the never-ending bloodshed in China had accepted the bloc economy as a vital component of Japan's foreign trade and economic future. Some, such as Murata Shōzō and Kobayashi Ichizō, had tired of the fighting. They wanted it to stop but also desired that the development of the regional economy continue. Murata favored military withdrawal from China, if the Nationalist government consented to full economic cooperation with Japan. Kobayashi suggested that troops hold only strategic points in the North and on the coast. Both men hoped that peace would bring a reemphasis on trade with the West.[93] Inoya Zen'ichi, a director of the Osaka Chamber of Commerce, observed in January 1941 that building the self-sufficient regional economy would take a long time. Meanwhile, "the creation of third-nation trade [was] important." He confirmed, though, that the Yen Bloc would serve as the "axis" of the economy. Takashima Seiichi worried that the new economic order would lead to the East Asian bloc receiving too much attention at the expense of outside trade. As a model he cited Germany, which had pioneered the new European order and maintained an active trade outside of its bloc.[94]

After 1937 the business community's earlier apprehensions about huge military budgets and ambivalence toward a bloc economy dissipated. Executives had not clamored for the conquest of China, but once the war started, it earned their zealous support. Indeed, even as stubborn Chinese resistance flustered officials who had counted on a quick victory, the fervor of business leaders for the bloc economy grew. The appeal of a potentially large market that Japan could control proved powerful, perhaps too much so, because the military needed more raw materials from the West to feed the nation's munitions industries. Although officials refused to loosen export restrictions to the Yen Bloc after 1938, companies managed somehow to boost their shipment of goods to China.[95] The *zaikai*'s alacrity in pursuing the bloc economy helped support the war effort.

EPILOGUE
THE LEGACY
OF THE INTERWAR ERA

The 1920s and 1930s saw the *zaikai* emerge as a major interest group. Powerful organizations came to represent the concerns of important sectors of the economy as well as the business community as a whole. Influence flowed through various channels. Executives often served as heads of the Ministries of Finance and of Commerce and Industry. They also joined special conferences and councils that frequently assembled to discuss pressing issues with officials. Moreover, business groups directed a steady barrage of proposals to the government.

The business community took initiatives and played an active role in forming trade policy. During the 1920s and 1930s business leaders recommended a wide range of responses to what seemed to be a perpetual trade crisis for Japan. Only once, in September 1937, did the government enact trade legislation that business groups had not first suggested. One cannot accept a passive depiction of the *zaikai*, that, for example, "most of the ideas for economic growth came from the bureaucracy and the business community reacted with an attitude of . . . 'responsive dependence.' "[1]

The business community sought what scholars today might well label a corporatist relationship with the government—a formal structure that granted an equal voice to each side in the policy process. By the mid-1930s officials and executives had worked together on composing and implementing several trade measures, a partnership that approached what Richard J. Samuels has called "reciprocity." The Trade Council that the Diet approved in 1937 set the stage for an enshrinement of a corporatist interdependence.

The strains of mobilization for war, first in China and then against the Anglo-American powers, blocked the attainment of this goal. So did rivalries between different government ministries. One scholar has described the government-business relationship in interwar Britain as "bargaining between two weak entities which often did not know their own minds."[2] A variation of this statement could apply to Japan. There the business community usually ended up knowing its mind on a trade issue, but the government sometimes did not. The procedure for making economic policy became increasingly corporatist in the sense that interest groups outside of business and government exerted little influence. Still, the impact of the *zaikai* fluctuated greatly, because it had to vie with so many other participants in the policy-making process, principally the Cabinet Planning Board and the Ministries of Foreign Affairs, Finance, Commerce and Industry, and the Army. Up to the start of 1942, no one of these dominated trade policy.[3]

Any discussion of business influence on economic policy must confront the perception that before 1945 the large zaibatsu, especially the Mitsui and Mitsubishi combines, wielded the most power.[4] To be sure, many participants in economic conferences came from this type of firm, and their executives predominated as leaders of major business groups. Nakajima Kumakichi, Yasukawa Yūnosuke, Ikeda Seihin, Fujiwara Ginjirō, and Dan Takuma are a few who come readily to mind. Still, one cannot conclude that a few zaibatsu as a unified bloc dictated economic policy. Executives from different zaibatsu took conflicting stands on issues, as did executives of separate companies within the same combine. The debate over the gold standard in the 1920s provided one example of this kind of disunity. The Ministry of Commerce and Industry often sought opinions and data from many business groups. Even the Japan Economic Federation, a proud representative of big business, encompassed several hundred members. Both the Japan Industrial Club and the federation gathered information from all sectors of the economy to present to the government. The desire to create ever more comprehensive lobbies for trade policy mirrored the realization that proposals had the greatest impact when they had broad support from all major groups, including those that embraced small enterprises.

The *zaikai* showed impressive energy in pursuing its aim of a nationally coordinated trade strategy. The exasperating stagnation of foreign trade in the 1920s and the shocking spread of protectionism in the 1930s had etched a new insight on executives' consciousness: international trade had become a form of warfare. While each industrial sector organized to decide its tactics on the world market, business leaders and government officials also had to conceive a grand strategy. Nakajima Kumakichi was among the first to explain these ideas in the 1920s; by the next decade they had become common convictions. The challenge of fostering a productive trade in East Asia and maintaining markets amid the diplomatic tensions of the late 1930s made such an approach even more imperative.

Events after 1940 hemmed in the business community. The conflict in China became an eight-year quagmire; the nation declared war against the Anglo-American powers; by the end of the world war foreign trade had virtually ceased as American submarines devastated the merchant marine. Unconditional surrender and a seven-year occupation followed. Yet, as is well known, the Japanese engineered a remarkable recovery from the desperate straits of 1945. Within two decades or so they had again become a major trading power. The business community's attitudes toward foreign trade and the partnership with the government that arose during the interwar period survived and guided policies to promote the expansion of trade after the end of the Allied occupation in 1952.[5]

Both officials and executives sought the creation of a national trade strategy. In 1949 the Ministry of International Trade and Industry (MITI) formed and soon assumed sweeping legal authority to regulate Japanese imports and hence to set trade policies in general. In 1953 the successor to the Japan Economic Federation, Keidanren (the Federation of Economic Organizations), recommended an economic program that reiterated the consensus that the business community had reached by the 1930s. Perceiving a "trend toward the intensification of export competition by each nation," Keidanren urged "creating a basis for national economic policy, clarifying the goals and priorities of policy, eliminating [the making of policies] case by case according to each ministry as in the past, and imparting consistency and a comprehensive quality to [economic] administration." The Japanese should concentrate on slashing the cost of exported items in order to achieve the most important goal of competitiveness in the world market. Citizens should also pare the domestic consumption of imports so that companies could use precious foreign exchange for purchasing raw materials to manufacture exports. Officials and civilians should determine policies together; a top-level agency should coordinate the economic policies of different ministries; and the government should extend the "export credit and insurance system." Keidanren even revived the idea of a link system that would give firms that manufactured exports priority in receiving foreign exchange. Finally, the group proposed "revising the Anti-Monopoly Law in order to prevent excessive competition among enterprises and plan the rationalization of enterprises' management."[6]

As in the interwar era, such cooperation proved elusive at times. For example, the fractured Japanese response to the United States' demands to curb textile exports in 1969 resembled the domestic reaction to the trade dispute with British India in 1933. Although in 1969 the leaders of Keidanren and the Ministry of Foreign Affairs desired a rapid settlement of the issue in order to maintain harmony with Japan's largest trading partner, the textile producers petulantly refused to compromise. The situation became even more divisive than in 1933, because MITI's support for the textile industry countered the leverage of the Foreign Affairs Ministry. The dissension on the Japanese side helped prolong negotiations for three years before diplomats could piece together a settlement.[7]

Sometimes cooperation progressed smoothly. In the 1950s, as Keidanren desired, the government permitted cartels to help firms in various industries endure a recession and to promote rationalization.[8] Meanwhile, officials consulted with business leaders on ways to spur industries with good prospects for growth in exports. The Ships Bureau of the Ministry of Transportation worked effectively with shipbuilding executives to strengthen that sector. By the end of the decade Japanese companies could compete on the world market.[9] In the computer sector both business groups and government officials acted to increase collaboration. In the mid-1960s the Japan Electronics Industry Development Association induced MITI to organize joint research projects to advance technology in this new field. A report by MITI's Amaya Naohiro in 1969 recommended that Japan switch its whole economic focus from smokestack sectors to "knowledge-intensive industries." Two years later the ministry's Industrial Structure Council, comprising officials and private citizens, endorsed the policy and opened the way for more collaborative projects.[10]

After the textile embroglio officials and executives cooperated more effectively to settle conflicts with trading partners. In 1977, for example, the Japan Iron and Steel Federation asked MITI to devise an orderly marketing agreement with the government of the United States in order to blunt complaints about Japanese exports. The federation not only accepted the resulting trigger mechanism to ensure a minimum price for Japanese steel but also volunteered to hold exports to 5 percent of the American market.[11] The American demand in 1980 that Japanese companies reduce their exports of automobiles produced some bureaucratic friction. MITI tried to persuade the Ministries of Finance and of Transportation to appease the United States through eliminating some barriers to automobile imports. The Finance Ministry would not lower domestic tariffs on imported vehicles, and the latter refused to ease inspections of them. Still, MITI and the Ministry of Foreign Affairs managed to coordinate their efforts. Despite some bombastic rhetoric, automobile executives agreed to adhere to a plan for "orderly exporting" through unilateral restraints.[12]

Japan's relations with the People's Republic of China (PRC) provided another example of close collaboration. When the Allied occupation ended in 1952, the business community eagerly awaited the resumption of contacts with the PRC. When the United States pressured Japan not to recognize the new communist regime of Mao Zedong, officials and business leaders had to adjust. They had to find a way to open commercial contacts on the continent without offending the Americans, who guaranteed Japan's defense under a Treaty of Mutual Security and who bought more Japanese exports than anyone else. Individual companies were allowed to increase trade with the PRC quietly to the extent that by 1970 Japan had become that nation's largest trading partner. Meanwhile, Keidanren refrained from criticizing Japan's policies toward China in order to avoid embarrassing the government. Only after the United Nations accepted the PRC as a member in 1972 and the United States signaled a change in its policy did the federation commence an active campaign for a normalization of relations. Within a year the government took that step.[13]

Determining policies to deal with declining industries has yielded both cooperation and friction between executives and officials. Even in the 1950s the government realized that some sections of the textile industry had lost a competitive edge. Officials have tried in various ways to phase out or reduce the least efficient sectors; determined resistance from producers, though, has slowed the process. The devastation of the aluminum industry in the late 1970s and early 1980s caught MITI by surprise. No one had anticipated how a rapid rise in the cost of electricity could so abruptly render the industry uncompetitive. The Japan Aluminum Federation joined forces with officials to save at least a part of the industry.[14]

Overall, the small number of limited case studies that exist indicate that business groups have continued to play an active role in forming trade policies with government officials. The idea that industries should approach international commerce as an intense competition, perhaps even as a type of war, requiring national-level planning and collaboration with government officials remains strong. Rivalries between ministries have still complicated the policy process; no one interest group has come to dominate trade policy. As before, it has resulted from a complex interaction between external stimuli, such as overseas competition or complaints from trading partners, and domestic participants—the different ministries and members of the business community.

NOTES

INTRODUCTION

1. Yanaga, *Big Business*, and Ōtake, *Keizai kenryoku*.

2. For example, Takeuchi, "Dokusen shihonka dantai" and "Shihonka dantai," I and II, and Miwa, "Rigai ishiki."

3. A recent example is Sakamoto, "Sensō to zaibatsu," p. 85. See also Bix, "Rethinking 'Emperor System Fascism,' " pp. 13–16.

4. Mitani, "Kokusai kin'yū shihon," pp. 114–58; Mitani, "Nihon no kokusai kin'yūka," pp. 123–53; Morikawa, "1930 nendai," pp. 122–36; Chō, "An Inquiry," pp. 388–90; and Nakamura, "The Japan Economic Federation," pp. 416–20.

5. See Vogel, *Number One*; Vogel, *Comeback*; Johnson, *MITI*; and Ouchi, *The M-Form Society*.

6. Johnson, *MITI*, stresses this point as does Nakamura, *Tōsei keizai*, pp. 11–12, and Nakamura, *Postwar Japanese Economy*, p. 18.

7. Johnson, *MITI*, states occasionally that the zaibatsu, the large combines, were powerful but provides no specific analysis of business opinion and its impact on policy during the 1920s and 1930s. Nakamura Takafusa criticizes Johnson for focusing too much on MITI and ignoring analysis of the private sector. See Nakamura's review of Johnson's *MITI* in the *Japan Quarterly* 29 (October–December 1982): 486.

8. Scholars and the media in Japan have used the term *zaikai* since at least the 1920s. *Zaikai* means literally "financial circle." In this book the terms *zaikai* and business community are used interchangeably.

9. See Ōgata, "The Business Community," p. 176.

10. Philippe C. Schmitter noted the rise of a naturally evolving "social corporatism" in nations such as the Netherlands after World War I. See Schmitter, "Still the Century of Corporatism?" pp. 105–12. Charles S. Maier has argued that the development of corporatism became a major political and economic trend within Germany, France, and Italy after 1919. See Maier, *Recasting Bourgeois Europe*, especially pp. 514, 543–45, 562–63, 578, and 580–81.

11. Middlemas, *Politics in Industrial Society*, pp. 13–21, 192, 243, and 373–83. Chapter 9, an analysis of the mobilization of Britain's aircraft industry to produce military planes, provides perhaps the clearest example of Middlemas's argument.

12. McConnell, *Private Power*, pp. 254–68, 275, and 289–95. See also Kaufman, *Efficiency and Expansion*. He argues that in the early twentieth century American businessmen who advocated "efficiency and expansion" pressured the government into creating the Department of Commerce and Labor in 1903. They later succeeded in convincing the administration of President Woodrow Wilson to pass legislation that eased antitrust restrictions on exporters and allowed special banks to finance exports.

13. For examples of such interpretations see Braunthal, *The Federation of German Industry*; Becker, *Business-Government Relations*; Turner, *Businessmen and Politics*; and Grant and Marsh, *The Confederation of British Industry*.

14. Grant and Marsh, *The Confederation of British Industry*, pp. 126 and 214. Braunthal, *The Federation of German Industry*, pp. 349–50, applies the pluralist model to the evolution of economic policy in West Germany.

15. Samuels, *The Business of the Japanese State*, p. 9, defines the concepts of "reciprocity" and "reciprocal consent." He uses them to describe government-business relations in the Japanese energy industries during the twentieth century.

ONE

1. Horikoshi, *Keizai dantai*, pp. 23–24, and Nihon Shōkō Kaigisho, *Kyūjū nen no ayumi*, pp. 37–39. Over the next six decades, the chambers of commerce assumed a variety of names—Shōhō Kaigisho (1878), Shōkōkai (1883), Shōgyō Kaigisho (1890), and finally Shōkō Kaigisho (1928). For convenience, this study will use only one English term, Chamber of Commerce. Ishida Takeshi discusses the creation of chambers of commerce in Japan in "The Development of Interest Groups," pp. 301–4.

2. Horikoshi, *Keizai dantai*, p. 25, and Nihon Shōkō Kaigisho, *Kyūjū nen no ayumi*, pp. 40–41.

3. Horikoshi, *Keizai dantai*, p. 26, and Tsūshō Sangyōshō, *Shōkō seisaku shi, sōsetsu*, pp. 20–21 and 57–59.

4. Nihon Shōkō Kaigisho, *Kyūjū nen no ayumi*, pp. 45–46, and Horikoshi, *Keizai dantai*, p. 27.

5. Wray, *N.Y.K.*, pp. 300 and 305.

6. Nihon Shōkō Kaigisho, *Kyūjū nen no ayumi*, p. 46.

7. Ibid., pp. 46–47, and Banno, *Taishō seihen*, p. 40.

8. Banno, *Taishō seihen*, pp. 42–44, and Nihon Shōkō Kaigisho, *Kyūjū nen no ayumi*, p. 47.

9. Banno, *Taishō seihen*, pp. 44–45.

10. Ibid., pp. 51–52, and Nihon Shōkō Kaigisho, *Kyūjū nen no ayumi*, p. 47.

11. Banno, *Taishō seihen*, pp. 133–34.

12. Tokyo Shōkō Kaigisho, *Sōran*, pp. 2–22.

13. Ibid., pp. 2–3; Yoda, *Hachijū-go nen shi*, pp. 947–60; and Noda, *Gō Seinosuke*, pp. 310–17.

14. Takeuchi, "Kōgyō kurabu," pp. 41–42, gives the data on the Tokyo council of 1917. He notes that the Tokyo Chamber of Commerce had determined that only members who paid a business tax of at least 100 yen could become candidates for the council. See too, Noda, *Gō Seinosuke*, p. 313. Nagata, *Keizai dantai*, pp. 154–56, implies that the chambers became primarily the representatives of small businesses.

15. See Kōbe Shōkō Kaigisho Hyaku Nen Shi Henshū Bukai, *Hyaku nen shi*, pp. 211–16.

16. Hamada, *Nihon bōeki kyōkai*, pp. 7–15 and 61.

17. Ibid., p. 62.

18. Ibid., p. 74.

19. Ibid., pp. 71–72.

20. Ibid., pp. 73–76.

21. Kojima, "Mengyō (I)," p. 9.

22. Miwa, "Karuteru," p. 176.

23. Kojima, "Mengyō (I)," pp. 17–18.

24. Miwa, "Karuteru," pp. 177–79, and Kojima, "Mengyō (I)," p. 9, provide the information for this and the following paragraph.

25. Miwa, "Karuteru," pp. 179–80.

26. Kojima, "Mengyō (I)," pp. 12 and 16–17.

27. Ibid., pp. 10–13 and 17.

28. Tokyo Shōkō Kaigisho, *Sōran*, pp. 171–73.

29. Ibid., pp. 151–52, and Hara, "Zaikai," pp. 180–81.

30. Nihon Kōgyō Kurabu, *Gojū nen shi*, pp. 20–21.

31. Ibid., pp. 22–27.

32. Takeuchi, "Kōgyō kurabu," pp. 27, 38, 43, and 45. The membership figure of 679 included five honorary members who did not pay dues.

33. Nihon Kōgyō Kurabu, *Gojū nen shi*, pp. 45–46.

34. Ibid., p. 46.

35. Shōkō Gyōsei Shi Kankōkai, *Gyōsei shi*, 2:64–67; Hamada, *Nihon bōeki kyōkai*, p. 74; and Takeuchi, "Keizai seisaku," pp. 130–31.

36. Nihon Kōgyō Kurabu, *Gojū nen shi*, pp. 47–48; Shōkō Gyōsei Shi Kankōkai, *Gyōsei shi*, 2:69–70; and Takeuchi, "Shihonka dantai (I)," pp. 87–96.

37. Shōkō Gyōsei Shi Kankōkai, *Gyōsei shi*, 2:91–94.

38. Nihon Kōgyō Kurabu, *Gojū nen shi*, pp. 57–59.

39. Ibid., pp. 77–82, and Horikoshi, *Keizai dantai*, pp. 74–75.

40. Mitani, "Kokusai kin'yū," pp. 117–26, and "Kokusai kin'yūka,"

pp. 137–49, for example, explain the close relationship between Inoue Junnosuke and Thomas Lamont of the Morgan Bank.

41. The so-called Iwakura Mission lasted from 1871 to 1873 and included most of the leaders of the new Meiji government. The trip convinced many of them that Japan had to industrialize in order to become a powerful nation.

42. The text of Dan's speech is given in Nakamura, *Nijū-go nen shi*, pp. 296–303.

43. Horikoshi, *Keizai dantai*, pp. 77–78.

44. Nakajima, *Seikai zaikai*, pp. 177 and 184.

45. Horikoshi, *Keizai dantai*, pp. 78–79.

46. Ibid., pp. 69–73.

47. Ibid., pp. 89–90.

48. See Chapter 2 for more details.

49. Horikoshi, *Keizai dantai*, pp. 88–90, and Takeuchi, "Keizai seisaku," pp. 127–29. Although Horikoshi gives the total membership as 330, his figures for the different categories of members add up to 326.

50. Horikoshi, *Keizai dantai*, pp. 92–94. The process for approving one proposal is outlined in pp. 124–30.

51. Ibid., pp. 86–87, 83, and 98–102. The federation initially cooperated with the National Federation of Chambers of Commerce to create the committee.

52. Nihon Kōgyō Kurabu, *Gojū nen shi*, pp. 106–9 and 111–12.

53. See Wray, *N.Y.K.*, for an analysis of the growth of the shipping industry.

54. Horikoshi, *Keizai dantai*, pp. 28–34, and Shōkō Gyōsei Shi Kankōkai, *Gyōsei shi*, 1:272–73 and 507–9.

55. Kōbe Bōeki Kyōkai, *Kyōkai shi*, p. 162.

56. Ibid., p. 160, and Horikoshi, *Keizai dantai*, pp. 33–34.

57. Miwa, "Keizai kōzō," pp. 275–95, provides an overview of trends in Japanese trade during the late 19th and early 20th centuries.

58. Duus, "Economic Dimensions," p. 148, and Tsūshō Sangyōshō, *Shōkō seisaku shi, sōsetsu*, pp. 34–38.

TWO

1. Miwa, "Keizai kōzō," pp. 290–93.

2. Horikoshi, *Keizai dantai*, pp. 78, 90, and 103–4.

3. Inoue, *Kokusaku keizai*, pp. 9–10. These remarks were originally part of an address given to the Tokyo Clearinghouse in January 1920. Nihon Ginkō Tōkeikyoku, *Statistics*, pp. 290–95, gives the trade statistics for this period.

4. Tokyo Shōkō Kaigisho Hyaku Nen Shi Hensan Iinkai, *Hyaku nen shi*, p. 110.

5. "Kokuri minfuku no daiichi wa . . . ," *Osaka jiji shinpō*, October 14, 1921, in *Shinbun*, 10:101.

6. "Shōgi bōeki shinkō seian," *Kōbe shinbun*, June 29, 1921, and "Yu-shutsu sokushin iken sho," *Yomiuri shinbun*, July 26, 1921, in *Shinbun*, 10:90–91 and 96–97.

7. "Yushutsu sokushin iken sho," *Yomiuri shinbun*, July 26, 1921, and "Shōgi bōeki shinkō seian," *Kōbe shinbun*, June 29–30, 1921, in *Shinbun*, 10:96–97 and 91.

8. "Bōeki shinchō saku to kyōdō hanbai," *Chūgai shōgyō shinpō*, June 6, 1921, "Yushutsu sokushin iken sho," *Yomiuri shinbun*, July 26, 1921, "Yu-shutsu shinkō saku," *Osaka jiji shinpō*, September 4, 1921, and Shōgi bōeki shinkō seian," *Kōbe shinbun*, June 29–30, 1921, in *Shinbun*, 10:86, 96–97, 99–100, and 90–91.

9. "Taigai bōeki shinkō saku," *Shin Aichi shinbun*, July 7–9, 1921, "Shōgi shōkō shinkō ketsugi," *Kōbe shinbun*, October 9, 1921, "Bōeki shinkō saku fugi," *Osaka jiji shinpō*, June 25, 1921, "Bōeki shinkō saku yōmoku," *Osaka asahi shinbun*, June 26, 1921, "Bōeki shinkō saku to kyōdō hanbai," *Chūgai shōgyō shinpō*, June 6, 1921, "Yushutsu sokushin iken sho," *Yomiuri shinbun*, July 26–27, 1921, and "Shōgi bōeki shinkō seian," *Kōbe shinbun*, June 29–30, 1921, in *Shinbun*, 10:92–93, 100–101, 89–90, 86, 96–98, and 90–91.

10. "Bōeki shinkō saku fugi," *Osaka jiji shinpō*, June 25, 1921, and "Shōgi bōeki shinkō seian," *Kōbe shinbun*, June 29–30, 1921, in *Shinbun*, 10:89–90 and 90–91.

11. "Bōeki shinkō saku fugi," *Osaka jiji shinpō*, June 25, 1921, "Yu-shutsu sokushin iken sho," *Yomiuri shinbun*, July 26–27, 1921, "Yushutsu shinkō saku," *Osaka jiji shinpō*, September 4, 1921, and "Shōgi bōeki shinkō seian," *Kōbe shinbun*, June 29–30, 1921, in *Shinbun*, 10:89–90, 96–98, 99–100, and 90–91.

12. "Kaigai bōeki shinkō kyōgi," *Shin Aichi shinbun*, May 20, 1921, "Yushutsu sokushin iken sho," *Yomiuri shinbun*, July 26–27, 1921, and "Shōgi bōeki shinkō seian," *Kōbe shinbun*, June 29–30, 1921, in *Shinbun*, 10:84, 96–97, and 90–91.

13. Quoted in Nihon Kōgyō Kurabu, *Gōjū nen shi*, pp. 93–94. The mission to the United States is discussed in more detail in Chapter 1.

14. This talk by Dan to the Industrial Club on May 10, 1922, is reprinted in Nakamura, *Nijū-go nen shi*, pp. 296–303. See p. 298 for comments on the budget. See "Bōeki shinkō saku fugi," *Osaka jiji shinpō*, June 25, 1921, "Yushutsu shinkō saku," *Osaka jiji shinpō*, September 4, 1921, "Yushutsu so-kushin iken sho," *Yomiuri shinbun*, July 26–27, 1921, "Shōgi bōeki shinkō

seian," *Kōbe shinbun*, June 29–30, 1921, in *Shinbun*, 10:89–90, 99–100, 96–98, and 90–91.

15. Nakamura, *Nijū-go nen shi*, pp. 301 and 297, and Tokyo Shōkō Kaigisho Hyaku Nen Shi Hensan Iinkai, *Hyaku nen shi*, pp. 113–14.

16. "Bōeki shinkō no tame yonshō kaigi o kaisai," *Tokyo asahi shinbun*, April 24, 1922, "Bōeki shisetsu," *Tokyo asahi shinbun*, April 12, 1922, "Bōeki shinkō saku," *Osaka asahi shinbun*, June 21, 1922, "Gaikoku bōeki," *Osaka asahi shinbun*, April 25, 1922, in *Shinbun*, 10:116–17, 114–15, 118, and 117.

17. "Sangyō bōeki no shinkō taisaku," *Kokumin shinbun*, January 13, 1923, "Bōeki shinkō hōsaku," *Osaka asahi shinbun*, May 13, 1924, "Bōeki shinkō," *Osaka jiji shinpō*, June 28, 1924, and "Bōeki sokushin kondan," *Kōbe shinbun*, August 22, 1924, in *Shinbun*, 10:120, 130–31, 132, and 135.

18. Bōekibu, "Dai nimen daini tokubetsu iinkai giji keika gaiyō," May 27, 1924; "Dai ichimen daiichi tokubetsu iinkai giji yōroku," May 22, 1924; and "Dai nimen daiichi tokubetsu iinkai giji yōroku," May 23, 1924, in Teikoku keizai kaigi giji yōroku.

19. Bōekibu, "Dai sanmen daiichi tokubetsu iinkai giji yōroku," May 24, 1924, in Teikoku keizai kaigi giji yōroku.

20. "Sangyō bōeki no shinkō taisaku," *Kokumin shinbun*, January 13, 1924, "Taigai bōeki shinkō saku," *Chūgai shōgyō shinpō*, March 1, 1924, "Iyoiyo yushutsu zōshin no ritsuan," *Kōbe yūshin nippō*, July 18, 1924, "Bōeki shinkō," *Osaka mainichi shinbun*, August 15, 1924, "Bōeki shinkō saku ritsuan," *Tokyo asahi shinbun*, September 2, 1924, "Seisan hōhō kaizen saku," *Osaka asahi shinbun*, September 6, 1924, and "Yushutsu bōeki sokushin saku," *Osaka jiji shinpō*, September 13, 1924, in *Shinbun*, 10:120, 126, 133, 135, 137, and 138–39.

21. "Bōeki to kōgyō no sokushin," *Osaka mainichi shinbun*, September 22, 1924, and "Yushutsu shikkin hōshō mondai," *Osaka asahi shinbun*, October 5, 1924, in *Shinbun*, 10:140 and 145–46.

22. "Yushutsu kumiai hōan," *Osaka asahi shinbun*, November 23, 1924, "Yushutsu kumiai no kazei menjo," *Osaka mainichi shinbun*, January 25, 1925, "Yushutsu shinkō saku," *Osaka jiji shinpō*, January 28, 1925, "Yushutsu kumiai kōgyō kumiai," *Tokyo asahi shinbun*, February 1, 1925, in *Shinbun*, 10:150, 153, 154, 155–56.

23. Shūgiin giji sokkiroku, *Kanpō gōgai*, February 6, 1925, pp. 169–75, and Shūgiin giji sokkiroku, *Kanpō gōgai*, February 18, 1925, p. 210. A full discussion of the issue of returning to the gold standard follows later in this chapter.

24. "Bōeki shikkin," *Osaka asahi shinbun*, February 6, 1925, "Rifu tegata rokubun ika," *Kokumin shinbun*, February 7, 1925, and "Kōgyō kumiai hō no nanten," *Jiji shinpō*, February 21, 1925, in *Shinbun*, 10:159 and 162.

25. "Yushutsu kumiai kōgyō kumiai," *Tokyo asahi shinbun*, February 1, 1925, in *Shinbun*, 10:155–56; Allen, "Japanese Industry," pp. 752–54; Asahi, *Japan's Trade*, p. 3; and Shūgiin giji sokkiroku, *Kanpō gōgai*, February 6, 1925, p. 164.

26. "Yushutsu kumiai kōgyō kumiai," *Tokyo asahi shinbun*, February 1, 1925, in *Shinbun*, 10:155–56, and Allen, "Japanese Industry," pp. 761–62.

27. Johnson, *MITI*, p. 98.

28. Horikoshi, *Keizai dantai*, pp. 124–30 and 136; and "Enka kaifuku ni doryoku," *Osaka asahi shinbun*, January 27, 1925, in *Shinbun*, 10:153–54. The committee actually formed on January 15.

29. Horikoshi, *Keizai dantai*, pp. 136–37; "Bōeki shinkō saku naitei," *Chūgai shōgyō shinpō*, February 26, 1925, and "Bōeki shinkō saku seian," *Osaka asahi shinbun*, March 8, 1925, in *Shinbun*, 10:162–63.

30. Arisawa, *Keizai shi*, pp. 50–53. See too Friedman and Schwartz, *A Monetary History*, pp. 192–93.

31. "Kin yushutsu kaikin sanpi," *Osaka jiji shinpō*, August 17–31, 1922, in Nihon Ginkō Chōsakyoku, *Shiryō*, 23:650, and Mutō Sanji, *Jitsugyō seiji*, pp. 181–83.

32. Nihon Rekishi Gakkai, *Mutō Sanji*, pp. 176–84.

33. Ibid., pp. 185–94.

34. "Kin yushutsu kaikin," *Osaka jiji shinpō*, October 31, 1924, in Nihon Ginkō Chōsakyoku, *Shiryō*, 23:425.

35. Mutō Sanji, *Jitsugyō seiji*, pp. 42–43, 46, 53, and 69–85.

36. Inoue, "Nao seiri kinshuku no jidai," November 25, 1922, in Takahashi Kamekichi, *Zaisei keizai*, 6:258–60, and Inoue, "Chūkan keiki o imashimu," (January 1922) in Inoue, *Kokusaku keizai*, pp. 27–32.

37. Inoue Junnosuke, "Onshitsu ura no zaikai" (1924), in Inoue, *Kokusaku keizai*, pp. 44–65.

38. "Kin yushutsu kaikin sanpi," *Osaka jiji shinpō*, August 17–31, 1922, in Nihon Ginkō Chōsakyoku, *Shiryō*, 23:650–57.

39. Ibid., pp. 652 and 655. This study will cite exchange rates in terms of dollars per one hundred yen, because observers at the time usually did so.

40. "Ichiki ōkurashō shusai kin kaikin mondai kondankai," *Chūgai shōgyō shinpō*, September 8–9, 1922, in Nihon Ginkō Chōsakyoku, *Shiryō*, 23:567–68. See also Aoki, "Kin kaikin," p. 1. These sources provide the basis for this paragraph and the next one.

41. Mutō Sanji, "Zaisei gyōsei keizai no soshiki kinō ni kansuru seiri kaizen mondai," July 2, 1924, and Hamaguchi Osachi, "Zaisei gyōsei keizai no seiri kaizen," July 2, 1924, in Takahashi, *Zaisei keizai*, 2:92–93 and 98–99.

42. "Dai yonmen kin'yū bukai giroku," May 7, 1924; "Kin'yūbu tokubetsu iinkai (kawase) dai ikkai kaigi yōroku," May 14, 1924; "Kin'yūbu tokubetsu iinkai (kawase) dai nikai kaigi yōroku," May 15, 1924; Teikoku keizai kai-

gi kin'yūbu tokubetsu iinchō, "Gaikoku kawase kaizen hōsaku oyobi kingin yushutsu kaikin . . . ," May 15, 1924, in Teikoku keizai kaigi, kin'yū bukai kaigi roku. For the final recommendation, see also "Shimon jikō no chōsa kōmoku oyobi tōshin an," in Takahashi, Zaisei keizai, 5:419.

43. "Yushutsu bōeki shinkō saku . . . ," Osaka asahi shinbun, May 20, 1921, in Shinbun, 10:84–85; Tokyo Shōkō Kaigisho, "Kin yushutsu kaikin ni kansuru kaigi," May 10, 1924, in Teikoku keizai kaigi, kin'yūbu shorui; and Zenkoku Tegata Kōkanjo Rengōkai, "Waga kuni zaisei keizai no genjō ni kansuru ketsugi," November 21, 1924, in Takahashi, Zaisei keizai, 4:366–67.

44. Imaizumi, Sengo Doitsu, pp. 4–6, 9, and 32–33.

45. Ibid., pp. 2–3 and 33. Ōkōchi's comments appear in the Foreward, pp. 1–2, to Imaizumi's pamphlet in Teikoku keizai kaigi, kōgyōbu shorui.

46. Nakajima, Dantaiteki kōdō, pp. 8 and 13–14.

47. Ibid., pp. 12 and 20–23.

48. Ibid., pp. 8–9 and 15–16.

49. Shōwa zaisei shi shiryō, 2-60, contains a list of participants.

50. Furukawa Kōgyō Kabushiki Kaisha and Furukawa Denki Kōgyō Kaisha, "Dai ikkai bōeki kaigi ni taisuru iken sho," September 1926, pp. 1, 2, and 6, and Mitsui Bussan Kabushiki Kaisha, "Dai ikkai bōeki kaigi tōshin sho," September 1926, p. 10, in Shōwa zaisei shi shiryō, 5-70.

51. Furukawa Kōgyō Kabushiki Kaisha and Furukawa Denki Kōgyō Kabushiki Kaisha, "Dai ikkai bōeki kaigi ni taisuru iken sho," September 1926, pp. 4–5, and Mitsui Bussan Kabushiki Kaisha, "Dai ikkai bōeki kaigi tōshin sho," September 1926, p. 9, in Shōwa zaisei shi shiryō, 5-70.

52. Tokyo Shōkō Kaigisho, "Dai ikkai bōeki kaigi no gidai ni taisuru iken," September 1926, p. 11; Osaka Shōkō Kaigisho, "Dai ikkai nan'yō bōeki kaigi ni taisuru iken," September 1926, pp. 6–7; and "Roku shōgyō kaigisho no kyōdō shuchō," 1925, pp. 1–3, in Shōwa zaisei shi shiryō, 5-70. The six largest chambers were those in Tokyo, Osaka, Yokohama, Nagoya, Kōbe, and Nagasaki.

53. "Dai ikkai bōeki kaigi giji yōshi," Yushutsu bukai, September 18 and 22, 1926, pp. 84, 97, 98, 119, and 120, in Shōwa zaisei shi shiryō, 5-69.

54. "Nan'yō bōeki kaigi no seika," pp. 545–48.

55. Horikoshi, Keizai dantai, pp. 143–45, and Nihon Keizai Renmeikai, Jigyō hōkoku, "Dai roku hōkoku sho," 1927, pp. 19–24.

56. Tokyo Shōkō Kaigisho, "Shōkō shingikai no gidai ni kansuru iken," pp. 97–99. This document is not dated, but the introduction states that the Tokyo Chamber of Commerce prepared the report for the Shōkō Shingikai.

57. Ibid., pp. 100–103.

58. Ibid., pp. 112–13 and 123–24.

59. Ibid., pp. 8–26.

60. Hamada, *Nihon bōeki kyōkai*, p. 95. The nature and purpose of the Council on Commerce and Industry are explained below.

61. Nihon Shōkō Kaigisho, "Sangyō bōeki no jōchō sokushin ni kansuru kengian," November 29–December 1, 1929, in Takahashi, *Zaisei keizai*, 4:166–69.

62. As president of the successful Osaka Shipping Company, Nakahashi had extensive experience in business.

In 1925, the Ministry of Agriculture and Commerce split into two ministries, the Ministry of Commerce and Industry and the Ministry of Agriculture and Forestry. Hereafter, the latter will be referred to as the Ministry of Agriculture.

63. Tsūshō Sangyōshō, *Seisaku shi*, 4:300–305 and 311–15.

64. Shōkō shingikai jūyō kōgyō ni kansuru shisetsu tokubetsu iinkai dai sankai giji sokkiroku, September 13, 1927, pp. 39–46.

65. Ibid., pp. 53–55. Shōkō Gyōsei Shi Kankōkai, *Gyōsei shi*, 2:288–89, explains the strength of the German competition.

66. Shōkō shingikai daiichi tokubetsu iinkai dai nimen kaigi giji yōroku, October 11, 1929; Shōkō shingikai daiichi tokubetsu iinkai dai sanmen kaigi giji yōroku, October 25, 1929; and Shōkō shingikai daiichi tokubetsu iinkai dai gomen kaigi giji yōroku, November 15, 1929, in Rinji sangyō shingikai shimon dai ichigo tokubetsu iinkai giji roku. This committee of the Council of Commerce and Industry focused on the topic of industrial rationalization.

Sakurai Gunnosuke served as the director of several companies, including the Chōsen Spinning Company (Chōsen Bōseki Kabushiki Kaisha), the Taiwan Savings Bank (Taiwan Uchiku Ginkō), and the Taiheiyō Coal Company (Taiheiyō Tankō Kabushiki Kaisha).

67. Reprinted in Tsūshō Sangyōshō, *Seisaku shi*, 4:317–20.

68. Reprinted in ibid., pp. 337–38.

69. Reprinted in ibid., pp. 320–23.

70. Reprinted in ibid., pp. 331–33.

71. See Ibid., pp. 322 and 337.

72. Kataoka, "Watakushi no kōsaku," pp. 16–17; Aoki, "Kin kaikin," pp. 1–2; and Tsūshima, "Takahashi Korekiyo," p. 11.

73. Inoue, *Kin kaikin*, pp. 1–40.

74. "Kin kaikin to honnen no zaikai," *Tōyō keizai shinpō*, January 1–15, 1927, and Matsunaga Yasusaemon, "Shin no kaifuku o kin kaikin go ni matsu," *Daiyamondo*, August 15, 1928, in Nihon Ginkō Chōsakyoku, *Shiryō*, 23:668–69, 671, and 40.

75. Yamamuro Sōbun, "Kin no kaikin ga hitsuyō," *Daiyamondo*, August

15, 1928, and Hirao Hachisaburō, "Jitsugyōka no mitaru kin kaikin," *Osaka kōgyō kurabu*, January 1929, in Nihon Ginkō Chōsakyoku, *Shiryō*, 23:41 and 50–53.

76. "Kin kaikin to honnen no zaikai," *Tōyō keizai shinpō*, January 1–15, 1927, and Yatsushiro Norihiko, "Kyōkō de sokushin sareta kin kaikin," *Ekonomisuto*, May 1, 1928, in Nihon Ginkō Chōsakyoku, *Shiryō*, 23:668–69 and 38–39.

77. "Kin kaikin to honnen no zaikai," *Tōyō keizai shinpō*, January 1–15, 1927, and "Kin yushutsu kaikin mondai kondankai," *Tokyo asahi shinbun*, June 24, 1928, in Nihon Ginkō Chōsakyoku, *Shiryō*, 23:670 and 569–70.

78. Nihon Kōgyō Kurabu Chōsaka, *Iken*, pp. 5–7, 17–18, and 19–20.

79. Ibid., pp. 9–13 and 19.

80. Ibid., pp. 14–15, 18, 19, and 31–32.

81. See Miwa, "Rigai ishiki," p. 188, and Nihon Kōgyō Kurabu, *Gojū nen shi*, pp. 252–53.

82. Inamiya, *Yano Tsuneta*, pp. 261–64, 294, and 296.

83. See "Kin yushutsu kaikin mondai kondankai," *Tokyo asahi shinbun*, June 24, 1928, in Nihon Ginkō Chōsakyoku, *Shiryō*, 23:570. For the figures on gold reserves, see Itō, "Zaisei kin'yū," p. 114.

84. See "Kaikin ni menshi gen naikaku ni nozomu shoten," *Ekonomisuto*, August 1, 1929, in Nihon Ginkō Chōsakyoku, *Shiryō*, 23:86–88, and Miwa, "Rigai ishiki," pp. 187–88.

85. Kōbe Shōkō Kaigisho Hyaku Nen Shi Henshū Bukai, *Hyaku nen shi*, pp. 234–36.

86. Tokyo Ginkō Kyōkai, *Kōkanjo*, p. 64, and Miwa, "Rigai ishiki," pp. 181–86.

87. Miwa, "Rigai ishiki," pp. 195–96.

88. Nihon Shōkō Kaigisho, "Kin yushutsu kinshi kaijo dankō ni kansuru kengi an," October 25, 1928, in Takahashi, *Zaisei keizai*, 4:132.

89. "Ronsetsu," pp. 2–4, and "Bōeki jigen," pp. 2–4.

90. Miwa, "Rigai ishiki," pp. 196–97; Nihon Kōgyō Kurabu, *Gojū nen shi*, p. 253; and "Kin kaikin undō . . .," *Kōgyō oyobi dai Nihon*, November 7, 1928, in Nihon Ginkō Chōsakyoku, *Shiryō*, 23:312. Miwa contends that resistance in the federation was led by Nakajima Kumakichi, but Miwa offers no evidence or citation to back this point.

91. Miwa, "Rigai ishiki," pp. 193–95, and "Kin yushutsu kaikin mondai kondankai," *Tokyo asahi shinbun*, June 24, 1928, in Nihon Ginkō Chōsakyoku, *Shiryō*, 23:570.

92. For example, Ōkawa had founded the Karafuto Industrial Company and the Fuji Paper Company; he had served as vice-president of the Tōyō Steamship Company and as president of the Nihon Steel Company. See Take-

koshi, *Ōkawa Heisaburō*. A glance at the appended "Ōkawa Heisaburō jigyō kankei nenpu" will indicate the impressive scope of his activity.

93. Keizai shingikai, Dai sanmen sōkai giji sokkiroku, December 21, 1928.

94. Dai nanamen shijun dai nigo tokubetsu iinkai, November 30, 1928; Dai hachimen shijun dai nigo tokubetsu iinkai, December 7, 1928; and Dai kyūmen shijun dai nigo tokubetsu iinkai, December 7, 1928, in Keizai shingikai, shijun dai nigo tokubetsu iinkai giji roku.

95. Dai jūmen shijun dai nigo tokubetsu iinkai, December 8, 1928, in Keizai shingikai, shijun dai nigo tokubetsu iinkai giji roku.

96. Noda, *Gō Seinosuke*, pp. 65–68, and TBS Brittanica, *Nihon no ridā*, pp. 272–73.

97. Keizai shingikai, Dai sanmen sōkai giji sokkiroku, December 21, 1928.

98. Tsūshō Sangyōshō, *Seisaku shi*, 4:334–38. This committee became part of the Council on Commerce and Industry.

99. Aoki, "Kin kaikin," p. 3.

100. Yoda, *Hachijū-go nen shi*, p. 975, and Chō, *Shōwa kyōkō*, p. 62. Calculations that I have made using figures given in Aoki, "Kin kaikin," p. 3, indicate that the budget cuts for 1929 amounted to 5 percent of the total budget and that those for 1930 increased to approximately 9.5 percent.

101. "Osaka keizaikai no joretsu shūkai," August 15, 1929, in *Osaka ginkō tsūshinroku*, September 1929, in Nihon Ginkō Chōsakyoku, *Shiryō*, 23:582–91.

102. Ibid., pp. 584 and 587–89.

103. Yoda, *Hachijū-go nen shi*, p. 977.

104. Shōkō Gyōsei Shi Kankōkai, *Gyōsei shi*, 2:244–45. "Yushutsu shinyō hoshō hō," *Jiji shinpō*, April 23, 1929, "Shōkōshō no ni dai teian," *Chūgai shōgyō shinpō*, September 15, 1929, "Yushutsu hoshō seido o," *Kokumin shinbun*, September 17, 1929, "Gendo wa shichi, hachi wari," *Osaka asahi shinbun*, September 27, 1929, "Yushutsu hoshō seido wa," *Kokumin shinbun*, October 16, 1929, "Yushutsu hoshō seido tōgi kaishi saru," *Tokyo asahi shinbun*, October 16, 1929, "Yushutsu hoshō seido no dai taian o chikaku sakusei," *Osaka asahi shinbun*, October 22, 1929, "Yushutsu hoshō ni ni shurui," *Chūgai shōgyō shinpō*, October 23, 1929, "Yushutsu hoshō seido no taikō," *Osaka jiji shinpō*, October 29, 1929, "Shōkō shingikai no tōshin," *Kōbe yūshin nippō*, January 19, 1930, "Tokubetsu gikai e teishutsu no yushutsu hoshō hōan kettei su," *Osaka asahi shinbun*, April 19, 1930, "Yushutsu tegata no hoshō hō," *Jiji shinpō*, April 24, 1930, "Yushutsu hoshō hō no teido to jiki," *Osaka asahi shinbun*, May 3, 1930, and "Tokubetsu gikai o tsūka shita yushutsu hoshō hō," *Osaka asahi shinbun*, May 15, 1930, in

Shinbun, 10:213, 217–25, and 230–34. For the discussion in the Lower House, see Shūgiin giji sokkiroku, *Kanpō gōgai*, May 1, 1930, pp. 113–15, and Shūgiin giji sokkiroku, *Kanpō gōgai*, May 8, 1930, pp. 184–85. In his report on the bill, Okazaki Hisajirō acknowledged the important role played by the Council on Improving International Debits and Credits (Kokusai Taishaku Kaizen Shingikai) in the drafting process.

105. Allen, "Japanese Industry," pp. 753–69, discusses the development of these associations.

106. Shōkō Gyōsei Shi Kankōkai, *Gyōsei shi*, 2:404–10. The process by which the Control Law evolved and its implementation will receive more detailed analysis in Chapter 3.

107. Ibid., pp. 246–47, and Allen, "Japanese Industry," p. 737.

108. Chalmers Johnson views the bureaucracy of the Ministry of Commerce and Industry as the incubator of the industrial rationalization movement in *MITI*, pp. 102–3. See Mutō, "Gōrika kara mita waga bōseki gyō," December 20, 1928, in Mutō Sanji, *Zenshū*, 7:668–69 and 671–72; Takahashi, *Gōrika*, pp. 8–18; Hikida, "Sangyō kōzō," pp. 72–75; and Miwa, "Keizai kōzō," p. 306.

109. See Awaya, *Shōwa no seitō*, pp. 154–56 and 163–69.

110. For such an interpretation, see Miwa, "Rigai ishiki," p. 199.

111. Johnson, *MITI*, pp. 109–10 and 113, on the other hand, argues that the basic aim of business leaders was "self-control" and the strengthening of monopoly zaibatsu in each industry.

THREE

1. Mitsuchi, "Zaikai kōsei saku," pp. 23 and 27. The article is a reprint of a lecture given by Mitsuchi.

2. Mutō in "Zaikai nan dakai saku," *Tōyō keizai shinpō*, May 24, 1930, in Nihon Ginkō Chōsakyoku, *Shiryō*, 23:747.

3. "'Kyū heika kaikin jizuku' ka, 'kaikin denaoshi' ka," *Keizai jōhō*, October 1, 1930, in Nihon Ginkō Chōsakyoku, *Shiryō*, 23:758, 760–62, and 764.

4. Ibid., pp. 760, 762–64, and 766–67.

5. Ibid., pp. 760, 764, and 767.

6. "Zaikai nan dakai saku," *Tōyō keizai shinpō*, May 24, 1930, in Nihon Ginkō Chōsakyoku, *Shiryō*, 23:740–43.

7. Nihon Kōgyō Kurabu and Nihon Keizai Renmeikai, *Saikin zaikai fukyō*, pp. 4–7, 114–15, 157–58, 320–26, and 340–41. For the recommendation of the Council on Tariffs, see Takahashi, *Zaisei keizai*, 5:634–35.

8. Mutō, "Kin yushutsu saikinshi o dankō se yo," *Chūgai zaikai*, October

15, 1931, Tsuda, "Mengyō wa kin saikinshi ga hitsuyō," *Daiyamondo*, October 21, 1931; Futagami, "Zaikai kōsei saku wa heika kirisage aru nomi," *Daiyamondo*, November 1, 1931; and Fujiwara, "Kanzei kaisei to kin yushutsu kinshi," *Chūgai zaikai*, October 15, 1931, in Nihon Ginkō Chōsakyoku, *Shiryō*, 23:199, 202–3, and 199–201.

9. Nakamura, *Shōwa kyōkō*, p. 171, and Aoki, "Kin kaikin," pp. 4–5. The discount rate rose from 5.11 percent to 5.84 percent on October 6 and to 6.57 percent on November 5. See Gordon, "Japan's Balance of Payments," p. 896.

10. Inoue, "Waga zaikai no kiso wa kenjitsu," *Chūgai zaikai*, October 15, 1931, in Nihon Ginkō Chōsakyoku, *Shiryō*, 23:201–2.

11. "Kin hon'i yōgō no tame doryoku ni iken itchi," November 5, 1931, and "Zaikai yūryokusha kin hon'i sei yōgō moshiawase," November 6, 1931, in Takahashi, *Zaisei keizai*, 6:1072–73.

Other participants in the meeting on November 6 were Ōkura Masatsune; Okazaki Kuniomi, director of the Tokyo Stock Exchange; Nezu Kaichirō, head of the Seibu and Tōbu Railroad Companies; Yano Tsuneta of the Daiichi Mutual Life Insurance Company; Itō Jirozaimon, active in many different companies; Okazaki Tadao from the Kōbe Chamber of Commerce; Ōzawa Fukutarō of the Katakura Filature and Spinning Company; and Watanabe Tetsuzō.

12. Kōbe Shōkō Kaigisho Hyaku Nen Shi Henshū Bukai, *Kōbe shōkō kaigisho*, p. 237.

13. Nakamura, *Shōwa kyōkō*, pp. 160–61, and Takahashi, *Henkaku no zaikai*, pp. 102–4. For a defense of the banks' actions, see Yanagisawa, *Ikeda Seihin kaiko*, pp. 159–62. Ōshima Kenzō, an officer in the Sumitomo Bank, blames both Inoue and Mitsui for the controversial incident. Ōshima says that Inoue should have realized that Britain's decision doomed the gold standard in Japan and he should have acted more quickly. The Mitsui Bank should have perceived Britain's economic problems earlier and not invested so much money there. See Ōshima, *Kaisō*, pp. 173–94, especially 181–82 and 184–85.

14. Nakamura, *Shōwa kyōkō*, pp. 164–65, 173, and 178, and Chō, *Shōwa kyōkō*, pp. 131–32.

15. Chō, *Shōwa kyōkō*, pp. 188–92. See also Inoue Junnosuke, "Riyū naki kin saikinshi to kin hon'i no hakai," January 21, 1932, in Takahashi, *Zaisei keizai*, 2:953–61.

16. Gō, "Jikyoku o kataru," pp. 1–6.

17. Takamura, *Mengyō to Chūgoku*, pp. 116 and 129–30.

18. Zenkoku Shōgyō Kaigisho Rengōkai, "Shina kanzei no hikiage ni kansuru kengi an," May 26, 1923, in Takahashi, *Zaisei keizai*, 4:105–7.

NOTES TO PAGES 72–77

19. Ibid., pp. 106–7; Hamada, *Nihon bōeki kyōkai*, pp. 82–83; and Takamura, *Mengyō to Chūgoku*, pp. 141–43.

20. Takamura, *Mengyō to Chūgoku*, pp. 153–54, and Inoya, *Osaka shōkō kaigisho*, pp. 237–41.

21. Takamura, *Mengyō to Chūgoku*, pp. 149–50.

22. See Nihon Shōkō Kaigisho, "Shina mondai ni kansuru ketsugi," May 17–18, 1928, in Takahashi, *Zaisei keizai*, 4:130–31. As explained below, the Japan Economic Federation and the Japan Spinners Association helped compose this declaration. See Horikoshi, *Keizai dantai*, p. 166.

23. Nihon Shōkō Kaigisho, "Kokusai renmei keizai iinkai ni okeru tsūshō bōeki nado no shōgai kenkyū ni kansuru iken sho," April 29, 1929, "Shina kakuchi ni okeru hainichi haika mondai ni kansuru kengi an," May 16, 1929, and "Nisshi tsūshō jōyaku kaitei ni kansuru iken sho," July 8, 1929, in Takahashi, *Zaisei keizai*, 4:143–49, 153–54, and 155–57.

24. Inoya, *Osaka shōkō kaigisho*, pp. 274–75.

25. See Horikoshi, *Keizai dantai*, p. 166, and Nihon Shōkō Kaigisho, "Shina mondai ni kansuru ketsugi," May 17–18, 1928, in Takahashi, *Zaisei keizai*, 4:131.

26. Horikoshi, *Keizai dantai*, pp. 166–70.

27. Takamura, *Mengyō to Chūgoku*, p. 156, makes this point. In support, Takamura refers to an article by Peter Duus.

28. Mutō, *Jitsugyō seiji*, pp. 39–43, 46, and 53.

29. See Nihon Shōkō Kaigisho, "Gunshuku ni yoru jōyo zaigen no shito ni kansuru kengi an," April 17, 1930, and "Kokumin funtan keigen ni kansuru kengi an," May 26–28, 1930, in Takahashi, *Zaisei keizai*, 4:175 and 180.

30. Nihon Shōkō Kaigisho, "Nichiman bōeki shinkō ni kansuru kengi an," June 28, 1926, and "Sangyō bōeki no jochō sokushin ni kansuru kengi an," November 29–December 1, 1929, in Takahashi, *Zaisei keizai*, 4:119 and 167; and Kōbe Shōkō Kaigisho, *Manmō mondai*, pp. 1–4, 30–35, and 47–48.

31. Kenpei Shireikan Tōyama Toyomi, "Manshū jihen ni taisuru Osaka zaikai hōmen no hankyō ni kansuru ken hōkoku," September 30, 1931, in Fujiwara and Kunugi, *Manshū jihen*, pp. 136–37. In future references, these reports for the Kenpeitai (military police) by officer Tōyama will be cited as "Hōkoku" with the appropriate dates.

32. "Hōkoku," October 1, 1931, in Fujiwara and Kunugi, *Manshū jihen*, pp. 140–41.

33. "Hōkoku," October 2, 1931, and October 6, 1931, in Fujiwara and Kunugi, *Manshū jihen*, pp. 142–44.

34. Yoda, *Hachijū-go nen shi*, p. 1009; Horikoshi, *Keizai dantai*, pp. 171–75; and Nakagawa, *Yōran*, pp. 217–21.

35. Takamura, *Mengyō to Chūgoku*, p. 196; and "Hōkoku," October 9, 1931, in Fujiwara and Kunugi, *Manshū jihen*, pp. 148–51.

36. "Hōkoku," October 9, 1931, in Fujiwara and Kunugi, *Manshū jihen*, p. 148.

37. "Hōkoku," October 10, 1931, in Fujiwara and Kunugi, *Manshū jihen*, pp. 153–55.

38. "Hōkoku," October 19, 1931, and October 24, 1931, in Fujiwara and Kunugi, *Manshū jihen*, pp. 158–59.

39. "Hōkoku," October 19, 1931, October 24, 1931, October 26, 1931, and October 31, 1931, in Fujiwara and Kunugi, *Manshū jihen*, pp. 158–65.

40. Sakamoto, "Sensō to zaibatsu," pp. 50–51.

41. "Tai Manshū keizai seisaku no sasshin oyo[bi] kakuritsu ni kansuru kengi," April 13, 1932, in Yoda, *Hachijū-go nen shi*, pp. 1010–12.

42. "Nichiman sangyō tōsei ni iinkai setchi," November 8, 1932, "Nichiman keizai teikei iinkai hiraku," November 18, 1932, "Manshū no keizaiteki rieki Nihon ga dokusen wa fuka," November 18, 1932, and "Nichiman keizai tōsei gutai kenkyū ni hairu," November 25, 1932, in *Tokyo asahi shinbun*. These sources provide the information for this paragraph and the next one. Members of the committee included Fujiwara Ginjirō, Yūki Toyotarō, Miyakegawa Momotarō, Itō Chūbei, Kadono Chokyūrō, Isaka Takashi, Mori Heibei, Miyajima Seijirō, and Yasukawa Yūnosuke. For information on the new tariff rates in Manchukuo, see The South Manchurian Railway, *Report on Progress*, pp. 267–69.

43. "Indo seifu ni teishutsu no chinjutsu sho," pp. 1–2 and "Nihon bōseki jigyō ni taisuru Indo no gokai ni kansuru chinjutsu sho," pp. 2–10. For figures on the overall trade balance, see Nihon Ginkō Tōkeikyoku, *Statistics*, p. 292.

44. Yamamoto, "Mengyō funsō," p. 13.

45. Horikoshi, *Keizai dantai*, p. 186.

46. Ishii, "Cotton Textile Diplomacy," p. 104; Yamamoto, "Mengyō funsō," p. 9; and Nihon Ginkō Tōkeikyoku, *Statistics*, p. 292.

47. Ishii, "Cotton Textile Diplomacy," p. 103, and Yamamoto, "Mengyō funsō," p. 16.

48. Telegram from Mr. Snow, April 27, 1933, in the records of the British Foreign Office, Japan Correspondence, 1930–1940, Vol. 17160, pp. 121–26. (Hereafter these microfilmed documents from the British Foreign Office will be cited as BFOJC.)

49. Telegram from Mr. Snow, April 27, 1933, BFOJC, Vol. 17160, pp. 121–26. Kurusu became more famous for his efforts in 1941 to help Foreign Minister Nomura Kichisaburō conduct intensive negotiations with the United States in order to prevent war between the two nations.

50. Yamamoto, "Mengyō funsō," p. 18.

51. "Nichiei mengyō no kōsō," *Tokyo asahi shinbun*, May 10, 1933, and Nakagawa, *Yōran*, p. 228.

52. "Indo men fukai," June 9, 1933, and "Bōren ketsugi ni sandō," June 10, 1933, *Tokyo asahi shinbun*.

53. "Saizen no michi wa Nichiin chokugo kōshō," *Tokyo asahi shinbun*, June 10, 1933; From Mr. Snow, Tokyo, Interview between Mr. Sansom and Mr. Kurusu, June 9, 1933, and Record of Conversation between Sir G. Mounsey and the Japanese Ambassador, June 27, 1933, BFOJC, Vol. 17160, pp. 217–22, 209–11, and 213.

54. Yoda, *Hachijū-go nen shi*, pp. 1061–62; Kōbe Shōkō Kaigisho Hyaku Nen Shi Henshū Bukai, *Hyaku nen shi*, p. 277; and Nakagawa, *Yōran*, pp. 229–30. The international economic conference in London is examined later in this chapter.

55. "Shimura kaishō ni bōren daihyō haken kettei," and "Taikō kyōgi ni," *Tokyo asahi shinbun*, June 27, 1933.

56. "Nichiin Shimura kaishō no konpon seisaku o kyōgi," July 21, 1933, and "Kanmin saigo no uchiawase," August 18, 1933, *Tokyo asahi shinbun*.

57. "Menka fukai no tekkai o waga bōren ni konsei su," July 7, 1933, and "Hōhin seiatsu saku o Indo seichō ga kōkyū," July 27, 1933, *Tokyo asahi shinbun*.

58. Letter from T. Ainscough to A. Edgcumbe on October 2, 1933, with official minutes for meetings on September 23, 25, 27, and 30 attached; Letter from Thomas Ainscough to A. Edgcumbe on October 9, 1933, with official minutes for meetings on October 3 and 5 attached; and Letter from Mr. Sansom to Mr. Orde on October 9, 1933, with Sansom's Official Diary of Mission to Simla Conference attached, in BFOJC, Vol. 17163, pp. 193–213, 57–69, and 15–23. Also, "Waga tōgyōsha wa fuman," *Tokyo asahi shinbun*, October 5, 1933.

59. Ishii, "Cotton Textile Diplomacy," p. 118; and Statement by Sir William Clare Lees, October 4, 1933; Letter of Thomas M. Ainscough to A. Edgcumbe, Tripartite Industrial Discussions, October 7, 1933; and Trade Discussions in India, October 19, 1933, in BFOJC, Vol. 17163, pp. 40–44, 34–39, and 25–27. These sources provide the basis for the rest of this paragraph.

60. Trade Discussions in India, October 19, 1933, and Telegram from Government of India, October 17, 1933, in BFOJC, Vol. 17163, pp. 25–29.

61. Telegram from Mr. Snow [in Tokyo], October 26, 1933, and from Viceroy of India, copy of telegram from George Sansom [in India] to Tokyo, October 25, 1933, in BFOJC, Vol. 17163, pp. 224–25 and 228–30.

62. "Minkangawa kiwamete kyōkō," October 31, 1933, and "Tōgyōsha yuzurazu," November 1, 1933, *Tokyo asahi shinbun*.

63. "Kanmin no iken itchi," *Tokyo asahi shinbun*, November 9, 1933. Five officials from the Ministries of Commerce and Foreign Affairs, including

Kurusu and Yoshino, participated.

64. Mr. Snow to Sir John Simon, November 20, 1933; Foreign Office to Mr. Snow [Tokyo], December 6, 1933; and Government of India, Commerce Department, to Secretary of State for India, December 5, 1933, in BFOJC, Vol. 17165, pp. 103–4, 34–35, and 40–47.

65. "Waga mengyō dantai no saiseimei hibiku," November 30, 1933, and "Kanebō saigo no ketsui," December 1, 1933, *Tokyo asahi shinbun*.

66. "Waga mengyō dantai no saiseimei hibiku," *Tokyo Asahi shinbun*, November 30, 1933; and Telegram from Mr. Snow, December 7, 1933, in BFOJC, Vol. 17165, pp. 57–58.

67. Telegram from Mr. Snow, December 12, 1933, BFOJC, Vol. 17165, p. 65.

68. Telegram from F. O. Lindley [Tokyo], December 26, 1933; Telegram from Sir F. O. Lindley, December 27, 1933; and Telegram, Government of India, Commerce Department, to Secretary of State for India, December 23, 1933, in BFOJC, Vol. 17165, pp. 90–93 and 95–99.

69. Telegram from Mr. Snow, December 7, 1933, in BFOJC, Vol. 17165, pp. 57–58.

70. "Menpu no yushutsu wariate," January 9, 1934, "Taiin menpu tōsei ni yushutsu shōgawa gen'an naru," January 12, 1934, "Taiin yushutsu tōsei ni konponteki na tairitsu," January 13, 1934, "Bōren wa dokuji no renmeian de susumu," January 14, 1934, "Yushutsu tōsei kikan setsuritsu kyōgi," January 19, 1934, "Taiin menpu yushutsu kumiai taikō kettei su," January 20, 1934, "Taiin menpu yushutsu no tōsei yōkō kettei su," January 21, 1934, "Taiin yushutsu menshikimono wariate kimaru," January 28, 1934, and "Wariate hiritsu," January 30, 1934, *Tokyo asahi shinbun*.

The main export groups were the Export Cotton Textile Traders Association and the Osaka Export Association for Cotton Cloth and Rayon Woven Goods (Osaka Menpu Jinken Shikimono Yushutsu Kumiai). Menkōren represented mostly small and medium-size producers. For an explanation of Menkōren, see Kojima, "Mengyō (II)."

71. Letter from T. Ainscough to A. Edgcumbe on October 2, 1933, with official minutes for meetings on September 23, 25, 27, and 30 attached, in BFOJC, Vol. 17163, pp. 193–213.

72. See Tsuda, "Menseihin no yushutsu," pp. 32–34, and "Mengyō tōsei," pp. 51 and 56.

73. "Ronsetsu," pp. 5–6.

74. "Kanzei kyūsen kyōyaku ni kansuru kengi," December 1929, in Yoda, *Hachijū-go nen shi*, pp. 1057–59, and Horikoshi, *Keizai dantai*, p. 194.

75. Asahi Shinbun Keizaibu, *Asahi keizai nen shi*, 1934, p. 323.

76. Nihon Keizai Renmeikai, *Jigyō hōkoku*, "Dai jūni kai hōkoku sho," pp. 1–2; Nakagawa, *Yōran*, pp. 140–41; and Suzuki, "Keizai kaigi," pp. 14–17.

77. "Kanzei kyūjitsu kyōtei oyo[bi] kanzei teigen ni kansuru kengi," June 1933, in Yoda, *Hachijū-go nen shi*, pp. 1059–60.

78. Nakajima, "Ishii daihyō," p. 76.

79. "Boikotto kinshi kokusaiteki ni torikiwame," June 10, 1933, "Boikotto kinshi no kokusai kyōtei o teian," June 13, 1933, and "Saikeikoku jōkan no kinō seigen o nozoke," June 20, 1933, *Tokyo asahi shinbun*.

80. This account relies on Asahi Shinbun Keizaibu, *Asahi keizai nen shi*, 1934, pp. 325–27, and Mutō Sanji, "Nihon seifu wa Bei seifu o shiji se yo," June 23, 1933, in Mutō, *Zenshū*, 7:209–10. An account of the conference in English is Feis, *1933*, pp. 170–258.

81. "Kyōchōshugi ima ya hatan," July 7, 1933, *Tokyo asahi shinbun, gōgai*, and Asahi Shinbun Keizaibu, *Asahi keizai nen shi*, 1934, p. 327.

82. Fujiyama, "Waga bōeki," pp. 6–7; Kadono, "Tsūshō seigen," pp. 2–3; Speech (Enzetsu) by Kikumoto Naojirō on October 3, 1933, pp. 2 and 7, in the Archives at the Mitsui Bank in Tokyo; "Kabushiki kaisha Mitsubishi ginkō gaikyō" (January–December 1933), *Mitsubishi shashi*, Vol. 36 for Shōwa 6–Shōwa 9 [1931 to 1934]: 809; and Nakajima Kumakichi, "Kokusaiteki kokkashugi no taitō to yushutsu shinkō no sho shisetsu," in Hamada, *Nihon bōeki kyōkai*, pp. 365–66.

83. Nakajima, "Rinji sangyō," pp. 22–27.

84. Ibid., p. 21.

85. Nakajima, "Sangyō gōrika," pp. 14, 21–23, 31, and 40. For a concise analysis of Rathenau's ideas, see Joll, *Three Intellectuals*, pp. 97–102.

86. *Sangyō gōrika*, no. 1 (December 1930): 156.

87. *Sangyō gōrika*, no. 2 (February 1931): 219–21; Shūgiin giji sokkiroku, *Kanpō gōgai*, March 1, 1931, pp. 505–14; Shūgiin giji sokkiroku, *Kanpō gōgai*, March 15, 1931, pp. 733–36; and Kizokuin giji sokkiroku, *Kanpō gōgai*, March 26, 1931, pp. 659–61. In his report on the bill to the House of Peers, Ōkubo Toshitake noted the important role of the Industrial Control Committee in the drafting process. See Chapter 2 for more details on the provisions of the law.

88. Yoshino, *Omoishutsu*, pp. 204–5. In an interview, Yoshino described a range of responses from the general business community. Some executives, he said, favored the law because they wanted "order in the industrial world," while others resented being forced to join a cartel. See Andō, *Shōgen*, p. 124.

89. *Sangyō gōrika*, no. 16 (March 1935): 177–78 and 179–81.

90. Shōkō Gyōsei Shi Kankōkai, *Gyōsei shi*, 2:413.

91. Nakajima, "Rinji sangyō," pp. 27–29.

92. Ibid., pp. 27–28, and "Shiryō," pp. 33–61, form the basis for this paragraph and the next one.

93. Nakajima, "Rinji sangyō," pp. 28–29, and "Shiryō," pp. 61–70.

94. Tsūshō Sangyōshō, *Seisaku shi*, 9:71–73.

95. "Shiryō," pp. 34, 60–61, and 70–71.

96. Yoshino, *Kōgyō seisaku*, pp. 257–59 and 313–16.

97. Tsūshō Sangyōshō, *Seisaku shi*, 9:79–81, and *Sangyō gōrika*, no. 3 (June 1931): 126–30.

98. Tsūshō Sangyōshō, *Seisaku shi*, 9:84–85.

99. *Sangyō gōrika*, no. 16 (March 1935): 172–73.

100. Tsūshō Sangyōshō, *Seisaku shi*, 9:91–95, and *Sangyō gōrika*, no. 16 (March 1935): 172 and 174.

101. The Introduction discusses the definition of the concept of reciprocal consent between the state and the business community.

FOUR

1. Nihon Kingendai Shi Jiten Henshū Iinkai, *Kingendai shi jiten*, pp. 13 and 482.

2. Nihon Ginkō Tōkeikyoku, *Statistics*, pp. 279 and 284–85. Data presented in Nakamura, *Senzenki*, p. 225, indicate that the trade deficit narrowed dramatically in 1935 but that Japan had a surplus of exports in no year between 1931 and 1937.

3. Ishii, "Cotton Textile Diplomacy," p. 268, and Farley, *Trade Expansion*, pp. 39–40.

4. Ishii, "Cotton Textile Diplomacy," pp. 194–96, 201–9, 272–84, 308–9, and 411–13, and Farley, *Trade Expansion*, pp. 40 and 49–60.

5. "Kanzei shingikai no tōshin an," November 21, 1929, in Takahashi, *Zaisei keizai*, 5:634–35.

6. "Kanzei seido ni kansuru iken sho," December 17, 1931, in Nakagawa, *Yōran*, pp. 106–11.

7. Ibid., pp. 112–13.

8. "The Commercial Council Attached to the Ministry of Foreign Affairs Set Up in September 1933," pp. 1–2, in Teikoku bōeki seisaku shi kankei zakken, Tsūshō shingikai iinkai kankei, pp. 1164–68. (Hereafter these documents will be abbreviated as TSIK.) Also Tsūshōkyoku Daiikka, "Sho gaikoku no yunyū bōatsu shudan gaiyō," September 14, 1933, TSIK, vol. 4.

Tsūshō Shingikai could also be translated as Commerce Council or Trade Council. This study will use the term Commercial Council, because the English language document of the Ministry of Foreign Affairs cited above uses this term.

Members included Abe Fusajirō, Yasukawa Yūnosuke, Tsurumi Sakio,

Hirao Hachisaburō, Inahata Katsutarō, Miyakegawa Momotarō, Kodama Kenji, Isaka Takashi, Miyajima Seijirō, and Murata Shōzō.

9. "Tsūshō shingi iinkai dai ikkai giji yōkō," October 14, 1933, TSIK, pp. 1209–14, and "Tsūshō shingi iinkai dai nikai kaigi giji roku," November 13, 1933, TSIK, pp. 1275–82.

10. See Tsūshō shingi iinkai dai ikkai giji yōkō," October 14, 1933, TSIK, pp. 1235–36, and "Tsūshō shingi iinkai dai nikai kaigi giji roku," November 13, 1933, TSIK, pp. 1300–1301.

11. See "Daini tokubetsu iinkai dai ikkaigi giji roku," December 12, 1933, TSIK, pp. 1450–59 and 1469.

12. "Daini tokubetsu iinkai dai ikkaigi giji roku," December 12, 1933, TSIK, pp. 1465, 1469–71, and 1480; "Daini tokubetsu iinkai dai sankai kaigi," February 23, 1934, TSIK, pp. 1521–30; "Tokubetsu iinkai rengō kyōgikai oyobi dai sankai sōkai," February 23, 1934, TSIK, pp. 1327–39.

13. "Shōkōshō de junbi o isogu," Osaka asahi shinbun, December 15, 1933, "Yushutsu tōsei no kyōka," Osaka mainichi shinbun, December 22, 1933, "Bōeki tōsei an nado," Osaka asahi shinbun, February 1, 1934, "Tsūshō bōei kengen an," Tokyo nichinichi shinbun, February 20, 1934, "Kyōryoku naru tsūshō yōgō hō," Chūgai shōgyō shinpō, March 11, 1934, "Muzei hin yunyū gekizō de," Jiji shinpō, January 16, 1934, in Shinbun, 10:283, 285, 290–93, and 287–88.

14. Shūgiin giji sokkiroku, Kanpō gōgai, March 21, 1934, pp. 732–39, and Kizokuin giji sokkiroku, Kanpō gōgai, March 25, 1934, pp. 467–68.

15. The text of the law is reprinted in Shōkō Gyōsei Shi Kankōkai, Gyōsei shi, 2:437–38.

16. "Kyōryoku naru tsūshō yōgō hō," Chūgai shōgyō shinpō, March 11, 1934, in Shinbun, 10:293.

17. "Yushutsu tōsei no kyōka," Osaka Mainichi shinbun, December 22, 1933, in Shinbun, 10:285; Shūgiin giji sokkiroku, Kanpō gōgai, March 11, 1934, pp. 495–97, 500, and 505; Shūgiin giji sokkiroku, Kanpō gōgai, March 21, 1934, p. 732; and Kizokuin giji sokkiroku, Kanpō gōgai, March 25, 1934, p. 468.

18. "Dai yonkai tsūshō shingi iinkai giji yōroku," May 30, 1934, TSIK, 3:195; "Tsūshō shingi iinkai dai gokai sōkai giji yōroku," April 26, 1935, TSIK, 3:356–58; and Shōkō Gyōsei Shi Kankōkai, Gyōsei shi, 2:439. The author converted the yen figure for the Canadian trade surplus by using the yen/dollar exchange rate for 1934: $29.51 per 100 yen. See Nihon Ginkō Tōkeikyoku, Statistics, p. 320.

19. Shōkō Gyōsei Shi Kankōkai, Gyōsei shi, 2:439–41, and "Tsūshō yōgō hō hatsudō," Osaka mainichi shinbun, May 26, 1936, in Shinbun, 10:381.

20. For example, Ogawa Gōtarō expressed this concern. See Shūgiin giji sokkiroku, *Kanpō gōgai*, March 21, 1934, pp. 732–33.

21. Nihon Keiei Shi Kenkyūjo, *Chōsen to sōzō*, pp. 117–19, and Nihon Keiei Shi Kenkyūjo, *Mitsui bussan*, pp. 557–58.

22. Nihon Keiei Shi Kenkyūjo, *Mitsui bussan*, pp. 628–29.

23. Nihon Keiei Shi Kenkyūjo, *Chōsen to sōzō*, p. 116, and Nihon Keiei Shi Kenkyūjo, *Mitsui bussan*, p. 632.

24. Nakamura, *Kahoku keizai shihai*, pp. 37 and 68–72, and Fujiwara, *Taiheiyō sensō*, p. 27.

25. Kurimoto, "Kokusaku," pp. 22–27, forms the basis for this paragraph and the following one.

26. Tsuda, "Waga sangyō," pp. 25–27, and Tsuda, "Kanebō," pp. 2–11.

27. Tsuda, "Waga sangyō," pp. 26–27; Tsuda, "Kanebō," pp. 11–13; and Tsuda, "Sen'i kōgyō," pp. 67–68.

28. Tsuda, "Sen'i kōgyō," pp. 67–68, and "Waga sen'i," pp. 30–31.

29. "Tsūshō shingi iinkai dai gokai sōkai giji yōroku," April 26, 1935, TSIK, 3:352.

30. Tiedemann, "Big Business and Politics," p. 292; Sugiyama Kazuo, "Ikeda Seihin," p. 139; and Nihon Keiei Shi Kenkyūjo, *Chōsen to sōzō*, pp. 112–13.

31. Yasukawa, "Nisshi shinzen," pp. 110–11.

32. Itō, "Hokushi mondai," pp. 38–39.

33. Itō, "Menpu yushutsu," pp. 38–40, and Itō, "Waga menseihin," pp. 19 and 21.

34. Yasukawa, "Hatten ryoku," pp. 41–42.

35. Yasukawa, "Shin bōeki seisaku," pp. 92–102.

36. Nihon Shōkō Kaigisho, *Manmō keizai*, pp. 58–59 and 61.

37. Ibid., pp. 60 and 62.

38. Ibid., pp. 64–65.

39. Ibid., pp. 67–68.

40. Tokyo Shōkō Kaigisho, *Nihon zaikai*, pp. 93, 107–11, and 190–93.

41. Nakajima, "Tōsei keizai," pp. 9–10.

42. Miyake, "Bōeki tōsei," p. 35, and Fujiyama, "Waga bōeki," pp. 6–7.

43. Mukai, "Taigai bōeki," pp. 222–24.

44. Nakajima, "Tōsei keizai," p. 8.

45. Ibid., p. 10. For a discussion of the experience of the striped cloth and cotton crepe industries, see Chapter 3.

46. Kawai, *Hijōji*, pp. 1–3 and 63–70.

47. Kuhara, "Kokusaku," pp. 352–54.

48. Fujiwara, "Nihon zaikai," pp. 118–19 and 122.

49. Miyake, "Bōeki tōsei," pp. 35–41.

50. Mukai, "Taigai bōeki," pp. 221-24.

51. Katō, "Yushutsu bōeki," pp. 94-96, 104-11, and 123-24. Using trade figures from Nihon Ginkō Tōkeikyoku, *Statistics*, p. 279, the author made the calculation that exports of 400 million yen would represent an increase of roughly 20 percent.

52. Itō, "Waga menseihin," pp. 19-21.

53. Mori, "Sangyō kokusaku," pp. 15-19.

54. Fujiyama, "Kyōchō no seishin," p. 10.

55. Yasukawa, "Hatten ryoku," p. 42.

56. Katō, "Yushutsu bōeki," p. 104.

57. Kadono, "Tsūshō seigen mondai," pp. 13 and 25-27.

58. "Zadankai, gunji yosan," pp. 134-35.

59. "Mengyō tōsei," pp. 56 and 59-60.

60. Mitsubishi Economic Research Bureau, *Japanese Trade*, pp. 559-62 and 564-65.

61. "Memorandum of Understanding (January 22, 1937)," pp. 2-4.

62. "Japan Economic Mission: Report of the Cotton Subcommittee," June 15, 1937, in Honpōjin kaigai shisatsu ryōkō kankei zakken, ken Eibei keizai shisatsu dan kankei, vol. 1.

63. "Konshū no keizaikai," September 14, 1935, p. 31.

64. Horikoshi, *Keizai dantai*, pp. 214-25.

65. See Johnson, *MITI*, pp. 133-34.

66. "Bōeki gyōsei kikan no tōsei . . . ," *Osaka Jiji shinpō*, November 19, 1929, in *Shinbun*, 10:223. For a brief description of earlier proposals, see Chapter 2.

67. "Tsūshō shingi iinkai dai nikai kaigi giji roku," November 13, 1933, TSIK, pp. 1297-1302, and "Tsūshō shingi iinkai dai nikai kaigi ni oite Inahata iin yori teishutsu no iken," TSIK, 3:390-94.

68. Kōbe Shōkō Kaigisho, "Bōekishō setchi ni kansuru chinjō," June 30, 1934, in Bōekishō setchi mondai ikken.

69. Nihon Shōkō Kaigisho, "Bōeki gyōsei tōitsu ni kansuru kengi," November 1934, in Bōeki Kumiai Chūōkai, *Bōeki gyōsei*, pp. 13-14.

70. Hamada, *Nihon bōeki kyōkai*, pp. 103-4.

71. "Kyōka tōitsu o kengi," *Hōchi shinbun*, March 22, 1935, in *Shinbun*, 10:308.

72. "Waga kuni sangyō no tōsei ni kansuru iken sho," July 29, 1935, in Nakagawa, *Yōran*, pp. 183-91. For a description of how the report was compiled, see Horikoshi, *Keizai dantai*, pp. 208-10.

73. For the complaint of the textile producers, see "Taiin yushutsu no nyūsatsu sei," *Kokumin shinbun*, October 15, 1935, in *Shinbun*, 21:505-6. For a discussion of the issue by leaders from the Spinners Association and export associations, see "Mengyō tōsei," pp. 51-63.

74. Nihon Keizai Renmeikai, "Bōeki gyōsei chūsū kikan no setchi ni kansuru iken," July 1936, reprinted in Bōeki Kumiai Chūōkai, *Bōeki gyōsei*, pp. 8–10.

75. Tokyo Shōkō Kaigisho, "Bōeki shinkō saku ni kansuru kengi," August 1936, reprinted in Bōeki Kumiai Chūōkai, *Bōeki gyōsei*, pp. 20–21.

76. Yokohama Shōkō Kaigisho, "Bōeki tōsei ni kansuru ketsugi," July 1936, reprinted in Bōeki Kumiai Chūōkai, *Bōeki gyōsei*, pp. 26–28.

77. Nihon Shōkō Kaigisho, "Bōeki kokusaku jūritsu kikan narabi ni bōeki gyōsei chūsū kikan setchi ni kansuru kengi," August 1936, reprinted in Bōeki Kumiai Chūōkai, *Bōeki gyōsei*, p. 14.

78. Moji Shōkō Kaigisho, "Bōeki tōsei ni kansuru ketsugi," July 1936, reprinted in Bōeki Kumiai Chūōkai, *Bōeki gyōsei*, pp. 21–22, and Yokohama Shōkō Kaigisho Sōritsu Hyaku Shūnen Kinen Jigyō Kikaku Tokubetsu Iinkai Hyaku Nen Shi Hensan Bunkakai, *Hyaku nen shi*, pp. 504–5.

79. See Asahi Shinbun Keizaibu, *Shōwa zaikai shi*, pp. 169–72, for an analysis of the role of export associations.

80. Nihon Keizai Renmeikai, *Bōeki tōsei*, pp. 1, 12–18, 21–22, 53, and 59–60, and "Bōeki tōsei mondai ni kansuru rijikai," p. 86.

81. Nihon Keizai Renmeikai, *Bōeki tōsei*, pp. 14–15, 17–18, 37, 52, and 56.

82. Nihon Keizai Renmeikai, *Bōeki tōsei*, pp. 10–11.

83. "Bōeki tōsei o meguri," *Osaka jiji shinpō*, September 6, 1936, "Yushutsunyū to tōsei ryō kumiai," *Osaka jiji shinpō*, September 19, 1936, "Bōeki tōsei mondai," *Osaka asahi shinbun*, October 13, 1936, and "Bōeki hijōji taisaku . . . ," *Hōchi shinbun*, October 20, 1936, in *Shinbun*, 10:359–62.

84. Nihon Keizai Renmeikai, "Bōeki tōsei ni kansuru iken," pp. 7–13, and "Bōeki tōsei mondai ni kansuru rijikai," p. 86.

85. "Yushutsu, yunyū o fukumu," *Osaka asahi shinbun*, October 23, 1936, "Bōeki tōsei kumiai hō no rippō," *Chūgai shōgyō shinpō*, October 27, 1936, and "Bōeki tōsei no rippōka," *Osaka asahi shinbun*, November 14, 1936, in *Shinbun*, 10:363–64 and 366.

86. "Shōshō hajime no bōeki komon kaigi," *Osaka mainichi shinbun*, April 8, 1937, "Bōeki shingikai o mōke," *Osaka asahi shinbun*, March 6, 1937, "Fukyū hin yunyū no yokusei mo yamu o enu," *Osaka asahi shinbun*, May 8, 1937, and "Bōeki shinkō no ni rippō an," *Tokyo asahi shinbun*, May 12, 1937, in *Shinbun*, 10:417, 414–15, and 421–22. Also, Shūgiin giji sokkiroku, *Kanpō gōgai*, March 20, 1937, p. 684.

87. Shūgiin giji sokkiroku, *Kanpō gōgai*, March 20, 1937, pp. 683–84, and Shūgiin giji sokkiroku, *Kanpō gōgai*, August 3, 1937, pp. 135–37. Ashida, then a member of the Seiyūkai, would join the Progressive party after 1945 and serve as prime minister in 1948.

88. Shōkō Gyōsei Shi Kankōkai, *Gyōsei shi*, 3:76–77; Ashida, "Chōsei

mondai," pp. 25–26; and "Bōeki tōsei kumiai ryō hōan o," *Osaka asahi shinbun*, December 18, 1936, and "Yunyū wariate dankō ka," *Osaka mainichi shinbun*, August 8, 1937, in *Shinbun*, 10:370–71 and 430.

89. "Yunyū wariate dankō ka," *Osaka mainichi shinbun*, August 8, 1937, in *Shinbun*, 10:430.

90. Crowley, *Japan's Quest*, pp. 208–9, and Arisawa, *Keizai shi*, 1:153–55. Barnhart, *Japan Prepares*, Chapter 1, analyzes in detail the army's planning for a self-sufficient regional bloc.

91. See Awaya, *Shōwa no seitō*, pp. 163–69.

92. Hata Shinji, Kenpei Shireikan, "Gogatsu jiken ni kansuru Osaka hōmen no hankyō ni kansuru ken hōkoku," May 19, 1932, and "Gogatsu jiken ni taisuru Osaka zaikai yūryokusha no taido ni kansuru hōkoku," May 24, 1932, in Awaya, *Kokumin dōin*, pp. 7–9 and 20–21.

93. Yoshino Shinji Tsuitō Roku Kankōkai, *Yoshino Shinji*, p. 258.

94. Gō, "Seikyoku," p. 25.

95. Ibid., p. 25; Tokyo Shōkō Kaigisho, *Nihon zaikai*, pp. 85 and 98; Fujiwara, "Nihon zaikai," pp. 122–24; and Ishii, "Cotton Textile Diplomacy," pp. 413–14.

96. Gō, "Seikyoku," p. 25; Katō, "Waga kuni," p. 128; and Tokyo Shōkō Kaigisho, *Nihon zaikai*, pp. 191–92.

97. Takeuchi, *Tōsei keizai*, pp. 23–28.

98. Gō Danshaku Kinenkai, *Gō Seinosuke*, pp. 759–60.

99. Takeuchi, *Tōsei keizai*, pp. 19 and 22.

100. See Sakamoto, "Sensō to zaibatsu," p. 85; Bix, "Rethinking 'Emperor System Fascism,'" pp. 13–16; Chō, "An Inquiry," pp. 388–90; and Nakamura, "The Japan Economic Federation," pp. 416–20.

In studies of the start of Japanese imperialism in the late Meiji era, Peter Duus and William D. Wray point out the cautious and opportunistic attitudes of the business community. See Duus, "Economic Dimensions," pp. 141–47 and 161–63, and Wray, *N.Y.K.*, pp. 356–58 and 365–70.

FIVE

1. "Yunyū wariate dankō ka," *Osaka mainichi shinbun*, August 8, 1937, and "Senji taisei ni saihensei," *Osaka asahi shinbun*, August 18, 1937, in *Shinbun*, 10:430 and 432–33.

2. "Ni dai kokkan kettei su," *Osaka mainichi shinbun*, August 21, 1937, in *Shinbun*, 10:434–35, and Shōkō Gyōsei Shi Kankōkai, *Shōkō gyōsei shi*, 3:78–79.

3. Arisawa, *Keizai shi*, 1:194–97 and 207–10.

4. "Denryoku kokuei an ni taisuru iken," p. 4; Yoda, *Hachijū-go nen shi*, pp. 1276–77; and Inoya, *Osaka shōkō kaigisho*, pp. 367–68.

5. Arisawa, *Keizai shi*, 1:214. Pages 211–14 present an overview of the electrical power issue.

6. Tiedemann, "Big Business and Politics," pp. 291–93 and 310–11.

7. Schumpeter, "Industrial Development," p. 840.

8. Horikoshi, *Keizai dantai*, pp. 339–42, and "Sangyō bōeki kondan-kai," *Tokyo asahi shinbun*, October 10, 1937.

9. "Yushutsu zōshin no sekkyoku saku o nozomu," p. 1.

10. "Senji bōeki kanri wa bōeki kumiai hō ni yore," *Yomiuri shinbun*, August 24, 1937, in *Shinbun*, 10:436.

11. "Menka oyobi yōmō no yunyū seigen wariai kessu," *Osaka mainichi shinbun*, October 1, 1937, and "Minjūhin no yunyū keikaku," *Osaka asahi shinbun*, October 22, 1937, in *Shinbun*, 10:447 and 460.

12. Nangō, "Tokushu kikan," pp. 24–26.

13. "Yushutsu shōhinyō genryō no yunyū onwa ga senketsu," "Gimu yushutsu dankō," and "Mengyō bōeki kawase no dokuritsuka," *Yomiuri shinbun*, February 14, 1938, in *Shinbun*, 10:480–82.

14. "Yushutsu bōeki shinkō saku," *Osaka asahi shinbun*, March 2, 1938, and "Yushutsu fushin no dakai ni . . . ," *Osaka mainichi shinbun*, April 10, 1938, in *Shinbun*, 10:488–89 and 500–501. For the Japan Economic Federation's report, see also Horikoshi, *Keizai dantai*, pp. 309–13.

15. "Bōeki shinkō taisaku," *Chūgai shōgyō shinpō*, May 10, 1938, in *Shinbun*, 10:509, and Horikoshi, *Keizai dantai*, pp. 311–15. The Japan Trade Federation embraced the Japan Trade Council and several other regional organizations dedicated to promoting foreign trade.

16. "Tōsei kikō no ichigenka," May 16, 1938, and "Waga koku bōeki fushin taisaku no kentō," May 17, 1938, *Osaka asahi shinbun*, in *Shinbun*, 10:515–18.

17. "Waga koku bōeki fushin taisaku no kentō," *Osaka asahi shinbun*, May 17, 1938, and "Yushutsu shinkō taisaku ni izen iken tairitsu," *Osaka jiji shinpō*, May 19, 1938, in *Shinbun*, 10:515–18 and 520; and Kōbe Shōkō Kaigisho Hyaku Nen Shi Henshū Bukai, *Hyaku nen shi*, pp. 312–13.

18. "Bōeki shinkō saku," *Osaka asahi shinbun*, May 25, 1938, in *Shinbun*, 10:521. A full draft of this plan is in Bōeki Kumiai Chūōkai, *Bōeki gyōsei*, pp. 14–16.

19. The exclusion of nations in the Yen Bloc, especially China and Manchukuo, from the link system became a major issue, as this chapter explains later.

In a report issued in June 1938, "Hoten taisaku kyōka no teido to kore ga eikyō nara[bi ni] jikkōjō kōryo o yōsuru jikō," the Cabinet Planning Board voiced its support for a link system for the textile industry. See Nakamura and Hara, *Kokka sōdōin*, 1:316–17.

20. "Dai shihon no sōryoku dōin," *Osaka mainichi shinbun*, July 11,

1938, in *Shinbun*, 11:6–8, and Nakamura, *Kahoku keizai shihai*, p. 221.

21. Nangō, "Mengyō bōeki," pp. 14–15 and 19–23.

22. "Nikagetsu gimu yushutsu sei," *Osaka asahi shinbun*, July 16, 1938, in *Shinbun*, 11:13; "Yushutsu gimu kikan no teppai o nozomu," p. 1; and "Kōkyūteki mengyō taisaku o jūritsu se yo," p. 1.

23. Nihon Ginkō Tōkeikyoku, *Statistics*, p. 284.

24. Reports of the ministry's deliberations are in "Sōgō rinku sei no zanteiteki sōchi kettei," *Osaka mainichi shinbun*, August 5, 1938, "Bōeki sō-gō rinku sei," *Chūgai shōgyō shinpō*, September 6, 1938, and "Sōgō rinku sei no bōekikyoku gen'an naru," *Osaka mainichi shinbun*, September 28, 1938, in *Shinbun*, 11:31, 57–58, and 65–66. A description of the system is given by "Shōhin betsu no tokushu rinku sei e," *Osaka asahi shinbun*, October 21, 1938, in *Shinbun*, 11:92–93. "Sōgō rinku sei ni," October 7, 1938, and "Jibun to shite wa jisshi shitai," October 8, 1938, *Osaka asahi shinbun*, in *Shinbun*, 11:70–71 and 76, report Ikeda's enthusiasm for the link system.

25. "Jiji kaisetsu," p. 29.

26. "Sōgō rinku sei no bōekikyoku gen'an naru," September 28, 1938, and "Sōgō rinku sei an," October 21, 1938, *Osaka mainichi shinbun*, in *Shinbun*, 11:65–66 and 94; "Jiji kaisetsu," pp. 29–30; and Kobayashi, "Sōgō rinku sei," p. 22.

27. "Tokushu sōgō rinku an," *Kyōsei nippō*, December 24, 1938, in *Shinbun*, 11:120–21, and "Sōgō rinku," pp. 11–12.

28. "Shōhin betsu no tokushu rinku sei e," *Osaka asahi shinbun*, October 21, 1938, "Tokushu sōgō rinku an," *Kyōsei nippō*, December 24, 1938, and "Yushutsu genzairyō kakuhō ni tokushu rinku sei jisshi," *Osaka mainichi shinbun*, December 25, 1938, in *Shinbun*, 11:92–93 and 120–22.

29. "Tokushu rinku ni koō shi genzairyō haikyū kaisha kessei," *Chūgai shōgyō shinpō*, December 26, 1938, and "Tokushu rinku jisshi de haikyū tōsei kaisha o settei," *Kōbe shinbun*, January 7, 1938, in *Shinbun*, 11:123–24 and 127.

30. "Dai chūsū kikan setchi," November 11, 1938, "Bōeki shinkō kyō-gikai," November 12, 1938, and "Bōeki gyōsei kikan no tōitsu kyōka o yōbō," November 13, 1938, *Osaka asahi shinbun*, in *Shinbun*, 11:105–8, and Hori-koshi, *Keizai dantai*, p. 315.

31. "Bōekishō shinsetsu yōbō," *Osaka mainichi shinbun*, February 16, 1939, and "Yushutsu shinkō o hakare," *Osaka asahi shinbun*, April 6, 1939, in *Shinbun*, 11:171–72 and 191–92.

32. Bōeki Kumiai Chūōkai, *Bōeki gyōsei*, pp. 1–2, 10–13, and 16–17, and Inoya, *Osaka shōkō kaigisho*, p. 377.

33. "Bōekishō no shinsetsu," *Osaka mainichi shinbun*, October 22, 1938, and "Bōekishō setchi e," *Yomiuri shinbun*, October 31, 1938, in *Shinbun*, 11:95 and 100.

34. "Bōeki gyōsei kikō no tōgō wa kokka no kyū," *Osaka mainichi shinbun*, January 10, 1939, in *Shinbun*, 11:143–44.

35. "Bōekishō no setchi," *Osaka jiji shinpō*, June 8, 1939, in *Shinbun*, 11:214–15.

36. "Bōekishō no setchi an," June 13, 1939, and "Kanmin izure mo sansei," June 11, 1939, *Tokyo asahi shinbun*, in *Shinbun*, 11:213–14 and 216.

37. "Kanmin izure mo sansei," June 11, 1939, *Tokyo asahi shinbun*, in *Shinbun*, 11:216, and Shiraishi, "Shiken," pp. 31–33.

38. "Bōekishō no setchi an," June 13, 1939, and "Kanmin izure mo sansei," June 11, 1939, *Tokyo asahi shinbun*, in *Shinbun*, 11:213–14 and 216.

39. "Bōeki shinkō saku jūritsu ni," *Osaka mainichi shinbun*, June 11, 1939, and "Shu, shō ryōshō no iken itchi," *Chūgai shōgyō shinpō*, June 20, 1939, in *Shinbun*, 11:217 and 220–21.

40. "Aku made bōekishō yōbō," *Chūgai shōgyō shinpō*, June 20, 1939, and "Bōeki iinkai no shinsetsu," *Tokyo asahi shinbun*, June 21, 1939, in *Shinbun*, 11:222–23.

41. "Bōekishō setchi ron saimoyasu," *Osaka jiji shinpō*, June 23, 1939, and "Bōekishō mondai," *Kokumin shinbun*, June 29, 1939, in *Shinbun*, 11:225–26 and 230–31.

42. "Bōekishō an o kamei," *Hōchi shinbun*, June 23, 1939, in *Shinbun*, 11:227–28.

43. "Kyōryoku na jikkō suishin ga bōeki kokusaku no chūshin," *Hōchi shinbun*, June 27, 1939, and "Bōekishō setchi yōkō an," *Chūgai shōgyō shinpō*, July 19, 1939, in *Shinbun*, 11:229 and 241–42.

44. "Bōekishō setchi shingen," *Yomiuri shinbun*, July 30, 1939, in *Shinbun*, 11:245.

45. "Bōekishō no shinsetsu," *Osaka jiji shinpō*, August 4, 1939, and "Shushō no ketsui ugokazu," *Kōbe shinbun*, August 14, 1939, in *Shinbun*, 11:247–49.

46. "Bōekishō wa hitsuyō," *Osaka asahi shinbun*, August 31, 1939, in *Shinbun*, 11:255.

47. "Bōekishō iyoiyo kakugi e," September 26, 1939, and "Bōekishō setchi ni kesu," September 27, 1939, *Osaka mainichi shinbun*, in *Shinbun*, 11:265–66, and Gaimushō Hyaku Nen Shi Hensan Iinkai, *Hyaku nen*, pp. 99–102.

The ministry would include the Commerce Bureau from the Ministry of Foreign Affairs; the Exchange Bureau and Customs Section from the Finance Ministry; the Silk Yarn Bureau and parts of the Ocean Products Bureau of the Ministry of Agriculture; the Trade Bureau and parts of the Textile and Chemical Bureaus from the Commerce Ministry; and part of the Development Bureau of the Ministry of Development.

48. "Bōekishō no tanjō," p. 3.

49. "Minkan ken'isha kiyō se yo," *Osaka jiji shinpō*, September 27, 1939, in *Shinbun*, 11:267.

50. Gaimushō Hyaku Nen Shi Hensan Iinkai, *Hyaku nen*, pp. 95–102.

51. Ibid., pp. 102–46, gives an overview of the crisis. For details, see "Seifu daian o kentō," October 10, 1939, "Shōmukan ninmei ken no yōkyū," October 10, 1939, "Gaimushōin hanshō sezuba," October 11, 1939, "Hisō na shōsōha," October 11, 1939, "Zen kōtō kan o mōra," October 12, 1939, "Omoi ashitori de jihyō," October 12, 1939, *Tokyo asahi shinbun*.

52. See "Seifu, dakyō an o sakusei," October 13, 1939, "Naikaku jōhō ron yūryokuka," October 13, 1939, "Abe shushō ni zensho ichinin," October 14, 1939, "Kaku shō fuman hyōmei ka," November 4, 1939, *Tokyo asahi shinbun*.

For an example of such criticism of the selfish and reckless action of foreign ministry officials and of the Abe cabinet's lack of courage, see "Nanzan no bōekishō," p. 4.

53. "Tōsei keizai no konpon hōshin ni kansuru kengi," January 1940, and "Sekkyokuteki yushutsu shinkō saku ni kansuru kengi," January 1940, in Inoya, *Osaka shōkō kaigisho*, pp. 379–80 and 448–50.

54. "Shōhin betsu kumiai o shichū ni," *Chūgai shōgyō shinpō*, March 6, 1940, in *Shinbun*, 11:295–96.

55. "Keizai tōsei ni kansuru tōgyōsha no kujō nara[bi] ni kaizen iken," October 1938, in Nihon Keizai Renmeikai, *Kaizen iken*, pp. 309 and 310–15. One interesting feature of this report is the frankness with which the federation, a representative of big business, reported the concerns of small and medium-sized firms.

56. Horikoshi, *Keizai dantai*, pp. 290–97, and Nihon Keizai Renmeikai, *Kaizen iken*, pp. 176–78.

57. "Bōeki shinkō gutai an," *Tokyo nichinichi shinbun*, April 6, 1940, "Bōeki tōsei dankō e," *Osaka asahi shinbun*, June 18, 1940, Yushutsu shinkō kaisha o gōhei shi," *Osaka asahi shinbun*, June 19, 1940, "Bōeki iinkai setchi," *Osaka mainichi shinbun*, June 23, 1940, "Bōeki tōsei gen'an kaketsu," *Osaka mainichi shinbun*, June 30, 1940, "Yushutsu hin genzairyō o kakuhō," *Osaka mainichi shinbun*, July 2, 1940, in *Shinbun*, 11:300, 322–26, and 335–37. Horikoshi, *Keizai dantai*, p. 316, estimates that over 200 associations existed.

Shimoda, *Fujiwara Ginjirō*, pp. 287, 290–91, and 294–95, emphasizes Fujiwara's pragmatic approach to economic controls and his battles with the "new bureaucrats" and army officials who wanted extensive state supervision of private enterprise. For the market shares of the Ōji Company, see Nihon Kingendai Shi Jiten Henshū Iinkai, *Kingendai shi jiten*, p. 58.

58. The details of Konoe's campaign have been analyzed in Berger, *Parties*, pp. 251–351, and Fletcher, *Search*, pp. 139–54.

59. For background on Kobayashi, see Maeda, "Kobayashi Ichizō." For a detailed analysis of the role of Kobayashi as Minister of Commerce, see Miyake, *Kobayashi Ichizō*, pp. 262-82.

60. Horikoshi, *Keizai dantai*, pp. 299-302.

61. "Bōeki shinkō kyōkai sōritsu," *Tokyo asahi shinbun*, September 21, 1940, and "Nihon bōeki shinkō kyōkai setsuritsu," *Osaka mainichi shinbun*, December 21, 1940, in *Shinbun*, 11:369 and 413.

The name changed from the Nihon Bōeki Shinkō Kyōgikai to the Nihon Bōeki Shinkō Kyōkai. The amount that Gō raised was worth $234,000.00 at the exchange rate of $23.43 per 100 yen in 1940. See Nihon Ginkō Tōkei-kyoku, *Statistics*, p. 320, for the exchange rate.

62. "Bōeki hōkoku renmei sōritsu," *Osaka mainichi shinbun*, September 12, 1940, in *Shinbun*, 21:260. "Bōeki shokumin o teishō," November 20, 1940, and "Bōeki chūō iinkai," December 19, 1940, *Osaka mainichi shinbun*, in *Shinbun*, 11:402 and 413.

63. Horikoshi, *Keizai dantai*, pp. 302-4. For more details see Fletcher, *Search*, pp. 152-53.

64. "Bōeki shinkō taisaku," December 24, 1940, and "Bōeki kumiai saihen," March 23, 1941, *Osaka mainichi shinbun*, in *Shinbun*, 11:414-15 and 435.

65. Arisawa, *Keizai shi*, 1:270-71. Rice, "Economic Mobilization," describes some of these problems in a case study of the Electric Machinery Control Association.

66. "Bōeki keikakuka kakuritsu e," *Osaka asahi shinbun*, June 29, 1941, in *Shinbun*, 11:446-47.

67. Matsuyama, "Bōeki tōseikai," pp. 13-14.

68. "Nihon bōekikai no setchi," *Osaka mainichi shinbun*, October 9, 1941, and "Bōeki kumiai seiri o sara ni sekkyokuka," *Osaka asahi shinbun*, October 10, 1941, in *Shinbun*, 11:482-86.

69. "Bōeki keikakuka," *Tokyo asahi shinbun*, September 18, 1941, "Bōeki tōsei kikō seibi," *Nihon kōgyō shinbun*, October 25, 1941, "Bōekigyō tōseikai," *Kōbe shinbun*, October 28, 1941, "Dai shōsha henchō no kōsei," *Osaka asahi shinbun*, October 28, 1941, and "Bōeki tōsei kikō seibi kyōka," *Nihon kōgyō shinbun*, October 30, 1941, in *Shinbun*, 11:474, 491-94, and 496.

70. "Bōeki gyōsei kikō seibi," *Chūgai shōgyō shinpō*, November 7, 1941, in *Shinbun*, 11:502.

71. "Shin keizai," pp. 50 and 60-61.

72. Takashima, "Keizai dantai," p. 11.

73. "Nihon bōekikai," *Osaka mainichi shinbun*, December 24, 1941, and "Bōeki tōseikai kyō setsuritsu meirei," *Nihon kōgyō shinbun*, December 24, 1941, in *Shinbun*, 11:510-12.

74. "Nihon bōekikai, iyoiyo hassoku," *Nihon kōgyō shinbun*, January 28, 1942, in *Shinbun*, 11:519–20.

75. Shōkō Gyōsei Shi Kankōkai, *Gyōsei shi*, 3:323–25.

76. "Konoe naikaku," pp. 6–8, and "Shina jihen," pp. 1–3. For a description of the Kadono mission, see Chapter 4.

77. Tanaka, "Why Meddle in the Orient," pp. 30–31, and the speeches of Tsuda reprinted in Nishinojima, *Jitsugyō ō*, pp. 211–75. The quotes come from pp. 216, 218–19, 237, and 269–70.

78. "Eibeijin," p. 27.

79. Kobayashi, "Risō an," pp. 306–13; "Tōtaku sōsai Yasukawa Yūnosuke shi ni," pp. 30–35; Shibusawa, "Jikyoku," pp. 27–28; and Gō, "Hōkoku," pp. 10–13.

80. Kobayashi, *"Dai tōa kyōeiken,"* pp. 173–75.

81. Nakamura, *Kahoku keizai shihai*, pp. 162–65, and Gō Danshaku Kinenkai, *Danshaku Gō Seinosuke*, pp. 721–22. Nakamura, pp. 166–89, explains the projects that the companies carried out.

82. See Kobayashi, *"Dai tōa kyōeiken,"* p. 362, and Nakamura, *Kahoku keizai shihai*, pp. 220–25.

83. Nakamura, *Kahoku keizai shihai*, pp. 157–60 and 220.

84. "Nichimanshi mengyō kyōdō tōsei kikan no sōsetsu," p. 1.

85. "Jissen e no riron," p. 1; "Shinchō jikyoku ni taisho se yo," p. 1; " 'Kin' to 'yushutsu,' " p. 1; and "En buro kō menrui no yushutsu seigen o haisu," *Chūgai shōgyō shinpō*, July 26, 1939, in *Shinbun*, 11:243–44.

86. "Shōwa jūyon nen o okuru," p. 1.

87. "En burokku nai yushutsu seigen onwa nara[bi] ni genzairyō shutoku ni kansuru saiyōbō," February 22, 1939, reprinted in Inoya, *Osaka shōkō kaigisho*, pp. 438–41; "En burokku nai no yushutsu seigen taisaku," August 23, 1938, and "En burokku nai no bōeki wa mushiro sekkyokuteki ni," August 24, 1938, *Osaka mainichi shinbun*, in *Shinbun*, 11:52–54.

88. Proposals of July 1938, February 1939, June 1939, and December 1939, which are reprinted in Yoda, *Hachijū-go nen shi*, pp. 1304–7 and 1323–28.

89. "En burokku yushutsu ni mo rinku sei o saiyō se yo," July 21, 1938, "Nisshō an nari chikaku kengi," February 16, 1939, and "Nichimanshi bōeki kaizen," February 17, 1939, *Chūgai shōgyō shinpō*, in *Shinbun*, 11:16 and 172–74.

90. Horikoshi, *Keizai dantai*, pp. 292–93 and 318. Proceedings from one of the economic conferences on Japan, Manchuria, and China were printed in *Dai Nihon bōseki rengōkai geppō*, no. 554 (December 1938): 2–10.

91. "Tōa keizai kondankai daisan bunka kai tekiroku," pp. 41–44.

92. "En burokku bōeki oyobi tsūka no konpon seisaku," February 1939, reprinted in Yoda, *Hachijū-go nen shi*, p. 1306.

93. See Morikawa, "1930 nendai," pp. 131–33.
94. Inoya, "Bōeki seisaku," p. 15, and "Shin keizai," p. 53.
95. For the relevant figures, see Nihon Ginkō Tōkeikyoku, *Statistics*, p. 292. Exports to China remained steady between 1937 and 1938; by the author's calculations, these exports rose 40 percent between 1938 and 1939 and 7.5 percent between 1939 and 1940.

EPILOGUE

1. Johnson, *MITI*, p. 24.
2. Turner, *Businessmen and Politics*, p. 3.
3. This conclusion accords with that expressed in Rice, "Economic Mobilization," pp. 705–6. Rice emphasizes the conflict between different ministries and business leaders in the creation of the Electrical Machinery Control Association in the early 1940s.
4. Hara, "Zaikai," pp. 182–84.
5. In this respect, Richard J. Samuels's *The Business of the Japanese State* has relevance. Spanning the twentieth century, this study finds great continuity in the way that companies and government ministries interacted through a pattern of "reciprocal consent" to create policies for the coal and oil industries.
6. Keizai Dantai Rengōkai, Nihon Keieisha Dantai Renmei, and Kansai Keizai Rengōkai, "Kihon keizai seisaku ni kansuru iken," pp. 44–47. For another example of Keidanren proposing close cooperation between the government and the business community on trade policy, see Keizai Dantai Renmeikai, "Bōeki kihon seisaku ni kansuru yōbō," p. 23. The full name of Keidanren is Keizai Dantai Rengōkai (The Federation of Economic Organizations). The Diet passed the Anti-Monopoly Law in 1947 during the Allied occupation of Japan. The law aimed to prevent concentrations of economic power.
7. Ōtake, *Keizai kenryoku*, analyzes the textile dispute in detail with particular attention paid to the attitudes of Keidanren and the Japan Spinners Council (Nihon Bōseki Kyōkai). See pp. 84–88, 94–101, 104–5, 151, and 195–97. In English, see Destler, *The Textile Wrangle*.
8. Uchino, *Japan's Postwar Economy*, pp. 68, 103, and 120.
9. Vogel, *Comeback*, pp. 40–42 and 56–57.
10. Ouchi, *The M-Form Society*, pp. 50–56 and 103–9; Johnson, *MITI*, pp. 289–91; Vogel, *Comeback*, pp. 139–41 and 143–46; and Uekasa, "Industrial Organization," pp. 494–96.
11. Sato and Hodin, "Steel Issue," pp. 32–35, 48, and 57–63.
12. Winham, "The Politics," pp. 95–96, 100, 107, 111–12, and 114.
13. Ōgata, "The Business Community," pp. 175–203.
14. Ike, "Textile Industry"; and Samuels, "Destructuring."

BIBLIOGRAPHY

UNPUBLISHED MATERIALS

Chapel Hill, N.C., Davis Library at the University of North Carolina.
  British Foreign Office. Japan Correspondence, 1930–1940, Vols. 17160–
  17167 (available on microfilm).
Durham, N.C., Perkins Library at Duke University.
  Shūgiin giji sokkiroku [Shorthand Notes of the Proceedings of the Lower
  House] and Kizokuin giji sokkiroku [Shorthand Notes of the Proceed-
  ings of the House of Peers], 1925, 1930, 1931, 1934, and 1937. In
  Kanpō gōgai [Extra Edition of the Official Gazette]. These materials
  are available on microfilm, entitled Teikoku gikai giji roku [Proceedings
  of the Imperial Diet], compiled by Yūshōdō Shoten in Tokyo in 1974.
Tokyo, Gaimushō Shiryō Kan [Archives of the Ministry of Foreign Affairs].
  Bōekishō setchi mondai ikken [An Item Relating to the Problem of Estab-
  lishing a Ministry of Trade].
  Honpōjin kaigai shisatsu ryōkō kankei zakken, ken Eibei keizai shisetsu
  dan kankei [Items Relating to the Observation Trips of Japanese
  Abroad, Relating to the Group of Economic Envoys that Went to En-
  gland and America]. Vol. 1.
  Teikoku bōeki seisaku kankei zakken [Items Related to the Trade Policy of
  the Empire], Tsūshō shingi iinkai kankei [In Relation to the Commercial
  Council].
Tokyo, the Library of the Keizai Dantai Rengōkai [The Federation of Eco-
  nomic Organizations].
  Nihon Keizai Renmeikai, *Jigyō hōkoku* [Reports about the Activities of the
  Japan Economic Federation].
Tokyo, Kokuritsu Kōbunsho Kan [The National Archives of Japan].
  Keizai shingikai, kankei sho [Materials Related to the Economic Council].
    shijun dai nigo tokubetsu iinkai kankei shorui [Papers Related to the
    Special Advisory Committee Number Two].
    shijun dai nigo tokubetsu iinkai giji roku [Records of the Proceedings of
    the Special Advisory Committee Number Two].
    dai sanmen sōkai giji sokkiroku [Shorthand Notes of the Proceedings of
    the Third General Meeting].
  Kokusai taishaku kaizen shingikai, yōran [The Council on Improving In-
  ternational Debits and Credits, Outline].
    sōkai giji roku [Records of the Proceedings of the General Meetings].

Rinji sangyō shingikai, sōkai giji roku [The Temporary Council for Industry, Records of the Proceedings of the General Meeting].

shimon dai ichigo tokubetsu iinkai giji roku [Records of the Proceedings of Consultative Committee Number One].

Teikoku keizai kaigi [The Imperial Economic Conference], bōeki bukai giji yōroku [A Digest of the Proceedings of the Trade Section].

jirui [Various Items].

kin'yū bukai kaigi roku [Records of the Proceedings of the Finance Section].

kin'yūbu shorui [Papers Relating to the Finance Section].

kōgyōbu shorui [Papers Relating to the Industrial Section].

sankōtei [Items for Reference].

Tokyo, Archives of Mitsui Ginkō [The Mitsui Bank].

Enzetsu yōkō [Outlines of Speeches] of executive directors or company presidents.

Tokyo, Sangyō Seisaku Shi Kenkyūjo [Institute for Research on the History of Industrial Policy].

Shōkō shingikai [The Council on Commerce and Industry], jūyō kōgyō ni kansuru shisetsu tokubetsu iinkai dai sankai giji sokkiroku [Shorthand notes of the Proceedings of the Special Committee Number Three for Facilities Relating to Important Industries], September 13, 1927.

"Shōkō shingikai no gidai ni kansuru iken" [An Opinion on the Topics of the Council on Commerce and Industry], prepared by the Tokyo Shōkō Kaigisho [Tokyo Chamber of Commerce].

Tokyo, Zaisei Shi Shiryō Shitsu in the Ōkurashō [Archives of Source Materials Relating to the History of Public Finance in the Ministry of Finance].

Shōwa zaisei shi shiryō [Source Materials Relating to the History of Public Finance in the Shōwa Era], 2-60, 5-69, 5-70.

NEWSPAPERS AND PERIODICALS, 1920–1942

Bōeki [Trade]

Chūō kōron [Central Review]

Dai Nihon bōseki rengōkai geppō [The Monthly Report of the Greater Japan Spinners Association]

Daiyamondo [Diamond]

Ekonomisuto [The Economist]

Keizai renmei [The Economic Federation]

Sangyō gōrika [Industrial Rationalization]

Tokyo asahi shinbun [The Tokyo Asahi Newspaper]

Tōyō keizai shinpō [The Far Eastern Economic Review]

BOOKS AND ARTICLES

Allen, George C. "Japanese Industry: Its Organization and Development to 1937." In *The Industrialization of Japan and Manchukuo, 1930–1940*, edited by Elizabeth B. Schumpeter, pp. 477–786. New York: The Macmillan Co., 1940.

Andō Yoshio, ed. *Shōwa seiji keizai shi e no shōgen* [Testimony Related to the Economic and Political History of the Shōwa Era]. Vol. 1. Tokyo: Mainichi Shinbunsha, 1966.

Aoki Kazuo. "Kin kaikin to Inoue ōkurashō no omoishutsu" [Recollections of Finance Minister Inoue and the Removal of the Embargo on Gold]. In *Nihon kin'yū shi shiryō, Shōwa hen* [Source Materials for the Financial History of Japan, Volume for the Shōwa Era], edited by the Nihon Ginkō Chōsakyoku, vol. 22, pp. 1–10. Tokyo: Ōkurashō Insatsukyoku, 1968.

Arisawa Hiromi, ed. *Shōwa keizai shi* [The Economic History of the Shōwa Era]. Vol. 1. Tokyo: Nihon Keizai Shinbunsha, 1980.

Asahi Isoshi. *The Secret of Japan's Trade Expansion*. Tokyo: The International Association of Japan, 1934.

Asahi Shinbun Keizaibu, ed. *Asahi keizai nen shi* [The Asahi Economic Yearbook]. Tokyo: Asahi Shinbunsha, 1934.

———. *Shōwa zaikai shi* [The History of the Business Community in the Shōwa Era]. Tokyo: Asahi Shinbunsha, 1936.

Ashida Hitoshi. "Bōeki oyobi kankei sangyō chōsei mondai" [The Problems of Regulating Trade and Related Industries]. *Seiyū*, no. 443 (August 1937): 24–27.

———. "Keizai sensō no shinten" [The Progress of the Economic War]. *Chūō kōron* 50 (September 1935): 71–74.

Awaya Kentarō. *Shōwa no seitō* [The Political Parties of the Shōwa Era], *Shōwa no rekishi* [The History of the Shōwa Era]. Vol. 6. Tokyo: Shogakkan, 1983.

Awaya Kentarō and Ōtabe Yūji, eds. *Shiryō Nihon gendai shi* [Source Materials for the History of Modern Japan]. Vol. 9, *Ni-ni-roku jiken zengo no kokumin dōin* [National Mobilization before and after the February 26 Incident]. Tokyo: Ōtsuki Shoten, 1984.

Banno Junji. *Taishō seihen, 1900 nen taisei no hōkai* [The Political Change of the Taishō Era, the Destruction of the System of 1900]. Tokyo: Mineruva Shobō, 1982.

Barnhart, Michael A. *Japan Prepares for Total War: The Search for Economic Security, 1919–1941*. Ithaca: Cornell University Press, 1987.

Becker, William H. *The Dynamics of Business-Government Relations: Industry and Exports, 1893–1921*. Chicago: University of Chicago Press, 1982.

Berger, Gordon M. *Parties out of Power*. Princeton: Princeton University Press, 1976.

Bisson, T. A. *Japan's War Economy*. New York: Institute of Pacific Relations, 1945.

Bix, Herbert P. "Rethinking 'Emperor System Fascism': Ruptures and Continuities in Modern Japanese History." *Bulletin of Concerned Asian Scholars* 14, no. 2 (1982): 2–19.

"Bōeki jigen, heika kirisage zehi" [Comments on Trade, The Pros and Cons of Cutting the Parity]. *Bōeki* 29 (April 1929): 2–4.

Bōeki Kumiai Chūōkai, ed. *Bōeki gyōsei kikō tōitsu ni kansuru minkan sho dantai no yōbō* [The Requests of Some Private Groups Regarding the Unification of the Structure of Trade Administration]. Tokyo: Bōeki Kumiai Chūōkai, 1939.

"Bōeki tōsei mondai ni kansuru rijikai" [A Meeting of Directors Regarding the Problem of Trade Control]. *Keizai renmei* 7 (January 1937): 86.

"Boeki tōsei ni kansuru iken" [An Opinion Regarding Trade Control]. *Keizai renmei* 7 (January 1937): 7–13.

"Bōekishō no tanjō" [The Birth of the Ministry of Trade]. *Bōeki* 39 (October 1939): 3.

"Bōekishō shinsetsu ni manshin su beshi" [We Must Progress to the Creation of a Ministry of Trade]. *Bōeki* 39 (July 1939): 8.

Braunthal, Gerard. *The Federation of German Industry in Politics*. Ithaca: Cornell University Press, 1965.

Chō Yukio. "An Inquiry into the Problem of Importing American Capital into Manchuria: A Note on Japanese-American Relations, 1931–1941." In *Pearl Harbor as History: Japanese-American Relations, 1931–1941*, edited by Dorothy Borg and Shumpei Okamoto, pp. 377–410. New York: Columbia University Press, 1973.

———. *Shōwa kyōkō, Nihon fuashizumu zenya* [The Shōwa Depression: The Eve before Fascism in Japan]. Tokyo: Iwanami Shoten, 1973.

Crowley, James B. *Japan's Quest for Autonomy: National Security and Foreign Policy*. Princeton: Princeton University Press, 1966.

"Denryoku kokuei an ni taisuru tōkai iken" [The Opinion of This Federation Regarding the National Management of Electric Power]. *Keizai renmei* 6 (October 1936): 4.

Destler, I. M., Haruhito Fukui, and Hideo Sato. *The Textile Wrangle: Conflict in Japanese-American Relations, 1969–1971*. Ithaca: Cornell University Press, 1979.

Duus, Peter. "Economic Dimensions of Meiji Imperialism: The Case of Korea, 1895–1910." In *The Japanese Colonial Empire, 1895–1945*, edited by Ramon H. Myers and Mark R. Peattie, pp. 128–71. Princeton: Princeton University Press, 1984.

"Eibeijin ni atauru Tsuda honkai kaichō messeji" [The Message of the President of this Association, Tsuda, to the British and Americans]. *Dai Nihon bōseki rengōkai geppō*, no. 566 (December 1939): 27.

Farley, Miriam S. *The Problem of Japanese Trade Expansion in the Postwar Situation*. New York: Institute of Pacific Relations, 1940.

Feis, Herbert. *1933: Characters in Crisis*. Boston: Little, Brown & Company, 1966.

Fletcher, William Miles. *The Search for a New Order, Intellectuals and Fascism in Prewar Japan*. Chapel Hill: University of North Carolina Press, 1982.

Friedman, Milton, and Anna Jacobson Schwartz. *A Monetary History of the United States, 1867–1960*. Princeton: Princeton University Press, 1963.

Fujiwara Akira. *Taiheiyō sensō shi ron* [Essays on the History of the Pacific War]. Tokyo: Aoki Shoten, 1982.

Fujiwara Akira and Kunugi Toshihiro, eds. *Shiryō Nihon gendai shi* [Source Materials for the Modern History of Japan]. Vol. 8, *Manshū jihen to kokumin dōin* [The Manchurian Incident and National Mobilization]. Tokyo: Ōtsuki Shoten, 1983.

Fujiwara Ginjirō. "Nihon zaikai no ichikaku yori" [From One Corner of Japan's Business World]. *Chūō kōron* 48 (November 1933): 117–27.

Fujiyama Raita. "Waga bōeki to kyōchō no seishin" [Our Trade and the Spirit of Cooperation]. *Keizai renmei* 4 (April 1934): 6–10.

Gaimushō Hyaku Nen Shi Hensan Iinkai, ed. *Gaimushō no hyaku nen* [A Hundred Years of the Ministry of Foreign Affairs]. Vol. 2. Tokyo: Hara Shobō, 1969.

Gō Danshaku Kinenkai, ed. *Danshaku Gō Seinosuke kun den* [A Biography of Baron Gō Seinosuke]. Tokyo: Gō Danshaku Kinenkai, 1943.

Gō Seinosuke. "Jikyoku o kataru" [Discussing the Current Situation]. *Keizai renmei* 2 (March 1932): 1–6.

―――. "Nihon keizai no shinro to sono shidō seishin" [The Course of the Japanese Economy and Its Guiding Spirit]. *Daiyamondo* 24 (November 11, 1936): 132–35.

―――. "Seikyoku wa dō kawaru" [How Will the Political Situation Change?]. *Daiyamondo* 22 (March 1, 1934): 23–25.

―――. "Waga kuni sangyō gōrika no jūyō mondai" [The Important Problems of the Rationalization of Japan's Industry]. *Sangyō gōrika*, no. 1 (December 1930): 9–20.

―――. *Zaikai: fukyō jijō* [The Business Community: The Situation of the Depression]. Tokyo: Tokyo Shōkō Kaigisho, 1931.

―――. "Zaikaijin to shite no jinchū hōkoku" [Loyalty and Service to the Nation as a Member of the Business Community]. *Keizai renmei* 8 (April 1938): 10–16.

Gordon, Margaret S. "Japan's Balance of International Payments." In *Industrialization in Japan and Manchukuo, 1930–1940*, edited by Elizabeth B. Schumpeter, pp. 865–925. New York: The Macmillan Company, 1940.

Grant, Wyn, and David Marsh. *The Confederation of British Industry*. London: Hodder and Stoughton, 1977.

Hamada Tokutarō. *Nihon bōeki kyōkai gojū nen shi* [The History of Fifty Years of the Japan Trade Council]. Tokyo: Nihon Bōeki Kyōkai, 1936.

Hara Akira. "Senji tōsei keizai no kaishi" [The Start of the Wartime Control Economy]. In *Iwanami kōza: Nihon rekishi* [Iwanami Lectures: The History of Japan]. Vol. 20, *Kindai* [The Modern Era], no. 7, pp. 217–68. Tokyo: Iwanami Shoten, 1976.

_____. "Zaikai" [The Business Community]. In *Kindai Nihon kenkyū nyūmon* [An Introduction to Research on Modern Japan], edited by Nakamura Takafusa and Itō Takashi, pp. 170–92. Tokyo: Tokyo Daigaku Shuppankai, 1977.

Hikida Yasuyuki. "Sangyō kōzō" [Industrial Structure]. In *1920 nendai no Nihon shihonshugi* [Japanese Capitalism in the 1920s], edited by the 1920 Nendai Kenkyūkai, pp. 49–84. Tokyo: Tokyo Daigaku Shuppankai, 1983.

Hoashi Kei. "Senji keizaika no wagakuni bōeki seisaku" [Japan's Trade Policies under the Wartime Economy]. *Chūō kōron* 54 (July 1939): 60–69.

"Hokushi keizai o kongo dō suru ka?" [What Should We Do about the Economy of North China in the Future?]. *Chūō kōron* 52 (November 1937): 430–44.

Horikoshi Teizō. *Keizai dantai rengōkai, zenshi: Nihon keizai renmeikai shi, jūyō sangyō kyōgikai shi* [The Federation of Economic Organizations, a Pre-history: The History of the Japan Economic Federation and the Council of Important Industries]. Tokyo: Chūō Kōron Jitsugyō Shuppan, 1962.

Hosoya Chihiro. "1934 nen no Nichiei fukashin kyōtei mondai" [The Problem of the Non-Aggression Pact of 1934 between Japan and England]. *Kokusai seiji*, no. 58 (1977): 69–85.

Ike, Brian. "The Japanese Textile Industry: Structural Adjustment and Government Policy." *Asian Survey* 20 (May 1980): 532–51.

Ikeda Seihin Denki Kankōkai. *Ikeda Seihin den* [A Biography of Ikeda Seihin]. Tokyo: Keiō Tsūshin Kabushiki Kaisha, 1962.

Imaizumi Kiichirō. *Sengo Doitsu no sangyō soshiki: sangyōkai no shin gōdōhō rigai kyōyaku ni tsuite* [The Organization of German Industry after the War: Concerning the Industrial World's Interest Pacts under the New Merger Law]. Tokyo: Kōseikai, 1924. In Teikoku keizai kaigi kōgyōbu shorui [Papers Related to the Industrial Section of the Imperial Economic Council].

Inamiya Matakichi. *Yano Tsuneta, Ichigyō hitori den* [Yano Tsuneta, A Biography of One Person and One Industry]. Tokyo: Jiji Tsūshinsha, 1963.

"Indo seifu ni teishutsu no chinjutsu sho" [A Declaration for Presentation to the Indian Government]. *Dai Nihon bōseki rengōkai geppō*, no. 402 (February 1926): 1–2.

Inoue Junnosuke. *Kokumin keizai no tachinaoshi to kin kaikin* [The Removal of the Embargo on Gold and the Revival of the National Economy]. Tokyo: Chikura Shobō, 1929.

———. *Kokusaku keizai o kataru* [Discussing the Economy and National Policies]. Tokyo: Jitsugyō no Nihonsha, 1930.

Inoya Zen'ichi. "Bōeki seisaku no saikentō" [A Reexamination of Trade Policy]. *Ekonomisuto* 19 (January 13, 1941): 15–16.

———. *Osaka shōkō kaigisho shi* [A History of the Osaka Chamber of Commerce]. Osaka: Osaka Shōkō Kaigisho, 1941.

Ishida Takeshi. "The Development of Interest Groups and the Pattern of Political Modernization in Japan." In *Political Development in Modern Japan*, edited by Robert E. Ward, pp. 293–336. Princeton: Princeton University Press, 1968.

Ishii Osamu. "Cotton Textile Diplomacy: Japan, Great Britain, and the United States, 1930–1936." Ph.D. dissertation, Rutgers University, 1977.

Ishiyama Kenkichi. "Bōsekikai no zento ni yokotawaru ni mondai" [Two Problems that Obstruct the Future of the Spinners' World]. *Daiyamondo* 23 (December 1, 1935): 40–42.

Isomura Toyotarō. "Genka no zaikai ni taisuru kansō" [Thoughts on the Present Business World]. *Keizai renmei* 2 (March 1932): 7–9.

Itō Masanao. "Taigai keizai kankei" [Foreign Economic Relations]. In *1930 nendai no Nihon keizai: sono shiteki bunseki* [Japan's Economy in the 1930s: An Historical Analysis], edited by the Shakai Keizai Shi Gakkai, pp. 23–102. Tokyo: Tokyo Daigaku Shuppankai, 1982.

Itō Masanao. "Zaisei kin'yū" [Public Finance and the Circulation of Currency]. In *1920 nendai no Nihon shihonshugi* [Japanese Capitalism in the 1920s], edited by the 1920 Nendai Kenkyūkai, pp. 85–121. Tokyo: Tokyo Daigaku Shuppankai, 1983.

Itō Takenosuke. "Menpu ichiba to hokushi mondai" [The Market for Cotton Cloth and the Problem of North China]. *Daiyamondo* 23 (December 11, 1935): 38–39.

———. "Menpu yushutsu no shinten wa honnen mo jizoku sen" [The Expansion of Exports of Cotton Cloth Will Continue This Year Too]. *Tōyō keizai shinpō*, no. 1583 (January 20, 1934): 38–40.

———. "Waga menseihin bōeki ni tsuite" [About the Trade of Japan's Cotton Manufactures]. *Keizai renmei* 6 (October 1936): 16–21.

"Jiji kaisetsu, sōgō rinku sei to wa" [A Solution to the Current Situation, What About the Link System?]. *Ekonomisuto* 16 (October 21, 1938): 29–30.

"Jissen e no riron." *Dai Nihon bōseki rengōkai geppō*, no. 559 (May 1939): 1.

Johnson, Chalmers. *MITI and the Japanese Miracle: The Growth of Industrial Policy, 1925–1975*. Stanford: Stanford University Press, 1982.

Joll, James. *Three Intellectuals in Politics*. New York: Pantheon, 1960.

Kadono Chokyūrō. "Nihon hin no sekaiteki shinshutsu to tsūshō seigen mondai" [The World Advance of Japanese Goods and the Problem of Trade Limits]. In *Bōeki seisaku kōza* [Lectures on Trade Policy], edited by the Tokyo Shōkō Kaigisho, pp. 1–29. Tokyo: Tokyo Shōkō Kaigisho, 1934.

———. "Ōbei sho koku ni shishite" [Going on a Mission to Several Nations in Europe and America]. *Keizai renmei* 8 (January 1938): 2–8.

Kaplan, Eugene J. *Japan: The Government-Business Relationship*. Washington, D.C.: U.S. Government Printing Office, 1972.

Kataoka Naoharu. "Watakushi no kin kaikin junbi kōsaku" [My Actions to Prepare for the End of the Embargo on Gold], 1934. In *Nihon Kin'yū shi shiryō, Shōwa hen* [Source Materials for the Financial History of Japan, Volume for the Shōwa Era], edited by the Nihon Ginkō Chōsakyoku, vol. 22, pp. 16–17. Tokyo: Ōkurashō Insatsukyoku, 1968.

Katō Kyōhei. "Waga kuni yushutsu bōeki no shidō hōshin" [The Guiding Policy for Japan's Export Trade]. In *Bōeki seisaku kōza* [Lectures on Trade Policy], edited by the Tokyo Shōkō Kaigisho, pp. 85–128. Tokyo: Tokyo Shōkō Kaigisho, 1934.

Kaufman, Burton I. *Efficiency and Expansion, Foreign Trade Organization in the Wilson Administration, 1913–1921*. Westport, Conn.: Greenwood Press, 1974.

Kawai Yoshinari. *Hijōji no keizai taisaku* [Economic Policies for the Emergency]. Tokyo: Chikura Shobō, 1932.

———. *Nihon keizai o dō suru ka* [What Should We Do about Japan's Economy?]. Tokyo: Shōwa Tosho Kabushiki Kaisha, 1939.

Keizai Dantai Rengōkai, Nihon Keieisha Dantai Renmei, and Kansai Keizai Rengōkai. "Kihon keizai seisaku ni kansuru iken" [An Opinion on Basic Economic Policies]. *Chūō kōron* 68 (July 1953): 44–48.

Keizai Dantai Renmeikai. "Bōeki kihon seisaku ni kansuru yōbō" [Hopes Regarding Basic Trade Policies]. *Keizai rengō*, November–December, 1952, p. 23.

" 'Kin' to 'yushutsu' " ["Money" and "Exports"]. *Dai Nihon bōseki rengōkai geppō*, no. 565 (November 1939): 1.

Kō Dan Danshaku Denki Hensan Iinkai, ed. *Danshaku Dan Takuma den* [A Biography of Baron Dan Takuma]. Tokyo: Kō Dan Danshaku Denki Hensan Iinkai, 1938.

Kobayashi Hideo. *"Dai Tōa kyōeiken" no keisei to hōkai* [The Formation and Destruction of the "Greater East Asian Coprosperity Sphere"]. Tokyo: Ochanomizu Shobō, 1980.

Kobayashi Ichizō. "Hokushi keizai kensetsu no risō an" [An Ideal Plan for Constructing the Economy of North China]. *Chūō kōron* 52 (November 1937): 306–13.

―――. "Shosei isshin ka zenshinshugi ka" [Renovation of the Whole State of Affairs or Gradual Reform?]. *Daiyamondo* 25 (February 11, 1937): 21–22.

"Kobayashi Ichizō no 'Hokushi jihen tenyū' ron" [Kobayashi Ichizō's Theory that the 'North China Incident is Divine Assistance']. *Tōyō keizai shinpō*, no. 1776 (August 28, 1937): 10–11.

Kobayashi Yukimasa. "Sōgō rinku sei no hihan" [Criticism of the Comprehensive Link System]. *Ekonomisuto* 16 (October 21, 1938): 21–23.

Kōbe Bōeki Kyōkai, ed. *Kōbe bōeki kyōkai shi* [A History of the Kōbe Trade Association]. Kōbe: Kōbe Bōeki Kyōkai, 1969.

Kōbe Shōkō Kaigisho. *Manmō mondai no jissō* [The Real Situation of the Problems of Manchuria and Mongolia]. Kōbe: 1931.

Kōbe Shōkō Kaigisho Hyaku Nen Shi Henshū Bukai. *Kōbe shōkō kaigisho hyaku nen shi* [A History of One Hundred Years of the Kōbe Chamber of Commerce]. Kōbe: Kōbe Shōkō Kaigisho, 1982.

Kojima Kyōju Kenkyūshitsu. "Wagakuni mengyō ni okeru tōseiteki sho shisetsu (I)" [Some Facilities for Control in Japan's Cotton Industry (I)]. *Dai Nihon bōseki rengōkai geppō*, no. 510 (March 1935): 8–21.

―――. "Wagakuni mengyō ni okeru tōseiteki sho shisetsu (II)" [Some Facilities for Control in Japan's Cotton Industry (II)]. *Dai Nihon bōseki rengōkai geppō*, no. 511 (April 1935): 23–37.

"Kōkyūteki mengyō taisaku o jūritsu se yo" [Create a Permanent Policy for the Cotton Industry]. *Dai Nihon bōseki rengōkai geppō*, no. 555 (January 1939): 1.

"Konoe naikaku seiritsu shukuga bansankai ni okeru enzetsu" [Speeches at the Dinner Party in Celebration of the Creation of the Konoe Cabinet]. *Keizai renmei* 7 (July 1937): 1–9.

"Konshū no keizaikai" [The Economic World This Week]. *Tōyō keizai shinpō*, no. 1667 (August 17, 1935): 26–28; no. 1671 (September 14, 1935): 29–31.

Kuhara Fusanosuke. "Hijōji kokusaku konpongi" [The Basic Principles of National Policies during the Emergency]. *Chūō kōron* 48 (December 1933): 349–58.

Kurimoto Yūnosuke. "Jishuteki bōeki kokusaku kakuritsu no kyūmu" [The Urgency of Creating Independent National Policies for Trade]. *Keizai renmei* 6 (October 1936): 22–27.

McConnell, Grant. *Private Power and American Democracy*. New York: Alfred A. Knopf, 1967.

Maeda Kazutoshi. "Kobayashi Ichizō (Hankyū gurūpu sōsetsusha), Shōhisha shikō no daisanji sangyō kigyō shūdan no sōsetsu" [Kobayashi Ichizō (the Creator of the Hankyū Group), The Creation of an Enterprise Group of Tertiary Industry Directed at Consumers]. In *Nihon no kigyōka* (3) [Industrialists of Japan (3)], edited by Morikawa Hidemasa, pp. 89–131. Tokyo: Yuikaku Shinsho, 1978.

Maier, Charles S. *Recasting Bourgeois Europe: Stabilization in France, Germany, and Italy in the Decade after World War I*. Princeton: Princeton University Press, 1975.

Makino Ryōzō, *Nakahashi Tokugorō den* [A Biography of Nakahashi Tokugorō]. Tokyo: Nakahashi Tokugorō Denki Hensankai, 1944.

Matsuda Gen. "Kakukuni sengyō no kinjō, Nihon o osoreru Ōbei no bōseki" [The Recent Situation of Each Nation's Textile Industry, the European and American Spinners Who Fear Japan]. *Daiyamondo* 25 (January 21, 1937): 50–54.

Matsuyama Fujirō. "Bōeki tōseikai no setsuritsu mondai" [Problems in Establishing a Trade Control Association]. *Ekonomisuto* 19 (August 18, 1941): 13–14.

"Memorandum of Understanding (January 22, 1937)." *Keizai renmei* 7 (March 1937): 1–5.

"Mengyō tōsei mondai ni tsuite iken o kiku" [Requesting Opinions about Problems Regarding the Control of the Cotton Industry]. *Tōyō keizai shinpō*, no. 1650 (April 27, 1935): 51–63.

Middlemas, Keith. *Politics in Industrial Society, The Experience of the British System since 1911*. London: André Deutsch, Ltd., 1979.

Mitani Taichirō. "Kokusai kin'yū shihon to Ajia sensō—shumakki ni okeru taichū shikoku shakkan dan" [International Finance Capital and War in Asia—The Four-Power Consortium for China in the Period of Termination]. In *Kindai Nihon to tō Ajia* [Modern Japan and East Asia], edited by the Kindai Nihon Kenkyūkai, pp. 114–58. Tokyo: Yamakawa Shuppansha, 1980.

_____. "Nihon no kokusai kin'yūka to kokusai seiji" [Japan's International Financiers and International Politics]. In *Kindai Nihon no taigai taido* [The Attitudes of Modern Japan toward Foreign Nations], edited by Roger Dingman and Satō Seisaburō, pp. 123–58. Tokyo: Tokyo Daigaku Shuppankai, 1974.

Mitsubishi Economic Research Bureau. *Japanese Trade and Industry: Present and Future*. London: Macmillan & Co., 1936.

Mitsubishi Shashi Kankōkai, ed. *Mitsubishi shashi (Shōwa)* [Documents of the Mitsubishi Company (for the Shōwa Era)], vol. 36. Tokyo: Tokyo Daigaku Shuppankai, 1981.

Mitsuchi Chūzō. "Zaikai kōsei saku" [Policies to Revive the Business World]. *Bōeki* 30 (May 1930): 21–27.

Mitsui Ginkō 100 Nen no Ayumi Henshū Iinkai, ed. *Mitsui ginkō 100 nen no ayumi* [Mitsui Bank: The Course of a Hundred Years]. Tokyo: Mitsui Ginkō, 1976.

Miwa Ryōichi. "Daiichiji taisengo no keizai kōzō to kinkaikin seisaku" [The Economic Structure after the First World War and the Policy of Ending the Gold Embargo]. In *Nihon keizai seisaku shi ron* [A History of Japan's Economic Policy], edited by Andō Yoshio, vol. 1, pp. 259–329. Tokyo: Tokyo Daigaku Shuppankai, 1973.

————. "Kin kaikin seisaku kettei katei ni okeru rigai ishiki" [The Consciousness of Interests in the Process of Deciding the Policy to End the Embargo on Gold]. *Aoyama keizai ronshū* 26 (November 1974): 173–200.

————. "Nihon no karuteru" [Cartels in Japan]. In *Nihon no kigyō to kokka* [The State and Enterprises in Japan], edited by Morikawa Hidemasa, pp. 167–96. Tokyo: Nihon Keizai Shinbunsha, 1976.

Miyake Gōta. "Bōeki tōsei wa ikana ni kōsei su beki ka" [How Can We Improve the Control of Trade?]. *Keizai renmei* 7 (January 1937): 35–42.

Miyake Seiki. *Kobayashi Ichizō den* [A Biography of Kobayashi Ichizō]. Tokyo: Tōyō Shokan, 1954.

Mori Nobuteru. "Genka no sangyō kokusaku" [The Present National Policies for Industry]. *Keizai renmei* 6 (March 1936): 15–19.

Morikawa Hidemasa. "1930 nendai ni okeru kigyōjin no ishiki" [The Consciousness of Businessmen in the 1930s]. *Shisō*, no. 624 (June 1976): 122–36.

Mukai Tadaharu. "Waga taigai bōeki no genjō" [The Current Situation of Japan's Foreign Trade]. In *Bōeki seisaku kōza* [Lectures on Trade Policy], edited by the Tokyo Shōkō Kaigisho, pp. 205–26. Tokyo: Tokyo Shōkō Kaigisho, 1934.

Mutō Sanji. *Jitsugyō seiji* [Business and Politics]. Tokyo: Nihon Hyōronsha, 1926.

————. *Mutō Sanji zenshū* [The Complete Works of Mutō Sanji]. Vol. 7. Tokyo: Shinkisha, 1964.

Nagata Masaomi. *Keizai dantai hatten shi* [A History of the Development of Economic Organizations]. Tokyo: Kōtō Shoten, 1956.

Nakagawa Jirō, ed. *Nihon keizai renmeikai jigyō yōran* [A Survey of the Activities of the Japan Economic Federation]. Tokyo: Nihon Keizai Renmeikai, 1938.

Nakajima Kumakichi. *Beikoku no jitsugyōka no dantaiteki kōdō* [The Activities of Organizations of Businessmen in America]. Tokyo: Tokyo Seihen Gōshitsu Kaisha, 1926.

———. "Ishii daihyō o okuru" [Sending Off Ishii the Delegate]. *Ekonomisuto* 11 (May 15, 1933): 75–77.

———. "Rinji sangyō gōrikyoku no jigyō ni tsuite" [About the Activity of the Temporary Industrial Rationalization Bureau]. *Sangyō gōrika*, no. 1 (December 1930): 21–31.

———. "Sangyō gōrika ni okeru san dai kichō" [Three Fundamental Points in Industrial Rationalization]. *Sangyō gōrika*, no. 2 (February 1931): 10–40.

———. *Seikai zaikai gojū nen* [Fifty Years in the Political and Business Worlds]. Tokyo: Dai Nihon Yūben Kōdansha, 1951.

———. "Tōsei keizai" [The Control Economy]. *Keizai renmei* 2 (December 1932): 7–10.

Nakamura Hideichirō. "The Activities of the Japan Economic Federation." In *Pearl Harbor as History: Japanese-American Relations, 1931–1941*, edited by Dorothy Borg and Shumpei Okamoto, pp. 411–20. New York: Columbia University Press, 1973.

Nakamura Mototada, ed. *Nihon kōgyō kurabu nijū-go nen shi* [A History of Twenty-five Years of the Japan Industrial Club]. Tokyo: Nakamura Mototada, 1943.

Nakamura Takafusa. "Nihon no kahoku keizai kōsaku—Tanku kyōtei kara Rokōkyō jiken made" [Japan's Economic Operations in North China—from the Tanku Treaty to the Incident at the Marco Polo Bridge]. In *Kindai Nihon to tō Ajia* [Modern Japan and East Asia], edited by the Kindai Nihon Kenkyūkai, pp. 159–204. Tokyo: Yamakawa Shuppansha, 1980.

———. *Nihon no keizai tōsei, senji sengo no keiken to kyōjun* [Japan's Economic Controls, The Experience and Lessons of the Wartime and Postwar Eras]. Tokyo: Nihon Keizai Shinbunsha, 1974.

———. *The Postwar Japanese Economy: Its Development and Structure*. Tokyo: University of Tokyo Press, 1981.

———. *Senji Nihon no kahoku keizai shihai* [Japan's Economic Dominance of North China in Wartime]. Tokyo: Yamakawa Shuppansha, 1983.

———. *Senzenki Nihon keizai seichō no bunseki* [An Analysis of Japanese Economic Growth in the Prewar Period]. Tokyo: Iwanami Shoten, 1971.

———. *Shōwa kyōkō to keizai seisaku* [The Depression of the Shōwa Era and Economic Policy]. Tokyo: Nihon Keizai Shinbunsha, 1978.

Nakamura Takafusa and Hara Akira, eds. *Gendai shi shiryō* [Source Materials for Modern History]. Vol. 43, *Kokka sōdōin* [National Mobilization], 1. Tokyo: Misuzu Shobō, 1977.

Nangō Saburō. "Mengyō bōeki sokushin saku ni tsuite" [About Policies to

Promote Trade in the Cotton Industry]. *Keizai renmei* 8 (August 1938): 11–23.

———. "Tokushu kikan setsuritsu no hitsuyō" [The Need for Establishing a Special Organ]. *Keizai renmei* 7 (November 1937): 24–26.

"Nan'yō bōeki kaigi no seika" [The Results of the Conference on Trade with the South Seas]. *Ekonomisuto* 4 (October 15, 1926): 545–48.

"Nanzan no boekishō" [The Trade Ministry Which Is Having a Difficult Birth]. *Bōeki* 39 (November 1939): 4–5.

"Nichimanshi keizai kondankai (jūichi gatsu nijū-roku nichi)" [The Economic Conference for Japan, Manchuria, and China (November 26)]. *Dai Nihon bōseki rengōkai geppō*, no. 554 (December 1938): 2–10.

"Nichimanshi mengyō kyōdō tōsei kikan no sōsetsu" [The Creation of a Cooperative Control Organ for the Cotton Industry in Japan, Manchuria, and China]. *Dai Nihon bōseki rengōkai geppō*, no. 553 (November 1938): 1.

"Nihon bōseki jigyō ni taisuru Indo no gokai ni kansuru chinjutsu sho" [A Declaration Regarding India's Misunderstanding of Japan's Cotton Spinning Operations]. *Dai Nihon bōseki rengōkai geppō*, no. 402 (February 1926): 2–10.

Nihon Ginkō Chōsakyoku, ed. *Nihon kin'yū shi shiryō, Shōwa hen* [Source Materials for the Financial History of Japan, Volume for the Shōwa Era]. Vol. 23. Tokyo: Ōkurashō Insatsukyoku, 1969.

Nihon Ginkō Tōkeikyoku. *Hundred-Year Statistics of the Japanese Economy*. Tokyo: Bank of Japan, 1966.

Nihon Keiei Shi Kenkyūjo. *Chōsen to sōzō—Mitsui bussan 100 nen no ayumi* [Challenge and Imagination—The Course of One Hundred Years for the Mitsui Trading Company]. Tokyo: Mitsui Bussan Kabushiki Kaisha, 1976.

———. *Kōhon: Mitsui bussan kabushiki kaisha 100 nen shi* [A Manuscript: A History of a Hundred Years of the Mitsui Trading Company]. Vol. 1. Tokyo: Nihon Keiei shi Kenkyūjo, 1978.

Nihon Keizai Renmeikai. *Doitsu ni okeru tōsei keizai no jitsujō* [The Real Situation of the Control Economy in Germany]. Tokyo: n.p., 1940.

———. *Genkō sangyō tōsei no kekkan jitsujō nara[bi] ni kore ni taisuru gyōshu betsu kaizen iken* [The Real State of Affairs Regarding the Faults of the Current Controls for Industry and Opinions for the Reform of These Faults for Each Industry]. Tokyo: Nihon Keizai Renmeikai, 1940.

———. *Waga kuni bōeki tōsei ni kansuru kankei tōgyōsha no iken nara[bi] ni sankō shiryō* [Reference Materials and the Opinions of Businessmen Concerning the Control of Japan's Trade]. Tokyo: Nihon Keizai Renmeikai, 1936.

Nihon Keizai Renmeikai, Nihon Kōgyō Kurabu, Nihon Shōkō Kaigisho, Nikka Jitsugyō Kyōkai. "Kokusai renmei Shina chōsa dan hōkoku sho ni taisuru iken sho" [An Opinion Regarding the Written Report of the China Investigation Group from the League of Nations]. *Keizai renmei* 2 (December 1932): 2–6.

Nihon Kingendai Shi Jiten Henshū Iinkai, ed. *Nihon kingendai shi jiten* [A Historical Dictionary for Modern Japan]. Tokyo: Tōyō Keizai Shinpōsha, 1978.

Nihon Kōgyō Kurabu Chōsaka. "Kin yushutsu mondai ni kansuru Nihon kōgyō kurabu kaiin no iken" [The Opinions of Members of the Japan Industrial Club on Problems Relating to the Export of Gold]. Unpublished report, November 1928, in Keizai shingikai, shijun dai nigo tokubetsu iinkai kankei shorui [The Economic Council, Papers Relating to the Special Advisory Committee Number Two].

Nihon Kōgyō Kurabu Gojū Nen Shi Hensan Iinkai, ed. *Nihon kōgyō kurabu gojū nen shi* [A History of Fifty Years of the Japan Industrial Club]. Tokyo: Nihon Kōgyō Kurabu, 1972.

Nihon Kōgyō Kurabu, Nihon Keizai Renmeikai, ed. *Saikin zaikai fukyō no jitsujō nara[bi] ni kore ga gen'in to taisaku* [The Real State of Affairs of the Recent Depression of the Business World: The Causes of the Depression and Policies to Cope with It]. Tokyo: Nihon Kōgyō Kurabu, 1931.

Nihon Rekishi Gakkai, ed. *Mutō Sanji*. Tokyo: Yoshikawa Kobunkan, 1964.

Nihon Shōkō Kaigisho, ed. *Manmō keizai shisatsu dan hōkoku nara[bi ni] iken sho* [The Written Report and Opinions of the Group That Observed the Economy of Manchuria and Mongolia]. Tokyo: Nihon Shōkō Kaigisho, 1934.

_____. *Meiji hyaku nen to shōkō kaigisho kyūjū nen no ayumi* [The Course of a Hundred Years of Meiji and Ninety Years of Chambers of Commerce]. Tokyo: Nihon Shōkō Kaigisho, 1968.

Nishinojima Kyōzō. *Jitsugyō ō, Tsuda Shingo* [The King of Enterprise, Tsuda Shingo]. Tokyo: Kyō no Mondaisha, 1938.

Noda Reiji. *Ningen Gō Seinosuke* [Gō Seinosuke, the Person]. Tokyo: Kyō no Mondaisha, 1939.

Ōgata Sadako. "The Business Community and Japanese Foreign Policy." In *The Foreign Policy of Modern Japan*, edited by Robert A. Scalapino, pp. 175–203. Berkeley: University of California Press, 1977.

Ōshima Kenzō. *Ichi ginkōka no kaisō* [Recollections of One Banker]. Tokyo: Nihon Keizai Shinbunsha, 1963.

Ōtake Hideo. *Gendai Nihon no seiji kenryoku keizai kenryoku* [Political Power and Economic Power in Modern Japan]. Tokyo: San'ichi Shobō, 1979 and 1980.

Ouchi, William S. *The M-Form Society: How American Teamwork Can Re-*

capture the Competitive Edge. Reading, Mass.: Addison-Wesley Publishing Company, 1984.

Rice, Richard. "Economic Mobilization in Wartime Japan: Business, Bureaucracy, and Military in Conflict." *Journal of Asian Studies* 38 (August 1979): 689–706.

"Ronsetsu, Bōeki shinkō jō no ni dai shōgai" [Editorial, Two Large Obstacles for the Progress of Trade]. *Bōeki* 28 (March 1928): 2–6.

Sakamoto Masako. "Sensō to zaibatsu" [War and the Large Combines]. In *Taikei, Nihon gendai shi* [A Series: A History of Modern Japan], edited by Nakamura Masanori. Vol. 4, *Sensō to kokka dokusen shihonshugi* [The War and State Monopoly Capitalism], pp. 47–91. Tokyo: Nihon Hyōronsha, 1979.

Samuels, Richard J. *The Business of the Japanese State: Energy Markets in Comparative and Historical Perspective*. Ithaca: Cornell University Press, 1987.

———. "The Industrial Destructuring of the Japanese Aluminum Industry." *Pacific Affairs* 56 (Fall 1983): 495–509.

Sato Hideo and Michael W. Hodin. "The U.S.-Japanese Steel Issue of 1977." In *Coping with U.S.-Japanese Economic Conflicts*, edited by I. M. Destler and Hideo Sato, pp. 27–72. Lexington, Mass.: Lexington Books, 1982.

Schmitter, Philippe C. "Still the Century of Corporatism?" *The Review of Politics* 36 (January 1974): 85–131.

Schumpeter, Elizabeth B. "Industrial Development and Government Policy, 1936–1940." In *Industrialization in Japan and Manchukuo*, edited by Elizabeth B. Schumpeter, pp. 789–861. New York: The Macmillan Co., 1940.

Shibagaki Kazuo. *Mitsui, Mitsubishi no hyaku nen, Nihon shihonshugi to zaibatsu* [A Hundred Years of Mitsui and Mitsubishi, the Large Combines and Japanese Capitalism]. Tokyo: Chūō Kōron Shinsho, 1968, 1978.

Shibusawa Masao. "Jikyoku to seitetsu jigyō" [The Current Situation and the Operations of the Steel Manufacturing Sector]. *Keizai renmei* 8 (August 1938): 24–28.

Shimoda Masami. *Fujiwara Ginjirō kaiko hachijū nen* [Eighty Years of the Recollections of Fujiwara Ginjirō]. Tokyo: Dai Nihon Yūbenkai Kōdansha, 1949.

"Shin keizai taisei o kataru zadankai" [A Symposium on the New Economic Order]. *Ekonomisuto* 19 (January 6, 1941): 49–63.

"Shina jihen ni kansuru tai Eikoku keizai dantai seimei sho" [A Declaration to British Economic Organizations Regarding the China Incident]. *Keizai renmei* 7 (November 1937): 1–3.

Shinbun kiji shiryō shūsei [A Collection of Materials from Newspaper Arti-

cles]. Edited by the Kōbe Daigaku Keizai Keiei Kenkyūjo. Vols. 10 and
11, *Bōeki hen* [A Volume on Trade], nos. 1 and 2. Tokyo: Shinseisha,
1974.

Shinbun kiji shiryō shūsei [A Collection of Materials from Newspaper Arti-
cles]. Edited by the Kōbe Daigaku Keizai Keiei Kenkyūjo. Vol. 21, *Bōeki
hen* [A Volume on Trade], no. 12. Tokyo: Shinseisha, 1975.

"Shinchō jikyoku ni taisho se yo" [Respond Cautiously to the Current Situa-
tion]. *Dai Nihon bōseki rengōkai geppō*, no. 563 (September 1939): 1.

Shiraishi Kōzaburō. "Bōekishō setchi mondai ni kansuru shiken" [A Personal
Opinion on the Problems of Creating a Ministry of Trade]. *Keizai renmei* 9
(October 1939): 28–33.

_____. "Senjika mengyō tōsei no kaiko" [A Review of the Control of the
Cotton Industry in Wartime]. *Keizai renmei* 8 (December 1938): 8–11.

"Shiryō: Shima sanryō oyobi menjiki tōsei no hanashi" [Source Materials: A
Discussion of the Control of Striped Cloth and Cotton Crepe]. *Sangyō gōrika*, no. 1 (December 1930): 32–72.

Shōkō Gyōsei Shi Kankōkai, ed. *Shōkō gyōsei shi* [A History of the Administration of Commerce and Industry]. Vols. 1–3. Tokyo: Shōkō Gyōsei Shi
Kankōkai, 1955.

"Shōwa jūyon nen o okuru" [Sending Off 1939]. *Dai Nihon bōseki rengōkai
geppō*, no. 566 (December 1939): 1.

"Sōgō rinku ni taisuru ōkurashō tachiba" [The Position of the Finance Ministry Regarding the Comprehensive Link System]. *Tōyō keizai shinpō*, no.
1836 (October 15, 1938): 11–12.

South Manchurian Railway. *Fourth Report on Progress in Manchuria to
1934.* Dairen: 1934.

Sugiyama Kazuo. "Ikeda Seihin, tenkanki ni okeru zaibatsu kaikakusha"
[Ikeda Seihin, A Reformer of the zaibatsu in a Period of Change]. In *Ni-
hon no kigyōka (3)* [Industrialists of Japan (3)], edited by Morikawa
Hidemasa, pp. 133–75. Tokyo: Yuikaku Shinsho, 1978.

Suzuki Shimakichi. "Sekai keizai kaigi to Nihon" [The World Economic
Conference and Japan]. *Keizai renmei* 3 (May 1933): 14–17.

Takahashi Kamekichi. *Henkaku no zaikai to sono taisaku* [The Changing
Business Community and Its Policies]. Tokyo: Chikura Shobō, 1932.

_____. *Nihon shihonshugi no gōrika* [The Rationalization of Japanese
Capitalism]. Tokyo: Shun'yōdō, 1930.

_____. *Zaisei keizai nijū-go nen shi* [A History of Twenty-five Years of the
Economy and Public Finance]. Vols. 2, 4, 5, and 6. Tokyo: Jitsugyō no
Sekaisha, 1932.

Takamura Naosuke. *Kindai Nihon mengyō to Chūgoku* [China and the Cotton
Industry of Modern Japan]. Tokyo: Tokyo Daigaku Shuppankai, 1982.

Takashima Seiichi, "Keizai dantai saihensei no hōkō" [The Direction of the

Reorganization of Economic Organizations]. *Ekonomisuto* 19 (May 5, 1941): 11.

Takekoshi Yosaburō. *Ōkawa Heisaburō kun den* [A Biography of Ōkawa Heisaburō]. Tokyo: Ōkawa Heisaburō Kun Denki Hensankai, 1936, reissued by the Ikuei Shuppansha in Tokyo in 1983.

Takeuchi Kenji. *Tōsei keizai to dokusen* [The Control Economy and Monopoly]. Tokyo: Tokyo Shōkō Kaigisho, 1934.

Takeuchi Shōichi. "Dokusen shihonka dantai no setsuritsu to keizai seisaku" [The Establishment of Monopoly Organizations of Capitalists and Economic Policy]. *Rekishigaku kenkyū*, "Bessatsu tokushū" [A Special Collection in a Separate Volume], November 1976, 126–36.

―――. "Nihon kōgyō kurabu setsuritsu no haikei to sono shutai" [The Background of the Establishment of the Japan Industrial Club and Its Main Constituency]. *Chiba shōdai ronsō* 13 (June 1975): 25–50.

―――. "Shihonka dantai to keizai seisaku (I)—1920 nen kyōkōki ni okeru tekkō seisaku jūritsu katei" [Organizations of Capitalists and Economic Policy (I)—The Process of Creating Policies for Iron and Steel in the Depression Era of the 1920s]. *Chiba shōdai ronsō* 17 (September 1979): 77–96.

―――. "Shihonka dantai to keizai seisaku (II)—1920 nen kyōkōki ni okeru tekkō seisaku jūritsu katei" [Organizations of Capitalists and Economic Policy (II)—The Process of Creating Policies for Iron and Steel in the Depression Era of the 1920s]. *Chiba shōdai ronsō* 17 (December 1979): 147–64.

Tanahashi Toragorō. "Kokka hijō jikyoku ni kanshite" [Regarding the Emergency Situation of the Nation]. *Keizai renmei* 8 (August 1938): 35–38.

Tanaka Kanzō. "En burokku nai bōeki no genjō" [The Present Situation within the Yen Bloc]. *Keizai renmei* 9 (April 1939): 1–5.

―――. "*Why Meddle in the Orient?* o susumu" [I Recommend "*Why Meddle in the Orient?*"]. *Keizai renmei* 8 (August 1938): 28–32.

Tanaka Shin'ichi. *Nihon keizai sensō hisshi* [A Secret History of Japan's War Economy]. Tokyo: Nihon Keizai Sensō Hisshi Kankōkai, 1974.

TBS Brittanica, ed. *Nihon no ridā* [Leaders of Japan]. Vol. 8, *Zaikai kakushin no shidōsha* [Leaders of the Renovation of the Business World]. Tokyo: TBS-Brittanica, 1983.

Tiedemann, Arthur F. "Big Business and Politics in Prewar Japan." In *Dilemmas of Growth in Prewar Japan*, edited by James B. Morley, pp. 267–316. Princeton: Princeton University Press, 1971.

"Tōa keizai kondankai daisan bunkakai tekiroku," [A Summary of a Meeting of Section Number Three of the East Asia Economic Conference]. *Dai Nihon bōseki rengōkai geppō*, no. 566 (December 1939): 41–44.

Tokyo Ginkō Kyōkai. *Tokyo tegata kōkanjo kyūjū nen no ayumi* [The Course

of Ninety Years of the Tokyo Clearinghouse]. Tokyo: Tokyo Tegata
Kōkanjo, 1977.

Tokyo Shōkō Kaigisho. *Keizai dantai sōran* [An Outline of Economic Orga-
nizations]. Tokyo: Fukuyamabō, 1941.

Tokyo Shōkō Kaigisho, ed. *Nihon zaikai no gensei* [The Situation of Japan's
Business World]. Tokyo: Kaizōsha, 1935.

Tokyo Shōkō Kaigisho Hyaku Nen Shi Hensan Iinkai. *Tokyo shōkō kaigisho
hyaku nen shi* [A History of One Hundred Years of the Tokyo Chamber of
Commerce]. Tokyo: Tokyo Shōkō Kaigisho, 1979.

"Tōtaku sōsai Yasukawa Yūnosuke shi ni hokushi keizai kōsaku o kiku"
[Asking the President of the Oriental Development Company, Yasukawa
Yūnosuke, about Economic Activities in North China]. *Tōyō keizai shin-
pō*, no. 1787 (November 13, 1937): 27–35.

Tsuda Shingo. "Gaikoku no hinan ni taishite sangyōka no torubeki taido"
[The Attitude that Industrialists Must Take toward Criticism from Foreign
Nations]. *Daiyamondo* 22 (August 11, 1934): 75.

————. "Kanebō no genjō to shōrai" [The Present Situation of the Kanegafuchi Spinning Company and Its Future]. *Tōyō keizai panfuretto*, no. 3.
Tokyo: Tōyō Keizai Shuppanbu, May 1936, pp. 1–21.

————. "Menseihin no yushutsu wa taigekigen o kitasan" [Exports of Cotton Manufactures Will Produce a Large Decline]. *Tōyō keizai shinpō*, no.
1583 (January 20, 1934): 32–34.

————. "Sen'i kōgyō no zento" [The Future Course of the Textile Industry].
Daiyamondo 25 (February 11, 1937): 66–68.

————. "Waga sangyō no hatten to hokushi kōsaku—mengyō, mōshikigyō
no hatten saku" [The Development of Our Industry and Activities in North
China—Policies to Develop the Cotton Industry and Wool Weaving Indus-
try]. *Tōyō keizai shinpō*, no. 1692 (February 8, 1936): 25–27.

————. "Waga sen'i kōgyō no shōrai" [The Future of Our Textile Industry].
Tōyō keizai shinpō, no. 1693 (February 15, 1936): 30–31.

Tsūshima Shun'ichi. "Takahashi Korekiyo kō no koto" [Matters Regarding
Count Takahashi Korekiyo]. In *Nihon kin'yū shi shiryō, Shōwa hen*
[Source Materials for the Financial History of Japan, Volume for the
Shōwa Era], edited by the Nihon Ginkō Chōsakyoku, vol. 22, pp. 10–16.
Tokyo: Ōkurashō Insatsukyoku, 1968.

Tsūshō Sangyōshō, ed. *Shōkō seisaku shi* [A History of Policy toward Commerce and Industry]. Vols. 1 and 2, *Sōsetsu* [An Introduction]. Tokyo:
Shōkō Seisaku Shi Kankōkai, 1985.

————. *Shōkō seisaku shi* [A History of Policy toward Commerce and In-
dustry]. Vol. 4, *Jūyō chōsakai* [Important Investigation Committees]. Tokyo: Shōkō Seisaku Shi Kankōkai, 1961.

————. *Shōkō seisaku shi* [A History of Policy toward Commerce and Industry]. Vol. 6, no. 2, *Bōeki* [Trade]. Tokyo: Shōkō Seisaku Shi Kankōkai, 1971.

———. *Shōkō seisaku shi* [A History of Policy toward Commerce and Industry]. Vol. 9, *Sangyō gōrika* [Industrial Rationalization]. Tokyo: Shōkō Seisaku Shi Kankōkai, 1961.

Turner, Henry Ashby, Jr. *German Big Business and the Rise of Hitler.* New York: Oxford University Press, 1985.

Turner, John, ed. *Businessmen and Politics: Studies of Business Activity in British Politics, 1900–1945.* London: Heinemann, 1984.

Uchino Tatsurō. *Japan's Postwar Economy, An Insider's View of Its History and Its Future.* Tokyo: Kōdansha International, Ltd., 1983.

Uekasa Masu. "Industrial Organization: The 1970s to the Present." In *The Political Economy of Japan*, vol. 1, *The Domestic Transformation*, edited by Kozo Yamamura and Yasukichi Yasuba, pp. 469–515. Stanford: Stanford University Press, 1987.

Vogel, Ezra F. *Comeback.* New York: Simon and Schuster, 1985.

———. *Japan as Number One: Lessons for America.* Cambridge: Harvard University Press, 1979.

"Waga bōeki seisaku no tenkan" [The Conversion of Our Trade Policies]. *Ekonomisuto* 19 (July 14, 1941): 24–26.

"Waga kuni yushutsu bōeki no shinkō sokushin ni kansuru iken" [An Opinion Regarding the Encouragement of the Progress of Japan's Export Trade]. *Keizai renmei* 8 (April 1938): 1–6.

Watanabe Katsumasa, ed. *Shinbun shōroku taishō shi, Taishō 15* [A History of the Taishō Era through Excerpts from the Newspapers, 1926]. Tokyo: Taishō Shuppan Kabushiki Kaisha, 1979.

Winham, Gilbert R., and Ikuo Kabashima. "The Politics of U.S.-Japanese Trade." In *Coping with U.S.-Japanese Economic Conflicts*, edited by I. M. Destler and Hideo Sato, pp. 73–119. Lexington, Mass.: Lexington Books, 1982.

Wray, William D. *Mitsubishi and the N.Y.K., 1870 to 1914: Business Strategy and the Japanese Shipping Industry.* Cambridge: Harvard University Press, 1984.

Yamamoto Mitsuru. "Nichi-In (Ei) mengyō funsō" [The Cotton Industry Dispute between Japan and India (England)]. In *Taiheiyō, Ajia ken no kokusai keizai funsō shi* [A History of International Economic Disputes in the Asian and Pacific Region], edited by Hosoya Chihiro, pp. 3–40. Tokyo: Tokyo Daigaku Shuppankai, 1983.

Yanaga Chitoshi. *Big Business in Japanese Politics.* New Haven: Yale University Press, 1968.

Yanagisawa Takeshi, ed. *Ikeda Seihin, zaikai kaiko* [Ikeda Seihin, Recollections of the Business World]. Tokyo: Sekai no Nihonsha, 1949.

Yasukawa Yūnosuke. "Kontei aru honpōhin no kaigai hatten ryoku" [The Power of Japanese Products with a Basis to Develop Overseas]. *Tōyō keizai shinpō*, no. 1583 (January 20, 1934): 41–42.

―――. "Nisshi shinzen ron shokan" [An Impression Regarding Friendship between Japan and China]. *Daiyamondo* 23 (March 21, 1935): 110–11.

―――. "Shin bōeki seisaku no konpon hōshin" [The Basic Direction of the New Trade Policies]. Tōyō Keizai Shinpōsha ed., *Shin Nihon no sangyō seisaku* [Japan's New Industrial Policies], *Tōyō keizai panfuretto*, no. 4. Tokyo: Tōyō Keizai Shuppanbu, May 1936, pp. 92–102.

Yoda Shintarō, ed. *Tokyo shōkō kaigisho hachijū-go nen shi* [A History of Eighty-five Years of the Tokyo Chamber of Commerce]. Vol. 1. Tokyo: Tokyo Shōkō Kaigisho, 1966.

Yokohama Shōkō Kaigisho Sōritsu Hyaku Shūnen Kinen Jigyō Kikaku Tokubetsu Iinkai Hyaku Nen Shi Hensan Bunkakai, ed. *Yokohama shōkō kaigisho hyaku nen shi* [A History of One Hundred Years of the Yokohama Chamber of Commerce]. Yokohama: Yokohama Shōkō Kaigisho, 1981.

Yoshino Shinji. *Nihon kōgyō seisaku* [Japan's Industrial Policies]. Tokyo: Nihon Hyōronsha, 1935.

―――. *Shōkō gyōsei no omoishutsu—Nihon shihonshugi no ayumi* [Recollections of the Administration of Commerce and Industry—The Course of Japanese Capitalism]. Tokyo: Shōkō Seisaku Shi Kankōkai, 1962.

Yoshino Shinji Tsuitō Roku Kankōkai, ed. *Yoshino Shinji*. Tokyo: Yoshino Shinji Tsuitō Roku Kankōkai, 1974.

"Yushutsu gimu kikan no teppai o nozomu" [We Want the Elimination of the Obligatory Period for Exports]. *Dai Nihon bōseki rengōkai geppō*, no. 552 (October 1938): 1.

"Yushutsu zōshin no sekkyoku saku o nozomu" [We Want Positive Policies to Increase Exports]. *Dai Nihon bōseki rengōkai geppō*, no. 536 (June 1937): 1.

Yutani Kenzō. "Jikyoku shūshū no taisaku" [Policies for Coping with the Current Situation]. *Keizai renmei* 8 (August 1938): 32–34.

"Zadankai, gunji yosan no bōchō to sono eikyō" [A Symposium, the Expansion of the Military Budget and Its Influence]. *Tōyō keizai shinpō*, no. 1740 (January 1, 1937): 129–53.

www.ingramcontent.com/pod-product-compliance
Lightning Source LLC
Chambersburg PA
CBHW020348270326
41926CB00007B/350